A
Perception
of
Reality

The Teachings of Joshua

A Perception of Reality

By Gary Temple Bodley

Copyright © 2015 by Gary Temple Bodley

All rights reserved. This book or any portion thereof
may not be reproduced or used in any manner whatsoever
without the express written permission of the publisher
except for the use of brief quotations in a book review.

Printed in the United States of America

First Printing, 2014
Second Printing, 2015

ISBN 978-1500531416

This book would literally not have been possible without my wife, Lili. Her powerful asking and allowing made it flow from me onto these pages. Without her support and understanding I would never have come to the place where this book could have been written.

It was Lili who introduced me to Abraham and to the idea that we are more than we understand and that there is more to understand than we can imagine.

*I love and have loved many people, but Lili is the only one I have ever **loved and adored**. And so it is with all the love in my heart that I dedicate this book to Lili*

Contents

Acknowledgments	ix
My Story	xi
Introduction	
The Teachings of Joshua	xvii
Chapter One	1
The Laws of the Universe and Universal Forces	
Chapter Two	18
Emotions, Feelings, and Thoughts	
Chapter Three	32
Manifestation Events	
Chapter Four	49
Intention	
Chapter Five	64
Emotions	
Chapter Six	78
Inspiration, Motivation, and Action	
Chapter Seven	94
Parenting, Education, and Intelligence	
Chapter Eight	114
The Flow of Life	
Chapter Nine	129
Focus	
Chapter Ten	140
The Power of Abundance	
Chapter Eleven	158
The Art of Simplicity and Balance	
Chapter Twelve	182
Self-Awareness and Intuition	
Chapter Thirteen	204
The Perception of Vibration Through Your Beliefs	
Chapter Fourteen	225
The Magical Power of Creation Through Intention	
Chapter Fifteen	251
The Reality of Imagination	
Chapter Sixteen	265
Expectation	
Special Section	273
Questions and Answers	

Acknowledgments

I am blessed to have so many supportive friends and teachers. The first people I was fortunate to share this book with were Debra Jo and Frank Bright. When I read them the first few pages that had been written in those early days, the excitement they showed was even more powerful than my own. Debra Jo has been with me on this ride from the very beginning, and she continues to be an inspiration as we continue this process.

Jennifer Arsenault was also along with us at the very beginning. She was one of the first to ask Joshua a question. Even though many of the questions were personal, she wanted to make sure they would be available to everyone. Her questions, which have been many, offer so much insight into universal questions about parenting and the after life. I am sure that many, many people will be eased by Joshua's answers to her questions.

I would also like to thank all of the wonderful people who contributed to the design and production of this book. From all of the proofreaders to the editor, from the production designer to the cover artist; thank you all.

Most of all I would like to thank Esther and Jerry Hicks. Without Esther and Jerry, who brought the world the teachings of Abraham, I could not have imagined co-creating this book with Joshua. It was Esther who allowed me to know that a normal person could do this, and that anyone could do it. Without her, I would never have believed it to be possible. Without Abraham, I would never have been led to this level or awareness. And so I thank them all and acknowledge their contribution to this material and these teachings that have already helped so many lives.

My Story

I have come to know that I am the creator of my own reality. It has taken me over fifty years of life on this planet to be led to this fact. Looking back on my life from my present perspective, I can see all of the occasions where my thoughts preceded my reality. Though I've had many ups and downs, the fact that I created each situation, including my present reality, is now obvious.

The knowledge that I am the creator of my own reality has brought me incredible freedom and relief. I am now much less concerned with the opinions and judgments of others and I am free to be myself, just as they are free to be themselves. I have released others from my negative judgment and I have released myself from a lot of my own self-judgment. I have come to know that I live a completely unique life that can't be compared to any other life that has ever existed.

Everything changed for me when, in 2011, I attended my first Abraham-Hicks seminar in Asheville, NC. Abraham spoke to me like no other teacher had, and I immediately resonated with the material. But what really started it all was my decision to meditate. I began meditating every morning to the guided meditations of Abraham as presented by Esther Hicks. At first, I struggled to get through the fifteen-minute exercises. In the beginning, I could not last longer than five or six minutes at a time, all the while my thoughts were fluttering about as they normally do. However, I was soon able to complete the full fifteen minutes. Though my mind continued to wander, there were true moments of silence and calm.

I began to look forward to and enjoy each meditation. My wife Lili and I would lie in bed each morning and play the meditations over her phone with our dog, Rocky, lying between us. As I picked up the unique cadence of breathing (three beats in and five beats out), I got better and better at focusing inward. My thoughts turned away from the problems of the day to questions about the nature of the universe, the Law of Attraction, and the mechanism of physical reality.

After months of consistent meditation, I started to notice that many of my inner questions were answered immediately. I suspected it was just me answering my own questions since the inner voice that was posing the queries was identical to the one providing the answers. I had assumed that if I was asking God, or Abraham, or my inner self a question, the entity answering the question would sound different. But eventually I came to the realization that I was tapping into something larger than myself.

I began asking all kinds of questions and receiving answers that seemed to make a whole lot of sense. Instead of discounting the validity of the answers, as I would have done in the past, I chose to believe they came from somewhere or someone inside. It wasn't me answering my own questions; it was communication from another realm. In Abraham vernacular, I believed the communication was coming from the "nonphysical." I was tapping into infinite intelligence, as Abraham calls it.

Okay, that's great. Infinite intelligence is now communicating with me. Abraham has always said it is available to everyone, but I was the last one who ever thought I could actually get to that vibration. I certainly wasn't going to tell anyone about it, but I was going to play with it.

If I lost my keys, I would simply ask, "Where are my keys?" and the location would pop into my head. I made a habit of saying "Thank you" on each such occurrence. I have always had tremendous difficulty remembering names, so much so that it was nearly a full-blown phobia. Suddenly, though, all I had to do was ask and the name would come to me. "Thank you again," I would say to whoever was giving me the answers.

Sometime in October 2013, I thought I would ask this entity its name. I immediately received the answer "Joshua." I know channeling and such things exist, but believe me when I tell you I was skeptical of whatever was happening to me. I was sure I was simply inventing the name. When I shared the name with Lili, she responded, "It sounds right to me. It certainly fits in with Seth and Abraham."

As my meditations continued, I started inviting Joshua in to see what would happen. Soon, I felt a presence inside my body as I lay there meditating. It started slowly, first in my jaw and then in the right side of my head, then it moved into my entire body. The degree of this sensation varied during each meditation. One day it would be subtle and take a long time to progress, another day it would happen instantly and be obvious. It always started in my jaw and the right side of my head and expanded throughout my body from there.

On November 18, 2013, during a meditation, I heard Joshua clearly as they said, "Write, write, write!" I felt compelled to write like never before. Immediately after meditation that day I sat down at my computer and started typing. What you read in the first two pages of this book are the exact words that came out that day. The rest of the book contains the words that flowed from Joshua through me for eight weeks ending on Sunday, January 12, 2014.

Every time I read these pages, I am just as amazed as anyone by the clarity, wisdom, and knowledge that has come forth. I know only one thing: it did not come **from** me, it came **through** me. The information revealed in this book tells the story of reality from a completely new perspective. It opens up an entirely fresh and unique perspective on reality and our ability to create our lives in the most desirable manner possible. It teaches us how we create our lives and how we expand as a result of our creation.

On Monday, January 13, I was inspired to continue writing and a new book was started. This book, titled *Health, Wealth & Love*, was also written in exactly eight weeks and is almost the same number of words as the first book. This next book deals with more information on the topics that most of us find so important. The first book is like Understanding Reality 101 and this next book would be Understanding Reality 102.

The writing process is fascinating. I would meditate in the morning, make a quick protein shake, and shut myself in my home office. I would sit at the computer, clear my thoughts, and then start typing. Often I would know the first line I was going to write beforehand. Once I typed that line, the rest would just flow. I type with two fingers on my left hand and one on my right. I'm certainly not a fast typist by any stretch of the imagination, but as Joshua flowed from my mind to my fingers, it all came out at amazing speed. I could not look up from the keyboard to see if I was making any mistakes. It just came out so quickly. I could go like this for about an hour before I got tired. That's when the session would end for the day and would resume the next day. I only missed two days in the first eight weeks. Each day produced between three and five pages. There was no outline; it just came out in one perfectly formatted book. It's like the whole book was written at once. I cannot tell where one day's writing stopped and the next began.

Two complete books were written by Joshua in sixteen weeks. A lot of typos were corrected and a few grammatical changes were made at the insistence of my editor. However, what was typed in those eight weeks is what you read in this book.

In addition to writing the books, I have received lots of questions from friends, friends of friends, and even total strangers that I present to Joshua and Joshua has answered each question. The process is the same as writing the books. I receive the question in an email the day before. I meditate in the morning and then sit down to write and Joshua's words flow through me effortlessly onto the page.

This has been an extremely rewarding aspect of this whole experience. The answers to the questions are so amazing and everyone has really loved and appreciated their answers. Some people ask several questions and you can see their growth from one question to the next. Some of the answers are extremely complex and must be read several times for the recipient to get everything there is to get. Many of those who asked questions have read this book, so they have an understanding of the technical aspects of universal forces and the mechanism of physical reality. Joshua answers these people using more technical information. Other people have no experience with any of this and Joshua is able to provide great insight without using any of the language we are used to.

I have included three questions and answers in the Special Section in the back of the book, which I'm sure you'll find interesting. You can read many more questions and answers at www.theteachingsofjoshua.com. You may also ask a question yourself and receive an answer directly from Joshua that will be personal to you, but will also help many others who have similar questions.

In the beginning, very few people in my life knew about my experiences with Joshua. I have gone from thinking all of this was very weird to accepting my role in the dissemination of this important information. But I'm just a normal person with a normal life. This is very hard for me to believe, let alone for most other people. So I have decided to accept this information as the ultimate truth and live it as fully as I can. Those who will resonate with and understand this information will be drawn to it. I'm not going to preach

Joshua to anyone who doesn't want to hear it. But for those of us who are awakening to the reality behind reality, we going to start living on a whole new level. There is so much more coming, I can just feel it, and I'm exhilarated in anticipation.

Introduction

The Teachings of Joshua

Everything is right. There is no wrong anywhere in the universe. Anything perceived as wrong is an illusion. It only seems wrong through the narrow perception of your physical reality. From the broader viewpoint, whether it's the perception of nonphysical or the broader view of history, nothing is ever wrong. It is always, always right.

From your perception in your physical state right now, you can easily think of many events in history that seem wrong to you. All wars, all deaths, all injustices seem wrong. But these events were all part of the larger reality you now experience. If not for these events, you would be living a different reality altogether. In fact, quite literally, **you** would not exist.

Your actual, physical existence as you see it is absolutely the result or product of all the events that have ever happened in the history of your earth. If any single event had not happened exactly the way it did, you would not exist. This may seem unbelievable to you right now, but once you understand the mechanism that controls universal forces, you will understand our meaning. Everything is right.

We have come to teach you the broader perspective that we see. If you could view your world as we see it, you would love everything. You would love your planet. You would love your government. You would love the wealthy and the poor equally. You would be filled with joy at the existence of the most talented among you as well as the most troubled among you. All equally. It is all the same to us. All wonderful. All beautiful.

We say these things so that you can see your world as we see it, for once you do, your world will change, incredibly, for the better. We come to teach you these things we *KNOW*, so you can live a wonderful life while you are here. You will come to *KNOW* what we *KNOW* eventually. When you die, you will know what we know. We hope you come to know it as fully as you are able, now.

You are a creator. Your creation is you. You can be anything you want. It is all up to you. You may not understand this to be the truth in your life, but it is. You think other forces control your fate, but they do not. You are absolutely in charge of your life. It doesn't matter what has happened in your life up to this exact moment. Everything that has happened up to this moment has perfectly unfolded to bring you to these pages and to the awareness that there is something more. You create your life.

You are an eternal being who has lived countless lives. That is true of everyone you know. You are eternal. That means there is no death as you understand it. You are experiencing what you call "reality" right now. In this moment, what you see around you, what you sense, what you perceive is called reality. However, it is just a perception of reality. It seems physical, but it is the nonphysical simply organized into a state of reality. There seem to be walls, and tables, and rivers, and mountains, and the sun, etc. These are all just vibrations you are interpreting as reality. It's all beautiful and it's fun to experience this reality. It's fun to be alive, to see beautiful things, to have wonderful relationships, to taste food, to drink water. You come to this experience of physical reality for the joy of it and for the expansion of you.

Physical reality is not really physical at all. All molecules are held together by nonphysical energies that create whatever you perceive. If you perceive a chair, the one you are sitting on right now, for example, it's a chair that is completely unique, created in your mind and perceived as real through your senses. You did not manufacture the chair, but you did attract it into your existence. You know it is a chair. Because you know it is a chair, you can sit on it. You can move it. You might be able to destroy it or sell it or give it away. The knowing is what makes it real.

If you did not know it was a chair, it would not exist in your reality. If someone led you to knowing it was a chair, then it would exist in your reality. The only things that exist in your reality are the things you know. You could use the term "believe," but that is less powerful than knowing. Knowing is absolute.

When you were a baby, you did not know very much. That's why it is difficult to remember much from that time in your life. As you learned to perceive, your world filled in. The more you knew, the more you perceived.

You cannot perceive anything you do not know. However, you can know anything if you can be led to the knowing of it. This is the sticking point for most humans. You are conditioned by your experience to believe in certain things. These beliefs form your world as you alone perceive it. Everyone has a unique set of variable beliefs, and thus each person lives quite a unique experience. These beliefs hold you back as much as they help you. If you believe the poor are lazy or the rich are greedy, you will live a certain life based on those beliefs. If you believe the world is wonderful, that there is no danger, that joy and abundance are your birthright, then you will live that experience.

Beliefs shape your perception of the world. The wonderful thing is that your beliefs can change more easily than you think. Don't worry about that now, because it is our intention to lead you in a way that will help you mold your beliefs. You are the creator of your existence and you create your beliefs. You could construct a sculpture of magnificent beauty if you were led to the skills needed to create such a work. It might take a little time, but if you had the interest and patience, you would be able to create a work of art. We will give you the tools, and if you have the interest and a little patience, you will create a masterpiece that is the highest version of you.

II.

Everything is right and everyone is right. There is no wrong anywhere in the universe. There are no wrong people. Everyone is living their existence as best they can. You must come to understand that everyone is striving for the best life for them. But all of you are blocking yourselves from your most wonderful possible life in some fashion. Some of you live amazing, incredible lives, but all of you are doing things that prevent you from reaching higher, more wonderful life experiences.

The belief that others have control over you or can impact your life is one of the ways in which you hold yourselves apart from your finest possible life experience. From our perspective, your life is wonderful, but you are holding yourselves apart from an even richer experience. You are the absolute creator of you. No one can create you, but you. All other people create in their own experience and have no ability to create in your experience.

Your belief that they can is an illusion. It is a very powerful illusion, and few have come to realize they control their life 100 percent. Your parents, your spouse, your children, your employers, your police, your government, have absolutely no power to create in your life. You allow them to affect your own creation, which is you and your life. They have no power unless, by your focus and attention, you allow them to affect your experience.

As a child, you were conditioned by your parents, teachers, and others, and that is why you think they have control. However, they never did. In fact, when you were young and understood the laws of the universe, you impacted their lives in a far greater way. Over the years, they wanted you to conform to their understanding of life, rules, behavior, etiquette, judgment, etc. They wanted you to conform. No running, no laughing, no loud noises, sit up straight, eat everything on your plate, don't talk back, don't fight, go to school, be good, and so on.

Conformity is not natural for a child. You rebelled every step of the way until you became a teenager and would not tolerate it anymore. The time of rebellion does not last long, however, and most of you soon conformed to social norms. You were not allowed the time or freedom to discover your inner selves. You knew this inner self as a child, but you forgot it along the way. The inner self is where all of your guidance in life is found.

You are unique to all of the world and to all of history. There has never been another like you in all of existence. You, as the creator of your life, are the center of the universe. Since you are the creator, the universe does revolve around you. This is an important truth that, quite likely, you were never told. It's a truth you may have difficulty believing at this time. If you are the center of the universe, then what about everyone else? They, too, are the center of their universes. This truth means that there are infinite universes, all unfolding simultaneously. This concept may be hard for you to grasp at the moment, but we ask you to play with us for a bit and see how it unfolds for you.

The universe has a primary law that holds it together called the Law of Attraction. Like is drawn to like. What you think manifests in your reality. What another thinks manifests in their reality. It's simply the way of the universe and it is absolute and consistent. If it works for one, it works for all.

So, if you are the creator of your life, and all others are the creators of their lives, then you are the center of your universe and each and every other individual is the center of their universe. Therefore, there are multiple universes all entangled, unfolding, and working together at the same time.

If you can believe this one aspect of reality, you can set yourself free. You no longer need to be involved in the lives of others. Since they create their own reality and you create your own reality, and because they cannot create in your reality and you cannot create in their reality, then it really doesn't matter what you do and it doesn't matter what they do. You are free. They are free. You can be who you want to be and they are free to be who they want to be.

You have an inner guidance system directed by your inner self who understands you. There is a you that you do not fully know at this time. You have an understanding that there is more to you, but you have little knowledge of that part of you. We would like you to get to know the entire you. You have the perspective of the individual in your body. You live through your senses by what you observe of the outside world. But there are vast resources within. These resources can be utilized by looking inward. Discovering who you are on the inside is as valuable, if not more valuable, than understanding who you are on the outside.

Who you are on the outside at this present moment is the product of your experiences up to this point. Much of those experiences developed from events and circumstances that trace your life. But unseen in those experiences are the feelings and emotions you had at the time. Those feelings and emotions are much harder to remember than the actual events. However, they played a very large part in the unfolding of those events. Your feelings and emotions are resources from your inner self. They are part of your guidance system. They form your experiences. What you think and what you feel creates your reality. But there is also the aspect of time. Your reality does not instantly materialize. It is molded over time. It is created through your thoughts, feelings, and emotions and unfolds based on what your feelings indicate.

You are the product of your overall set of variable thoughts, emotions, and feelings. What you predominantly think and feel you predominantly live.

Can you think of a happy event in your life: your first kiss, your wedding, the birth of a child, or maybe your first car? These were all predetermined by your desires. You had consistent feelings that led to the outcome of these events. You thought about each event in your mind countless times before it materialized. You came to know that the event was possible, and then you felt hope that it could come to you. It became likely, and then you knew it would come and it materialized into your physical reality. It was not difficult and seemed natural.

Your life unfolds, good or bad, based on your thoughts and feelings. However, your memory is of the manifestation and not the thoughts and feelings that led to the manifestation. You might have been aware that you created each event or you might have thought fate led you to the outcome. But it was consistent thought that led you from possibility to hope to likelihood to actualization. The time lag between the initial idea and the outcome is directly related to the pace in which you travel from possibility to hope to likelihood to knowing.

Once you know something, it has manifested.

Memory, therefore, is not particularly helpful, because you cannot identify the thoughts and feelings that led to the event. You only remember the event. Usually, you cannot trace the path of thoughts that led to the outcome. Memory is but a blurry shadow of the event.

If you can understand the mechanism of manifestation, you can create your life in whatever fashion you desire. You can move from possibility to hope to likelihood to knowing quickly and easily.

Doubt is what keeps you from achieving your dreams. It slows the pace of manifestation. It holds you in place, stalled, without the power of momentum. There is a natural momentum that leads from idea to manifested reality. Doubt hinders that momentum. Fear and doubt are the same thing. They are projections of unwanted future outcomes of an idea. They are also potential manifestations that are as valid as the desire. When you desire something, you do so in the future tense. Doubt and fear are also based on a future outcome or possibility. The desire is one outcome and the doubt is another. Since only one outcome can occur, the one with the strongest momentum will be the likely result.

If you desire a mate, you have come through life experience to know what you prefer at a given point in time. You have identified what you like and don't like. You might think about the type of person you're looking for, what attributes that person possesses, maybe their body type, personality, intelligence, and many other facets of their overall being. You might have idealized versions of this person based on characters from your past, either real or fictional. But your desire is clear. You need not write it down. It is known by the universe entirely as you feel it.

The universe will deliver the physical manifestation of your exact desire. It will be perfect in every way. The one person who is identical to your actual desire will come to you. The universe knows the full you and the full version of your ideal mate. The universe will present that person to you - absolutely.

However, there is momentum that must occur for this to happen. As you consistently think and feel about the possibility of a mate, universal forces are at work, and the manifestation is in progress. If you are aligned with your desire, it will come quickly.

If, however, you have doubt, the manifestation stalls. You might think many thoughts that stall the manifestation, such as:

"I'm not worthy of this person."

"I might not be physically attractive enough for this person."

"I might not live in the same area as this person."

"This person might be in another relationship."

"I want this exact person who is not interested in me."

"I enjoy the freedom of being single."

"The new person might not like my family."

"The new person may believe in different things."

You see, there are endless ways in which doubt enters your thoughts and stalls momentum right at the beginning of the desire.

Let's say you have an idea for your new mate. This idea is the first phase of manifestation, and you are aligned with it. You feel ready for and comfortable with the idea of a new relationship. You are not experiencing any doubt at this stage and you create the feeling of possibility or hope. You look around with anticipation, wondering who the person will be and how they will show up. You are soon introduced to someone who is also ready for a new relationship. You successfully meet and begin your relationship. Fear and doubt once again have the potential to enter your thoughts. You might start to worry about where the relationship will end up. You might project negative possibilities into the future. At this stage, the negative possibilities also have momentum and can just as easily manifest. It all depends on your predominance of feelings and thoughts.

Remember, you create your reality. It has nothing to do with the thoughts and emotions of your new mate. They cannot create in your reality. They can only create in their reality. If you have negative thoughts about future outcomes and they seem to align with those thoughts, it's because you created them and your mate is just going along with your version of reality.

The opposite is also true. If you can maintain positive expectations of the relationship, your new mate will align with your positive expectations. This is the mechanism of reality, and it cannot be otherwise. It is the basis of the universe.

Positive and negative expectations are both legitimate and equally able to create probabilities in the universal system of manifestation. They are alike in certain ways; however, well-being is the basis of the universe, and probabilities tend towards well-being in general. The lesson here is that you have control over every outcome through your conscious awareness of the mechanism of manifestation.

Fear is thought projection of an unwanted outcome. It is a path toward an end that is unpleasant based on your current understanding of what you do and do not want. You have control over fear. Fear and worry are the same. Worry, however, tends to be a repetitive thought form, even more so than fear. Fear is often the result of analysis at the point of a decision. Worry is a thought form that tends to be repeated over and over again. Therefore, it carries more intrinsic possibilities for future outcomes than fear. A fearful thought is brief; worry can be chronic.

Once worry is initiated, it gains momentum and becomes a real possibility on its own. Worry is obsessive, compulsive, and more difficult to correct once the momentum takes hold.

The opposite of worry is knowing. Trust is a factor of knowing. You may not see the air you breathe, but you know it's there and you trust that it will be there for your next breath. At the moment of your next breath, you know the air is there and again trust that it will be there for each subsequent breath.

The tool for overcoming fear and worry is trust. If you trust the laws of the universe as much as you trust the law of gravity, you will be able to overcome fear and worry. If you understand that you are the creator of you, and that you are at the center of your universe, you will gain trust in the laws of the universe.

III.

You are a magnificent, worthy being and this world has been created for your pleasure, expansion, and joy. You were not given complete memory of the laws and mechanisms of the universe when you were born. This would have hindered your growth. As you come into alignment with your inner self, you will gain much joy, understanding, and expansion as you create wonderful experiences in your life. The purpose of this life is expansion. Expansion without joy is not meaningful expansion. You cannot have joy without alignment with your inner self. Therefore, the first step to joyous expansion is alignment with your inner self.

You live in a form of reality in which the external world takes up much, if not all, of your attention. You are designed to use your senses to navigate this wonderful planet on which you live. However, it was never intended for you to live fully outside yourself. Your life also has meaning within, as well. In fact, you must live a balanced life to have joyous expansion. You must align with your inner self.

The outer world is what you see, feel, smell, hear, taste, and even sense. The inner world exists in your mind, in your heart, inside your body, in your solar plexus. Your inner world is your thoughts, feelings, and emotions. There must be awareness of your inner world, as well, if there is to be alignment.

Once you achieve an understanding that your inner world shapes your outer world, only then will you have the freedom and ability to mold your life experience as you wish it to be. Without an understanding of your inner world, you are left to the whims of your random thoughts. If you understood how your thoughts, feelings, and emotions create your outer world experience prior to its manifestation in your reality, then the world would exist exactly as you would want it to. Your inner world creates your outer world.

This is not how you and almost all of humanity see life. The opposite seems true in your experience. You believe your thoughts, feelings, and emotions are based on what has occurred in the outer world. If someone is rude to you, you feel an unpleasant emotion. Maybe that emotion can be called that of a victim or of someone unworthy. You think the rude person made you feel the emotion because the emotion occurred after the rude comment. Therefore, the emotion was the result of the rude comment.

However, the rude comment was simply reinforcing your belief that you are a victim or that you are unworthy. Reality is a mirror of your inner feelings and predomination of thought. To the extent that you have those feelings, the universe will provide evidence to validate the feelings. This is simply the universe creating your version of reality.

If, on the other hand, you have consistent thoughts of beauty, worthiness, confidence, etc., then the universe will fill in your world with more confirmation of those feelings. You are the product of the life you've lived through the predomination of your thoughts to this point. If you can change your thoughts, feelings, and emotions, you will change your life. It is as simple as that. The change may not be simple, but the mechanism is simple.

The stronger your beliefs, the harder it will be to change your thoughts. If you believe the world is blessed with well-being, love, freedom, and joy, it will be difficult to change your beliefs because you see nothing but love, well-being, freedom, and joy.

If you believe that people are unkind, that life is hard, that resources are scarce, it will be difficult to change your beliefs because all you've known is cruelty, hardship, and scarcity. How can you change your beliefs for the better if the universe has proven you to be right all these years?

The path to change is through the knowledge of the laws of the universe and the mechanism by which these laws operate. The tool to changing beliefs is in gaining a new perspective on life.

The first step toward change is the idea that change is possible. Can you change your beliefs? Is it possible in any way? Can you know something different than that which you have lived every day of your existence? We know you can. We know you will. We will lead you if you are willing.

Chapter One

The Laws of the Universe and Universal Forces

There is the physical and the nonphysical, which exist simultaneously. There are laws that affect the physical realm, such as time and gravity, and there are laws that affect the nonphysical realm, as well. However, there is one law that affects all realms in much the same manner. That is the Law of Attraction. The Law of Attraction is the basis of all laws of existence, and without it, existence would not be possible. The Law of Attraction is the supreme law in your physical reality and guides everything that unfolds in your life and the lives of all consciousness in your world.

The Law of Attraction states that like is brought to like. You have control over this law through your thoughts, feelings, and emotions. The law is designed to work for you, not against you. You have come here to more fully understand this law. Once you do, your life experience will be forever changed.

The Law of Attraction allows you to live the life you desire now. You, through your life experiences, have come to know what you prefer. You have the Law of Attraction to bring you the things you want. The Law of Attraction knows how to bring them to you. You do not need the answers, for they will be given to you by the Law of Attraction.

If you want more money, you do not have to figure out how the money will come to you. In fact, if you try to create a path to money on your own, you will stall the money flow. You do not have the perspective required to see the magical way in which the money will flow to you. If, however, you have clarity of focus, without doubt or fear, and you trust that the money will come, the Law of Attraction will elegantly flow more money to you than you ever could have imagined.

A Perception of Reality

It is the Law of Attraction's purpose to bring you all that you desire. It is your work to allow the law to follow its natural course and bring to you whatever you truly desire. You do not have to write it down or speak it; the Law of Attraction knows what you want through the feelings, thoughts, and emotions you emit from inside.

Your inner self has a complete understanding of the forces of the universe and will guide those forces to bring you what you desire in the most beautiful way, at the perfect time, as long as you maintain your clarity of focus.

It does not matter what you want. There is never any judgment on the part of the Law of Attraction. You could want to witness a beautiful event or a tragic event. It is simply up to you. You could choose an easy, joyous, happy life experience or one filled with hardship and struggle. The Law of Attraction will bring you whatever you are a match for. You are the one who chooses and you will always receive a match for what you ask for through your feelings, emotions, and thoughts.

When you feel good, good things will come to you. When you feel hate, hateful things will come just as easily. The Law of Attraction supports whatever you feel. Because most humans are unaware of how their feelings affect their lives, they do not practice their feelings. They do not exercise that muscle. They believe their feelings are the after effects of events and not the precursors to them. If you feel sad, you will be given more reasons to feel sad. If you feel joy and appreciation, you will be given more reasons to feel joy and to appreciate.

The feeling always precedes the physical manifestation.

Everything that happens in your life is a physical manifestation. You take these things for granted, but they are actually a mirror of your feelings. Your feelings create the conditions. The conditions do not create your feelings; they reinforce them. This is all accomplished by the Law of Attraction. Since it is law, it cannot work otherwise.

Being of the fact that your feelings, emotions, and thoughts create your reality is indeed a great gift. Just the knowledge of this mechanism is enough to change your life forever. But what if you could actually guide your feelings purposely in order to create the life of your dreams? What if you were able to use the Law of Attraction to work for you? How would your life be different? We will show you how you can practice thoughts that feel good and thereby minimize thoughts that feel bad so you can improve your feelings and your life.

When your feelings improve, your life improves. It is the law and cannot be otherwise. As you feel better about yourself, you change for the better, literally. As you feel better about others in your life, they will change for the better, literally. You will physically change and they will physically change. The same is true of your government, your environment, your job, your car, your parents, your children, your home, etc. The better you feel about every aspect of your life, the better those things will be on a physical level. There will be an actual change, a change you will easily perceive.

Your reality is simply your perception of reality and nothing more. When you perceive things to be better, they *are* better. They actually change physically for the better. The change is real, not imaginary. However, having said that, imaginary change is also real.

What you imagine will come to you in reality. Desire is the imagination of a future outcome that is pleasing to you. Therefore, imagination is one of the tools of creation. Imagination is a powerful tool, and when it is used with clarity of intention, it has a tremendously powerful effect on creation. If you can imagine something and focus that imagination free of doubt or fear, you will create it in your physical experience.

Your physical reality is an illusion, and if you were able to inspect the smallest molecule in your world, you would notice that it is mostly empty space. You are tuned to a physical world that seems so real to you. This reality is fun, beautiful, and life-giving, but you need not focus your attention so strongly on what is.

You all see the world as a combination of vibrations that appear real. These vibrations can be manipulated by your perception. If you knew how differently you see the world compared to other people, you would be amazed. You only know your perception of reality and you assume that everyone else has the same or similar perception. You think dark blue is dark blue and white is white and everyone else sees the same colors. They do not. Everyone's version of reality is witnessed through their own perception which is unique to them. It is a wonder you are able to function together as well as you do, given your completely different and unique views of reality.

It is meant to be this way. The earth is designed as a physical reality so that you can exercise your natural powers. You can fine-tune your desires and then fulfill them, whatever they may be. The great purpose in life is to have a desire, and then see it fulfilled. Once the desire has been manifested, you're on to the next desire. You think it's about the manifestation of desire, but the manifestation is only the last step in the process. The joy comes through the conscious, deliberate creation of the manifestation. The end product is merely the reflection or proof that you've achieved your object of desire.

People tend to be attached to their manifestations as though they were trophies. However, you will notice that once the object has materialized, it loses most of its appeal. The joy is in the process of manifestation and not the result of the manifestation. It's the journey that is fulfilling, not the destination.

You may notice that many successful people are able to manifest things easily, but become unhappy when the object of their desire no longer pleases them. Those who are able to understand that it's the process of manifestation that is the joy, not the object, will find greater meaning in their lives. The joy is in the process.

You were designed as physical beings to enjoy the process, not the end result. However, your culture guides you away from this. You have learned to become fixated on the manifested evidence rather than the path to the manifestation. You are here to learn how to travel the path to that which you desire. The materialization of your desire is simply the finish line and has no intrinsic qualities of its own.

You are allowed to desire whatever you want and you are allowed to change those desires at any time. However, many humans tend to amend their desires based on the illusion that they are not progressing to the end result. They are impatient and want the manifestation to occur immediately. This is not the reason for your physical existence. You are here to learn to guide yourselves along the path from desire to manifestation.

Unfortunately, because you have not aligned with your inner self and are predominantly focused on your outer world, you are thrown off-course by the influence of others. You often create your desires based on what others have that you do not have. You might envy someone for something they possess and you think you want. That is all right because all desire is worthy in and of itself. Generally, however, if the desire is not born from within, it is not a true desire and the journey to the manifestation of that desire will be less fulfilling.

It is more difficult for someone to stay on a path of desire that has not been born from within. You may not be inspired to the actions necessary to fulfill the desire and you may not have the patience to maintain your clarity of thought to create the manifestation. Therefore, you may become disillusioned with the desire and with the process of manifestation altogether.

If you have previously attempted to fulfill a desire that was not born from within and have failed to achieve that manifestation, it was due to the fact that you were not properly inspired. If one chooses to pursue a desire just because of outside influences and then fails to achieve the manifested evidence of that desire, one may feel incompetent at achieving anything and therefore may believe they are unable to manifest any desire.

As you look around at those you know, you may notice that younger people tend to have stronger desires than older individuals. Youth comes into this world with strong desire and a zest for life. This enthusiasm can be explained by their ability to conjure strong desire and their eagerness to follow the path to the manifestation of desire. Some older people lack desire because they have never been aligned with their inner selves and have pursued desires that may not have been inspired. They may have failed to achieve the manifestations of those desires and simply gave up on their dreams.

But this is the reason for existence. Following the path of one true desire to the next is life-giving.

Desire is created through the experiences of your life. You come to know what you like and what you do not like. The Law of Attraction cares not about the desire. It brings to you manifested evidence of the predominance of your thoughts, feelings, and emotions. While the Law of Attraction can and will fulfill your desires, it can and will fulfill anything you give your attention to, wanted or unwanted equally. What you give your attention to manifests. If you give your attention to a desire, that desire, given pure focus, will manifest. If you give your attention to something unwanted, that too, provided enough attention is given, will also manifest.

You cannot wish anything away. It is the Law of Attraction. What you think about grows. Therefore, focus requires attention to what is wanted in order to create wonderful life experiences.

It does no good to protest for change. Pushing against something only makes it larger. For example, your government's war on drugs only exacerbates the prevalence of drugs in your society.

The universe is comprised of pure positive energy, and in your natural state, you are also a pure positive being comprised of that same energy. In your natural state, without the influences of outside distractions, you would live a life of joy. Without influence, you would be free from fear and doubt. Since influences do exist, unwanted things capture much of your attention in your day-to-day lives. You need not focus on anything unwanted, for without your attention to these things, they would not exist in your reality.

If you did not know about terrorism, you could not experience it. You would not be a vibrational match to it. To the extent that you believe terrorism exists, you become a match to it either physically or emotionally. You may believe terrorism is not likely to affect you physically; therefore, it is unlikely to affect you physically. You may however, think terrorists are evil people and must be destroyed at all costs. By carrying these thoughts, you bring more images of terrorism into your daily life through the news and other sources. You are therefore emotionally affected by terrorism, though you need not be.

There is no wrong in the universe. Your perspective that terrorism is wrong brings the issue to you. How could terrorism not be wrong you ask? To answer that question you must gain the larger perspective of our non-physical point of view. If you push against terrorism, you attract it. If you soften your view of terrorism and instead wish for peaceful coexistence, you lessen its effect on you and your life.

You are the creator of your own reality. You cannot control the conditions of the world around you by wishing they were not there. You control your thoughts regarding the conditions and thereby create actual conditions that are different than those you now accept as real. Remember that you create your own reality. If you believe that terrorism, or anything else unwanted, has the power to affect your life, then you add it to the fabric of your life. If you believe terrorism is a far-off struggle between people who are in the process of finding alignment within, then terrorism no longer affects your life either physically or emotionally.

This is a function of the universe. It is designed so that you have the absolute freedom to explore all facets of reality whether you deem them positive or negative, good or evil. There is no wrong anywhere in the universe. It all depends on your perspective. You can see the positive in any situation or event and you can perceive the negative as well. You can make the best of a situation or the worst of a situation. You can make things better and better or you can make them even worse. It's all up to you.

Free will allows you to expand as a human and as a nonphysical being. Your exposure to this world not only expands the you that you know in physical reality, but it also expands the inner you that resides in nonphysical reality. You are both focused here in the present moment. Sometimes you are not consciously aware of each and every moment of your life. You may be thinking about the past or projecting thoughts about the future. However, your inner self is always focused with you here on Earth in each and every moment. Your inner self is completely aware of you and your life and is guiding you to the extent that you are consciously aware of that guidance.

You have a personality that is you in the physical world. Part of that personality was adopted through much of your life experience during this lifetime. But the larger part of your personality was brought with you from your nonphysical personality. The part of you that is shy, reserved, insecure, fearful, or negative has been adopted during *this* lifetime. The much larger part of your personality, which comes from the inner you, is confident, secure, loving, fun, happy, prosperous, intelligent, and beautiful. That personality is the real you. The extent to which you mask it depends on the personality you've adopted through your life experiences during this lifetime.

When you die, the larger personality returns to the nonphysical, leaving behind any trace of the limiting aspects of your physical personality. You are much more than what you see in the fleshy body that appears as a reflection in the mirror. You have complete access to the broader part of you anytime you desire. First, you must become aware of the existence of your inner self, which remains in the nonphysical realm. Your inner self is powerful beyond measure. You have all the abilities you need to create a wonderful life experience when you align with your inner self.

Once you realize that you are the creator of your reality that you are the center of your universe and that you have an inner self that grants you full access to incredible abilities, you will have the power to transform your life experience. The more you are able to expand in this lifetime, the more you will expand your inner, nonphysical self as well. The key to creating the life of your dreams is in understanding the laws of the universe, the purpose of existence, and how to use universal forces to work in your favor.

II.

Anything can be achieved by aligning with universal forces. These forces are absolute and available to anyone at any time. If you have ever witnessed miraculous feats, spectacular performances, wondrous beauty, or incredible technological inventions, you have witnessed universal forces at work. Have you noticed that these incredible feats become even more? Records for physical competition continue to be broken. Many barriers that were believed to be absolute, such as the record for the fastest mile run (four minutes), have been overcome. Once that record was broken, many others overcame the same barrier within a very short amount of time. This was achieved due to the Law of Expansion.

The Law of Expansion states that as attention is given, the subject of the attention becomes more. If you focus your attention on something that fascinates you, your interest and knowledge of that subject will grow.

The rich will become richer, the poor will become poorer, the healthy will become healthier, and the sick will become sicker. The Law of Expansion is defined within the parameters of the Law of Attraction. The Law of Attraction creates the Law of Expansion. It is the nature of the universe. More becomes more and less becomes less.

The more you believe you are a success, the more success you will experience, until you no longer see yourself as a success, at which point you will experience failure. Then more failure will come to you until you've reached the bottom, at which point you will once again rise to your success. If you could maintain feelings of success, prosperity, and health, you would continue to create those realities in your life. As long as you can sustain your focus on the things you want without giving your attention to the things you don't want, you can continue to have a wonderful life experience. Paying attention to unwanted things makes them grow larger and expand as well.

Almost all of humanity focuses attention on the wanted and the unwanted simultaneously. You may want a child and then experience the birth of a beautiful baby who, in your eyes, is perfect in every way. As the baby grows, you may find aspects of the child who, at times, you judge unpleasing and you try to control the child's behavior to make yourself feel better. The more you try to control the child's behavior through discipline, the more the child will rebel. Your view of that perfect baby is now distorted by the view you hold of an unruly, rebellious teenager. Quite different realities, indeed. Does the child change or does your perception of the child change?

You may find the perfect job. In the beginning, everything is wonderful and you enjoy the people and the environment. You relish the satisfaction of a job well done and the process of creating with others. Then, one day, your spouse wonders why you haven't yet received a raise. Doubt creeps in and you start to feel unappreciated. The Law of Attraction reinforces your feelings and suddenly, out of the blue, you receive a reprimand from your employer. Your co-workers treat you differently. You no longer see the work as fulfilling and you determine that the job has changed and you begin to search for another one. However, the job, your employer, your co-workers did not change until your perception of the job changed.

According to the Law of Expansion, if you can maintain the positive perception of anything, it will continue to become even more positive. When you introduce doubt or fear into any situation, you reverse the Law of Expansion so that once positive circumstances become more and more negative.

If you were skilled in the understanding and practice of the Law of Expansion, you could reverse any negative momentum and start regaining positive expansion.

The Law of Expansion explains the cycles of your life experience. Your financial markets, your economy, your history, and your entire life experience is affected by cycles up and cycles down. When things are going well, the Law of Expansion makes everything better. When things are going poorly, the Law of Expansion makes them worse. However, the Law of Expansion is just a small component of the Law of Attraction and the Law of Attraction always supersedes the Law of Expansion. You are in total control of your reality and can control the Law of Expansion through deliberate focus of your thoughts, feelings, and emotions.

III.

All laws of the universe work within the main law which is the Law of Attraction. Another law which speaks to the eternal nature of the universe is the Law of Continuity. There is no end to the universe, which is always expanding. The universe is perfect but not complete. It is expanding and will never be complete. The Law of Continuity defines the process of expansion.

You, an eternal being, are temporarily focused in physical reality. When you die, you will be focused in a nonphysical reality until you decide to refocus into this physical reality once again. You are also never complete. You are also expanding along a continuous path of growth. You become more with each life and with each experience within each life. As you begin to understand more about the mechanism of the universe, you will grow exponentially. The understanding of universal laws and forces while you are physically focused is one of the highest forms of learning and understanding. The fact that you have been led to these pages indicates that you are on the leading edge of creation. You are one of the few who understand the broader perspective of physical reality. This is the understanding that will enhance your life experience to the degree that you realize that life is much more than it seems.

If you can understand that through the Law of Continuity, you are an everlasting being who is born into a physical reality and then transcends to a nonphysical reality and then again into a physical reality, continually on a journey of discovery and growth through many lives and life experiences, you will realize that each life is but a small part of that journey. You can relax, find ease, and discover a strong sense of relief in the knowing that there is no great purpose to one single life, but that it is the journey through many, many lives that allows you to grow and expand. The life you are living now is meant to be pleasurable and joyous. It is not meant to be taken so seriously. Think of each lifetime as a single day in your current life. If you have a bad day, it is not the end of the world, for there will be many more days ahead. You can start fresh tomorrow, so to speak.

As you realize that your existence through many lifetimes is a journey with no end or conclusion, you will understand that there is nothing that must be accomplished in this lifetime. You live this life as you please. You need not amass fortunes, build empires, save the world, fight anything, or live to be a hundred years old. You have done all of those things in previous lives and you will do all of them again in future life experiences. There is no rush, no worries, and no need to fear anything, especially death itself. Death is actually a very joyous and pleasurable experience.

There will be no judgment for the life you've lived during this experience in physical reality. You may enjoy a period of reflection, but you will be more eager to continue your interests once you are in the nonphysical realm. If you have a strong interest in a particular subject while here on earth in this physical lifetime, you will continue that interest into the nonphysical experience. You will work to help others who have the same interests. You will be intimately involved in and appreciate the lives of your family and friends who remain in physical reality. And, if you choose, you will return to another physical life experience.

Your purpose in this life experience is to discover that which thrills you. The interest you hold for any subject is the continuity of interest you held in other lives and in nonphysical reality. Your interests move and evolve over lifetimes and even within single lifetimes. But they continue along a path of growth. It is very important that you find your passion in life as soon as possible. That which excites you, that draws you in, is that which you are here to explore.

Your system of education is not designed to allow you the freedom to discover your passion. It is more like a container to keep children from escaping while their parents are at work or play. As a child, you were force-fed information that was not necessarily of interest to you at the time the information was provided. All information must be conveyed at the right time, and since every individual is unique, timing is different for each person. Therefore, your education system, which is set up to deliver the same information to many individuals at a specific point in time, is not effective in helping you discover your passion. In fact, it is disruptive to the natural path of learning that is unique to each individual. It is the main force holding your society back from the great heights it hopes to reach. As a child, you must be free to discover the world on your own and therefore allowed to find your interests at the time that is right for you.

Fortunately, the Law of Attraction works regardless of the conditions of your society. You may find your passion in the first sentence of a book you are forced to read in school. You may find your passion during an after-school activity. Your passion may be revealed to you while in the dream state. As long as you are actively searching for that which interests you, you will be filled with life-giving energy, even in circumstances that might hinder such discovery.

The school system, as well as social conditioning, may lead you down a path toward an end that is socially acceptable but has no true interest for you. The desire for money and fame masks the true interests of many in your culture. For these individuals, the quest for money and fame will likely lead to frustration and disappointment until they give up the useless effort of trying to prove their worthiness and return to the things they truly find interesting.

You may have been told by your teachers or parents that you did not possess the aptitude for a particular interest you once held. There are many reasons why so many of you do not pursue your interests, passions, and dreams. However, since it is the reason for your existence in this lifetime, it is in your best interest to discover or rediscover those passions as soon as you can.

Another aspect of the Law of Continuity is relationships which are also eternal. All relationships made in this lifetime will last forever. You may find this a welcome fact or a troublesome one, depending on the particular relationship. However, the roles you play in this life experience do not carry over to nonphysical life experience. In this life, your mother is your mother and you are the child. In another life experience, you may have been brothers, or best friends or terrible foes. You explore the various aspects of your intertwined relationship over each life experience. You do this to learn, to expand, and because it's fun.

All of your relationships are eternal, no matter how intimate or brief. You are tied eternally to each and every person you know and many who you have not met in this life. The bond you hold in this lifetime makes no difference because you are truly bonded throughout eternity. Your best friend you may have lost contact with will again be your friend in the nonphysical. Your relationship with someone who has died is stronger now than it was when that person was with you in this physical reality, it's just that you notice that this person is no longer around. But if you knew how the universe works - through the Law of Continuity - you would realize that this person is closer to you than ever and that you have even more access to them now. You will come to learn this as you discover more about the mechanism of the universe.

Now that you know that each and every relationship you have and have ever had is eternal, don't you feel a sense of relief? Doesn't it make the subject of relationships easier for you? Since you cannot break a relationship, you don't have to try so hard to make them work. You can be easy about each relationship, knowing you are linked together forever and nothing you can do will harm the relationship. Others cannot harm you either, for you are eternally linked, whether they realize it or not. It's life conditions that work to undermine relationships. Once you understand this concept, you can create the relationships of your dreams.

IV.

Within the larger framework of the Law of Attraction is the Law of Vibrations. Everything that exists in the universe, whether it is physical or nonphysical, exists in vibrational terms. You are a vibrational being and so are all other humans, life forms, and objects on your planet. The chair you're sitting on is a vibrational representation of a chair that is unique to your vibrational perception of the chair. The food you eat is vibrational. It vibrates aromas you can smell, flavors you can taste, texture you can feel, colors you can see, sizzle you can hear, and mass you can sense.

Sound is the easiest vibration to recognize because you are already aware that it is vibration. You may also be aware that light is vibration and what you see is vibration emitting from or reflecting off of objects. Sight, like all of your senses, is an interpretation of vibration. Taste is the act of interpreting vibration though your taste buds and translating it into the flavors of the foods you eat. Likewise, the sense of smell is also the translation of vibration. These vibrations make up your physical reality.

Vibrations are not static. They are constantly in motion, shifting and evolving. No vibration is translated identically by any two people. The interpretation of each vibration is unique to the perception of each individual.

A Perception of Reality

Since all perception is unique, then all translation of vibration is unique. However, you have made agreements that form the basis of your reality. When you smell an orange slice, that aroma is unique to you, but since its vibration is relatively consistent, you agree that the smell is that of an orange, all while having no knowledge whatsoever about what others are really translating into the smell of an orange slice. You agree that the color you see as orange is the same color that everyone else sees. This is because the vibration, not the color, is consistent. Therefore, you can copy the color in ink or paint and call it orange and others will agree.

You agree that vibrations in general mean similar things, but these are just simplified versions of their meaning. The meaning or representation of any vibration depends on the perception of the individual. Therefore, each vibration means something different to each individual. That's why your method of verbal and written communication is so inadequate.

Words and ideas are also vibrations. Each word carries a vibrational signal and the word is translated by your brain as you receive it. However, unlike colors or flavors, word vibrations carry many different meanings depending on the delivery method of the words and the emotional states of the sender and receiver at the time the word is delivered and received.

If you are in an emotional state of depression and someone says "I love you," you will receive those words differently than if you were in an emotional state of joy. If you and the receiver are both in an emotional state of joy and you say "I hate you," it will most likely be taken humorously because your state of being does not vibrationally match those words. Communication depends entirely on the emotional state of the deliverer of the message and the receiver of the message. Therefore, all vibration is translated differently depending on one's emotional state of being.

Vibrations, through the Law of Attraction, are drawn to similar vibrations. Victims, through their vibration, are drawn to victimizers. Lovers are brought together in the same way enemies are brought together. Good thoughts attract more good thoughts and unpleasant thoughts attract other unpleasant thoughts. It's the vibration of the thing that is attracted to another similar or compatible vibration. This is the essence of the Law of Attraction and it is completed through vibration.

You are a vibration that is the sum of your feelings, emotions, and thoughts at this moment in time. In the next moment, your vibration will be slightly different. Your vibration, as you might have realized by the nature of vibrations, is not static. It is constantly moving, shifting, and evolving. If you feel joy in this moment, your vibration changes to include the joy you are feeling. Unless you can sustain that joy, your vibration will return to a baseline state of vibration.

You can raise and lower your vibration very easily at times. It requires more focus to shift your vibration to a new, higher frequency and to maintain that frequency so that it becomes the new standard or baseline. Your knowledge of the concept of vibration will be of great assistance to you when you are ready to raise your vibration. The first step is to understand the nature of vibrational reality and the second step is to consciously create the desire to raise your vibration. The Law of Attraction will do the rest.

V.

The basis of the universe is well-being. The basis of your life and the world you live in is also one of well-being. You may experience momentary periods of crisis, but if you look back on your life in general, it has been one of calm, ease, and comfort. Your memory of life may not lead you to this conclusion because your memory is that of the events in your life and not the periods between the events. The predominance of your life has been and will continue to be one of well-being.

Well-being is a natural state of being for you, your planet, the inhabitants of your planet, and the inhabitants of the nonphysical realm. It's the baseline state of all existence. It's a state of ease, comfort, and safety. Any movement from this state is temporary and it is always easy to return to it.

Your life is one of ease unless you focus on difficulty, frustration, or hardship. You are guided and provided for. There is no lack unless you focus on lack. There is no struggle unless you create struggle through your thoughts of fear or lack. Your life is to be enjoyed fully, and this can be easily accomplished when you realize you are worthy, loved, and the center of attention in your universe.

The memory of your past as you perceive it from that narrow, limited view holds you back from the feeling of well-being when you focus on memories that do not feel good to you. Your memory can be of assistance to you when you focus on memories that feel good. It is the feeling that guides you. The thoughts, feelings, and emotions that feel good help you to understand that well-being abounds. The thoughts, feelings, and emotions that feel bad let you know that you are holding yourself apart from the experience of well-being.

There is tremendous energy in the universe, and you have access to that energy. It is a power that lights up worlds, creates all beauty, and is the force behind all creativity. It is endless and infinite, and you can harness it for your own purposes. You are a creator, and your creation is you in this physical environment. You are given an inner self to guide you as you pursue your interests, your life's passions, and your dreams. The power of the universe is here to support you in whatever it is you desire. In order to use this power to your advantage, you must deliberately create your life. You must move toward desires and not push against things unwanted. The power of the universe is great, but it must be controlled like any such power.

Electricity is beneficial when used to power your lights and appliances. However, without proper care, it can start fires or shock you. This is an oversimplification of the power of the universe, but you get our meaning. When directed properly, electricity is extremely beneficial. When not handled correctly, it has the potential to bring unwanted things.

The concept that you can deliberately create a life experience that is pleasing may be a new one for you. You have been using the power of the universe to create your life up to this point whether you realized it or not. The deliberate creation of your life experience means you utilize these universal forces to act in your favor to bring life experiences and manifestations that you desire. It also means you are not thrown into situations that you do not desire.

Deliberate creation requires focus. It is the practice of directing thoughts, feelings, and emotions toward the things you desire and not against the things you do not want. Your focus must be unencumbered by doubt or fear. It must be clear on the path to your dreams without worry about future outcomes. You must be based in present time and not focused too far into the future.

If you could simply hold the good-feeling thoughts of things you want and pay less attention to the things you don't want or don't like, you would move quickly to a greatly improved life experience. There is never a positive reason to think about or discuss anything unwanted. The thoughts or discussions about things unwanted only engage the Law of Attraction to increase the potential for those unwanted things to be experienced in your life. Deliberate creation is the focus of attention on the wanted and the lack of attention to things unwanted.

Most humans talk more about unwanted things than wanted things. Anything that seems unjust is often the topic of passionate discussion. "We must fight this injustice!" you say. "We must rid the world of it!" You cannot rid the world of anything by giving your attention to it. It is the Law of Attraction, not the Law of Obliteration. The way to fight against anything is to desire its opposite. Instead of a war of drugs, you might desire tolerance, understanding, and compassion for those who are searching for a way to feel better. Instead of fighting to wipe out disease, you may desire alignment with well-being and health. The path to a world you prefer is found through your attention to that which you desire and not by pushing against anything unwanted.

The laws of the universe and the universal powers are there to assist you in deliberately creating the life you prefer. The laws work whether you want them to or not, whether you understand them fully or are ignorant of them entirely, whether you believe in them or don't. You can harness these powers with techniques we will explain in great detail. You will, through your desire, your focus, your intention, your patience and your practice, create the life of your dreams. This we *KNOW*.

Chapter Two

Emotions, Feelings, and Thoughts

You create your life through your thoughts, feelings, and emotions. The sum of these thoughts, feelings, and emotions make up your vibrational signal. You attract whatever matches your signal, both in the long and short term. If you are feeling angry today, you will be shown symbols that reflect that anger in the same day. If over your lifetime you predominantly feel like a victim, you will experience victimization over the course of your life. If you predominantly live a life of joy, you will experience far more joy in your life than someone who predominantly feels frustration.

Your emotions come from your inner self and help guide you through life. If you understand how they work, you can use them as guidance toward that which you desire. They let you know when you get off track. Your emotions can help you make the best of a good situation and they can let you know when you are making a bad situation even worse.

Your thoughts, feelings, and emotions precede your manifestations. Manifestations can be thought of as good or bad, depending on your perspective. A new car is a wonderful manifestation. An automobile accident is likely perceived in the moment as an unwanted manifestation. A smile from a stranger is a manifestation. A rude comment from your spouse is also a manifestation. Both wanted and unwanted manifestations are always preceded by thoughts, feelings, and emotions.

If you want to attract more positive manifestations into your life, simply think more thoughts of joy and practice feeling good. If you can feel the emotion of joy now, while sitting in your chair or lying in bed, you will encounter manifestations that reflect how you are feeling. They will be manifestations you deem positive. The opposite is true as well. When you think thoughts of hate, when you feel the emotion of hate, you will attract more hateful manifestations.

You have complete control over your thoughts in this exact moment. Think a thought now. What was the thought? Was it pleasant or unpleasant? That's all you need to know. Was the thought a good-feeling thought or a bad-feeling thought? Good-feeling thoughts bring good-feeling manifestations and thoughts that feel bad bring manifestations that feel bad. In this moment, you can choose a pleasant or an unpleasant thought. It's completely up to you. By the Law of Attraction, the more pleasant thoughts you think, the more pleasant thoughts you will attract. This is also true of unpleasant thoughts. The nice thing is that you have utter control of your thoughts.

Because you have absolute control of your thoughts, you have the complete control to deliberately create your life experience. Since no one else can control your thoughts, they cannot create in your experience. You may think others have some control over your thoughts, but they do not. You are in control, and you have a choice to make in each moment. Your thoughts are not as random as you may think. It's just that you have never thought to deliberately choose your thoughts. It is a skill to be practiced like any other.

Like most humans, you believe that each thought is created in your mind as an original thought. You see your mind as a "thought factory" constantly churning out thoughts one after the other. A more accurate representation of how your mind works is a radio. Thoughts are **received** by your mind. You reach for thoughts and they appear.

You can only receive the thoughts you are vibrationally ready to receive. You tune yourself to the frequency and then receive the thought. This is all done automatically without your conscious awareness. You receive random thoughts that swirl uncontrollably in your head. There are so many thoughts appearing and disappearing that you have trouble keeping track of them. You often find yourself losing thoughts that seemed important. You have yet to control how thoughts are received. Like most humans, you have never been taught to regulate the flow and quality of your thoughts.

Eastern civilizations in general have more knowledge and practice in the area of thought control. Meditation is a good method for learning the control of thoughts. Once you understand that thoughts are received and not created, you can deliberately choose which ones enter your mind. Meditation allows you to stop thought altogether for a period of time, even though, at first, it may be brief. Once you are practiced in meditation, you can achieve a state of prolonged absence of thought.

If you sit in your chair now and close your eyes, you can identify the next thought that enters your mind. What is the thought? Where did it come from? What does it mean? Who is thinking the thought? You are thinking the thought or, more accurately, you are experiencing the thought. Think of the thought as a very small movie in your mind. You did not create the movie; you are simply watching it. Since you are not the creator of the thought, simply the receiver, what does this mean to you?

If you can understand that you receive thoughts and you do not create them, your perspective can change. Because you believed you were the creator of thoughts, you believed you had less control. Your thoughts simply sprang fourth as if from a fountain. You had little control of what came from the fountain and the speed at which it came.

Since thoughts are received, you can receive any thought you wish. Through your vibration, you ask for thoughts. You attract thoughts. And those thoughts are actually manifestations of your feelings or emotional state of being.

If you are feeling fearful, you may attract fearful thoughts. These thoughts are then the manifestation of your feelings. They reinforce, through the Law of Attraction, your feelings. If you are feeling joyous, you will receive thoughts that reinforce your feelings of joy. Thoughts are therefore manifestations, and just like a new house or a new car, they come after the feeling.

You can greatly change the quality of your thoughts as you change your feelings. Thoughts are the first signs of what you're feeling. They come before physical manifestation. Thoughts are easy to receive and are the best mirror to reflect your overall feelings or current vibrational state.

You have the ability, whether you know it or not, to stop the reception of unpleasant thoughts and to receive good-feeling thoughts. The act of deliberately reaching for good-feeling thoughts will have an effect on your feelings and your vibrational signal. It is easier to change your thoughts than your feelings. Your feelings are like a large ship in the ocean and your thoughts are like the rudder. You move your thoughts in one direction, and the feelings will slowly move in that direction as well. If left without movement of the rudder, however, the ship will not change course.

Emotions, Feelings, and Thoughts

You cannot eradicate unpleasant thoughts from your mind. Once they are there, there's no use in getting rid of the thought. It has already arrived. Once you've opened the letter and read the contents, setting fire to it will do no good. You've already read it. Thoughts cannot be destroyed.

The tool for receiving fewer unpleasant thoughts is to ask for more pleasant thoughts. To strive for the best-feeling thought you can find at the moment is the practice of deliberate creation. The thoughts you consciously choose have the ability to change your life, just as the rudder has the ability to alter the course of a ship at sea.

Once you have noticed that an unpleasant thought has entered your mind and you are aware of it, you can ask for a better-feeling thought. After some practice, you will find that better-feeling thoughts come quickly and easily. It might help to have an idea of what better-feeling thoughts are ahead of time. Do you have a pet you love? If you think of your pet, is that a nice-feeling thought? Do you love nature? Thoughts of the blue sky, the ocean, mountains, trees, or wild animals may be good-feeling thoughts to you. Have these thoughts ready so that when an unpleasant thought has been drawn in, you can quickly and easily replace it with a better-feeling thought.

There is no need to dwell on unpleasant thoughts. You cannot eradicate them once and for all by thinking more and more about the subject. If it feels bad to think about it, then think about something that feels good. Due to the Law of Attraction, the more you receive unpleasant thoughts, the more unpleasant thoughts will arrive. The more you dwell on an issue, the larger it will get. Momentum is added to pleasant and unpleasant thoughts alike. You can't resolve a problem by dwelling on it. You are not in a position to receive the solution when you're plagued by the problem.

The higher your vibration, the more access you have to thoughts at this higher vibration. The reverse is also true. The lower your vibration, the more access you have to low-vibrational thoughts. It is easy to understand high and low vibration. A high vibration is one of joy, happiness, confidence, security, love, passion, excitement, understanding, clarity, etc. A low vibration is one that resonates with fear, hatred, despair, mourning, violence, rage, etc. Low vibrations attract thoughts (manifestations) of that frequency. High vibrations attract thoughts (manifestations) of that frequency.

You do not receive high-frequency thoughts when you have low-frequency feelings, and vice versa.

Your vibration can change quickly; in as little as a single minute, you can move from a lower-frequency feeling to a higher-frequency feeling. We will talk more about this later. For now just understand that the thoughts you receive are manifestations of the feelings, or frequency you emit.

If you are having a great time with friends and you trip and fall, you are likely to laugh. You are in a high-frequency state and the thoughts available to you in this state are high-frequency thoughts. If you are at a business function and are feeling nervous and insecure when you trip, you might feel the emotion of embarrassment. Your insecure feelings bring insecure thoughts. Your thoughts are the manifestation of your feelings. Change your state of being and you change the quality of thoughts you have access to.

Great discoveries and achievements have always been preceded by the individual attaining higher levels of vibration and therefore gaining access to thoughts at that new level. Acts of tragedy are always preceded by individuals who have access only to lower-vibrational thoughts. If you attain a high-vibrational state, the thoughts available to you in that state are full of creative potential and, through those thoughts, you can reach even higher levels of vibration. The thoughts available to you when you are in the throes of depression are those that reinforce your depressed emotional state. When in a high vibrational state, your thoughts can bring you even higher, and when in a low vibrational state, your thoughts can take you even lower.

We have just stated that when you are in a low vibrational state, you do not have access to thoughts that resonate at a higher vibration. So how is it that one can bring themselves, through thoughts they have no access to, up to a high vibrational state? The answer is that you can't move straight from a low vibrational state to a high vibrational state in one quick jump. You can, however, slowly steer the ship so that it turns in the general direction of the higher vibrational state. You can't go right from a state of fear to a state of joy. You could if you won the lottery, but that is not a vibrationally accurate statement. Someone who predominantly lives in fear is not going to win the lottery, and if they did they would not find it a pleasant experience. We will discuss this concept later. The point is that you must change your vibrational state incrementally.

II.

Your feelings create your reality. If you are able to harness the creative energy of your feelings, you can move your life toward the manifestations and life experiences you desire. Your feelings precede your life experiences. They foretell the life you will be living. Your feelings are translated first into thought manifestations and then into physical manifestations. Most humans do not understand this creative aspect of being physical, so they are not able to harness the power of their feelings to create the life experiences that please them.

Your feelings create your thoughts and your thoughts create your reality. It's as simple as that. Practice the feeling of what you want and you will attract thoughts that will lead you to what you desire. You must conjure the feeling of what you desire first. If you want a mate, you must imagine what it would be like to have the partner of your dreams. You must experience the feeling of that before the mate can arrive. What does the feeling of the perfect mate feel like to you? Don't think about the physical details of your perfect mate. Instead, think of how it would feel to have that person in your life.

Let's examine some of the feelings you might have when feeling for that person you desire:

Would you like to be loved?

Would you like to love another?

Would it be fun?

Would you feel secure?

Would you enjoy the co-creative process when being together with the person of your dreams?

Would you like to have someone to share life experiences with?

How do each of these things feel to you?

What is the basis of feeling behind each aspect of desire when contemplating a new mate?

If you can reach the innermost feeling aspect of that which you desire, it will appear in your physical experience.

A Perception of Reality

Let's look at the desire for money:

How would it feel to have enough money?

What feelings would you have when you have all the money you need?

Would you feel free?

Would you feel powerful?

Would you have fun with the money?

Would you create something with the money?

Would you share the money?

How would it feel in each of these questions to have the money you want?

Can you get to the feeling of freedom?

Can you achieve the feeling of abundance now?

This is your work. You can feel your way to anything you desire. It will manifest first in your thoughts, then in your physical experience. We will show you how to accomplish this in your life.

Now, let's examine the desire to have an improved physical body:

What would it be like to have a better-feeling body?

Would you also have freedom?

Would you also have joy?

Could you do more activities with a better-feeling body?

Would it be fun?

How does it feel to be healthy?

The process is the same with your body as it is with anything else you desire. Simply practice the feelings of the improvements you desire and the thoughts will follow. The manifestation of the improvements **will** arrive. It is somewhat easier to create a better-feeling body if you believe that the practice of feeling good will absolutely result in a better-feeling body because, for most of you, you once had a good-feeling body at some point in your life. If you can think back to a time when your body felt good to you, maybe a period in your youth, and if you practice those feelings you remember having as a child, your body will improve.

As a child you used your body for play. You allowed the energy of the universe to flow fully. While you were awake you had an excess of energy and you enjoyed it. While you were asleep you slept undisturbed. If you can focus on how that felt to you, and believe that by the practice of those feelings your body will improve, it ***will*** improve. This is the nature of physical reality.

However, if you believe that you are destined to live alone without the partner of your dreams, without enough money, and to succumb to the deteriorating body you see in the mirror, then those experiences will continue, just as you have designed. You see, feelings of loneliness, of lack of money, and of a declining body are just as valid to the universe as feelings of joy, happiness, and abundance. It matters not to the universe what you feel. You are free to feel anything, and the universe, through the Law of Attraction, will deliver the physical manifestations of your feelings.

Feelings come first, then thought, and then physical manifestation. We will discuss in a later chapter how all this works in greater detail, but for now please understand that the process is simple: *WHAT YOU PREDOMINANTLY FEEL CREATES THE PREDOMINANCE OF YOUR THOUGHTS WHICH CREATE YOUR REALITY.*

III.

Emotion is guidance from within. If you are an emotional person, you have an excellent guidance system. If you have little emotion, you will have to learn to understand the benefits of emotion. We will speak about the benefits of emotion in terms of your desires, not in terms of those unwanted experiences. When you have established a strong desire, your emotions act as a system of guidance to let you know how you are progressing.

Simply stated, your emotions let you know if you are on the path to that which you desire. The universe knows what you want by the feelings you have, not by your words. The universe knows what you truly desire by the vibration you emit through your feelings. Writing a list of wanted things is not the same, because you cannot possibly articulate either the essence or the entirety of what it is that you truly want. Your language lacks the necessary nuances to properly communicate that which you really desire. You could write an entire book on one specific thing you want and still not capture the fullness of your desire. It just isn't possible with language.

A Perception of Reality

Your specific desire emanates from your being through vibration and the universe understands the specific frequency you are emitting. That frequency is truly unique, and there are exact matches to your frequency all around you. You could not consciously identify the matches or the steps toward those matches by yourself. But the universe can see those matches, and it works to bring you together with that which you desire. The universe brings you the perfect match in the most elegant way, and the result will often exceed your wildest idea of what you consciously thought you wanted.

Your emotions help you stay on-track, moving toward your desire. When you understand how emotion works to bring you a match to your desire, you will know how to work with your emotions instead of against them. Simply stated, if you have a good-feeling emotion, you are on track, and if you experience a bad-feeling emotion, you are going off-track. The more you can keep on-track, the quicker your desire will manifest into your physical reality.

Good-feeling emotions include joy, interest, excitement, passion, love, happiness, pride, goose bumps, fun, laughter, hope, relief, abundance, confidence, security, harmony, peace, understanding, compassion, generosity, aptitude, acceptance, etc.

Bad-feeling emotions include frustration, judgment, fear, hatred, lack, envy, overwhelmment, doubt, malice, failure, scarcity, hopelessness, depression, sorrow, anger, etc.

Any emotion that feels good lets you know that you're moving in the direction of your desire. Any emotion that feels bad lets you know that you're moving away from your desire. Your desires manifest over time. Remember; it's the journey to the manifestation that is the fulfilling part, not the actual manifestation itself. Once you've achieved the manifestation, it will not hold the importance it once did. You will be off to the next desire. So really, the longer it takes to manifest your desire, the better. If your desires manifested instantly, you would not be as happy with the process as you would be with those that take some time.

The journey toward those things you desire is life-giving. It truly is not about the end result; it's about the satisfaction of using your powers to move toward and then actualize the manifestation. You will come to find that the larger the desire, the more satisfaction you will receive. Your emotions are guideposts along the way. Use them as such and you will enjoy the journey more fully.

Your emotions erupt within you as manifestations occur. The universe is working to bring you closer to that which you desire, and it must lead you there step by step, until you are ready for the physical manifestation. If you were to manifest what you desired instantly, you would not be ready for the ramifications of that desire and your life experience would actually be lessened as a result.

Let's say you wanted more money and bought a lottery ticket. If you were vibrationally ready for the winnings, you would have a wonderful experience. You would know all the ways to enjoy the money. You would have been led over time, step by step, to a place of readiness to receive the money. You would know how to handle the money, where to invest it, how to pay the taxes, how to plan for the future, what to buy, how to act, and how much to donate. You would know how to handle the relatives and friends who would come to you asking for money. You would know how to see the signs others emit when only interested in your money. You would not fear losing the money. You would not live to excess or try to be someone you are not. You would be completely ready in every way and your life experience would improve as a result. The money would be a welcome addition to your life and only there as another step toward the attainment of another, even larger desire. The money would come when needed to fulfill another desire. When you looked back, it would seem only natural that the money arrived in the manner in which it manifested.

If, however, you simply won the money without taking all the steps necessary for you to be ready for it, the money would create unhappiness in your life. You might think it would solve all of your problems, but it would actually cause more of them. If you were not vibrationally ready for the money, you would not know what to do with it to improve your life experience. You might feel guilt and end up giving it to family or friends who are also not ready for it. You might feel insecurity and try to buy your way to security, but unless you had vibrationally prepared yourself, you would experience even greater depths of insecurity. You might spend the money too quickly and incur the ridicule of others. You might have continued feelings of scarcity and horde the money, thereby incurring the hatred of your once close friends and family. Looking back, you would wish you never won the lottery in the first place.

The universe will take as long as necessary to lead you, incrementally, to that which you truly desire. You will never be unprepared for the manifestation of your dreams when it finally arrives as long as you have paid attention to your emotions along the way. The universe is busy preparing you, not the manifestation. If you are vibrationally far from your manifestation, there will be more steps to achieve before the desire is actualized into your reality. Please trust us. You want it to work this way.

If you miss a step along the way, the universe will quickly provide it again for you. You are constantly progressing toward your desire, even if at times it does not feel like it in the moment. When you perceive a setback and think of it as being wrong in the way it occurred, you will receive, as guidance from within, negative emotion. If it feels bad, then you're off-track. You must stop and realize it was not a setback; it was indeed a step on the path to your desire. As soon as you realize this, you will be flooded with positive emotion. Goosebumps are one of the most positive emotions. If you feel goosebumps, you are really on your way.

Why would the universe provide a step you perceive as wrong or as a setback of some kind? It's because the universe is morphing you into the version of you that will be ready when the manifestation arrives. You, in the current version of you, in your current state of being, in your current vibrational pattern, are not ready for that which you desire. You will be moved physically and spiritually into a form of being that matches your desire. Once you've transcended to that version of reality that is a perfect match to what you desire, you will be changed forever. The you that you knew then no longer exists. You will be able to look back and realize that fact. You might even say aloud, "I can't believe I was that person back then. I am so different now." It is the universe that worked its magic to transform you into the version of you that you needed to be in order to achieve the reality of your desire. Period.

As you have lived your life to this point, you have had many desires all intertwined simultaneously. Your guidance system is always working to assist you with each desire. You are receiving messages of emotion at every turn. One emotion is guiding you toward one desire and the next emotion is guiding you toward another desire. This can be confusing even if you have a clear understanding of how your emotional guidance system works. Don't worry about how a single emotion is affecting any particular desire. Instead, view each emotion as a sign that, in the moment, your feeling is contrary to your overall set of desires.

A good-feeling emotion means you're on-track toward all of your desires. The more good-feeling emotions you have, the faster you will arrive at all of the desires you're asking for. If you experience an emotion that feels bad, you know something has happened that is part of your progress toward your desire. It is not necessary to identify which desire is causing the unpleasant emotion, but you can if you want to.

If you were able to experience an unpleasant emotion and realize you had just had an experience that is an integral part of the metamorphosis that must take place in order for you to change so you will be ready for the manifested desire, you would thrive in this lifetime. You could actually see the manifestation event in progress and know you're on your way toward your desire. You would no longer see the event as a setback, but instead you would recognize the event for what it is: an integral part of the process. We will call these occurrences "Manifestation Events."

Manifestation events are those events, circumstances, thoughts, people, articles, news items, conversations, etc. that come to you along your path to your desire. Some manifestation events are fun and enjoyable, while others may seem quite painful. Think of your first relationship as a teenager. You might have been madly in love, but eventually the relationship ended. And while it was painful at the time, the relationship and the break-up changed you forever. It changed you in a way that was part of the progression to who you are now. If you are currently in a wonderful, loving relationship, the break-up of this initial romance was a manifestation event along the way. It was part of the transformation of you that allowed you to morph into the version of you that would be ready for the relationship you now enjoy.

If you are currently in a relationship that is not fulfilling, then this experience may be preparing you for the relationship of your dreams. This unfulfilling relationship is fine tuning you so you will be ready for the relationship that *is* fulfilling. You are experiencing what you do not like so you can determine more precisely what you do like. And when that preferable mate comes along, you will recognize it as the relationship you truly desire.

If you are not prepared for your desire vibrationally, you will not be able to recognize it when it comes. It will be wrapped up in a package that appears to be something other than that which you desire. Unless you are vibrationally tuned to the frequency of that which you desire, you will miss it when it comes. Don't worry, the universe will keep bringing you manifestation events until you become vibrationally ready to recognize and receive the object of your desire.

For now it is important that you understand how the universe works to bring you to your desire. You ask for that which you want through your feelings, not your words. The universe understands everything you want and works to bring about the changes in you necessary to make you vibrationally ready to recognize your desire when it comes. You are not vibrationally ready for what you desire at the time you want it; otherwise, it would already have manifested in your life.

If it is not already physically actualized in your life, then you are not vibrationally ready. If it is in your life, then you *are* vibrationally ready. You are vibrationally ready for the car you drive in this present moment, but you are not vibrationally ready for the car of your dreams. You are vibrationally ready for the dwelling you live in now, but you are not vibrationally ready for the home of your dreams.

You are, however, becoming vibrationally ready for everything you desire. The more easily you allow yourself to be molded into the version of you that is ready for each new desire, the faster your desires will physically manifest. You must be malleable like soft clay. You must be open to accepting the changes that must be made in order to become a vibrational match to what you want. One of the ways to make it easy for the universe to mold you is to be open to new ideas. We know this will be much easier for you than most humans because you are reading this book right now. You have attracted this book and are vibrationally ready for much (though not all) of the content contained within its pages. You are one who is open to new ideas.

If you want your desires to come to you easily, you must be able to accept new ideas easily. You must be able to accept the pleasant and unpleasant manifestation events equally. There really are no unpleasant manifestation events, but only your narrow perception of the events at the time of their occurrence. If you understand that each event is necessary to move you toward your goal, you can look at each event in a new light. You cannot see the path to your desires. You make up paths in your mind and when it seems like you're going backward, you are actually, truly moving forward. If you can accept this fact as reality, you can achieve anything you desire.

It would be fun to be in a relationship that ends badly and, while the other person is breaking up with you, to calmly say, "Thank you. This has been an incredibly enlightening experience and has moved me closer to finding the person of my dreams. By your unpleasant actions I have discovered in more detail what I really want, and it isn't you." If you could say that and be filled with positive emotion, you would find true love quickly and easily.

But alas, most humans do not see manifestation events for what they are. They see these events as reinforcing their feelings of unworthiness. We will discuss this topic in greater detail, but for now, we hope we have enlightened you about the nature of feelings, thoughts, and emotions. These are all part of your inner world. This is your inner reality, which you have not understood and may have even ignored or suppressed until now. These are the tools given to you at birth, but due to the life you have lived so far, with influences from parents, teachers, and society in general, you have forgotten how to use them. Now that you know how to use these tools to your benefit, you have unleashed the power of the universe, and your world has suddenly become a much more interesting place.

Chapter Three

Manifestation Events

Your life is meant to be filled with joy, fun, interest, and passion. You are meant to have strong desire. You are meant to fulfill your dreams. This is your reason for being. You enjoy the thrill of the chase, the moving toward the goal, the journey toward desire. The manifestation of the desire is but a small part of the joy of life.

We want you to have many large manifestations. We want you to have the home, car, money, and relationship of your dreams. Most of all, we want you to enjoy the process. It is the process that is life-giving, and the process is never ending. The process of moving from desire to manifestation never ends, not in this life, not in the afterlife, and not in the next life. You are constantly morphing into a new version of you as you move from desire to manifestation to new desire to its manifestation and so on.

There really is no point in holding a desire and thinking your life will be perfect once you attain that which you desire. Just as soon as it manifests, a new desire will appear and you'll be on to that one. Those who have accepted this principle enjoy wonderful lives filled with abundance and fun. They move easily toward bigger and brighter dreams. Those of you who believe that if you could just get a certain sum of money and your life would be easy have missed the point altogether and will struggle through this existence. You are meant to pursue your interests, passions, and dreams with zest and vigor. You are meant to roll with the punches and understand that they are not setbacks but only little taps on the shoulder guiding you directly toward your dreams.

Everything that happens is a manifestation event. Every thought, every contact, every idea, every conversation you overhear, every person you meet, everything you read, is leading you toward that which you desire. If your vibration is clear and focused on the thing you desire, then each manifestation event is leading you in the right direction. If you have doubt, then the manifestation events may be providing evidence of your uncertainty. This is why it is difficult for many people to change. Their reality is providing ample evidence of their vibration, which may include a fair amount of doubt. Know that the universe is helping you become a vibrational match to what you want. If doubt is included in the vibrational idea of your desire, you will receive manifestation events that include some doubt to the extent that it exists in the vibrational mix of your desire.

Every desire is an actualized reality in vibrational terms. Imagine for a moment that you birth a desire and you can see it emanate from your body and float up into the air in front of you. It actually exists, and you can see it. It has color and it shimmers and glows as it hovers there in the middle of the room. It is not static, but rather is constantly changing. It grows larger and smaller and larger again. It changes shape and color and intensity. It glows brighter and then dimmer. All of these things happen as you change the feeling of that desire. At one moment, you are in anticipation of the desire and the desire grows larger and brighter. In the next moment, you have doubt that it will ever manifest and the object gets smaller and dimmer. It is always a match to how you feel about it. You are always moving toward your desire. The better you feel about the desire and its manifestation, the easier your journey will be.

Doubt and fear keep you from manifesting anything you desire. The Law of Attraction responds to doubt and fear just as it does to the knowing and the confident aspects of your desire. Most of your desires are a mixed bag of knowing and doubt, of hope and fear. The clearer you can become about your desire, the easier it will be for you to transform into the vibrational version of you that is ready for the full manifestation of your desire.

Clarity is the key.

The idea of any desire can be general in nature or more specific. The more specific you get, the greater the possibility that doubt and fear will enter the vibrational pattern of your desire. The less specific or more general you become, the easier it is to be free from doubt and fear. The more specific you are, the faster the desire will manifest into your reality. The idea is to be as specific as you can without allowing fear or doubt to enter the vibrational pattern of the desire.

Being general means widening your focus. Thinking about the broader aspects of your desire makes it easier to leave out fear and doubt. To be general means to think in terms of thoughts that feel good as you think those thoughts. If fear and doubt creep into your thoughts, you are not being general enough.

For example, let's say you want a new car. In order to transform your desire into a vibrational pattern that the universe can be aware of and start working on, you fill the pattern with ideas of what you want. You know what you don't want because you are now driving a car you do not like. So you are careful not to include unwanted things in your desire. You can't get the car of your dreams by thinking about the aspects of your current vehicle you do not like. You can't say, "I want a car that doesn't break down every five minutes." You must only include those aspects you ***do*** want.

So now you have a car in mind. Your first thought is that it should be reliable and dependable. This is important to you because your last car was quite the opposite. You think, "I want a reliable car." If you leave it at that without fear or doubt, with the knowing that the universe will bring you a reliable car, the manifestation of such a car will happen quickly and easily. You are being general. To speed up your manifestation, you practice the feelings of what it would be like to drive a reliable car. You feel free, you feel ease, it feels good.

That was a general desire and while you are likely to get a reliable car, you're not going to receive the car of your dreams. Maybe you've had such a hard time with your unreliable car that any dependable car **would** be the car of your dreams. In that case, the universe delivered to you the perfect manifestation of your dreams. So you drive around in this dependable car and come to realize you would prefer a nicer-looking vehicle or a new model, or even a sporty convertible.

You birth a new desire for the universe to work on. This time your desire is more specific. You want a brand-new red convertible made in Europe. This is a more specific desire and you practice the feelings of what it would be like to own this shiny new vehicle. You see yourself driving it along the coast with full control and a rush of adrenaline as you stomp the accelerator to the floor. The vibrational pattern of your desire grows larger and brighter. Oh no, are you going too fast? Is there a policeman around the corner? Are you going to fly into the ocean? The vibrational pattern of your desire now shrinks and grows a little dimmer. The universe responds to the vibrational pattern of your new desire.

One day you experience several manifestation events. You see three cars that are identical to the one of your dreams. The people driving the cars seem happy and pleased with the car. Then, you see a cop at the side of the road giving some unfortunate person a ticket. You read an article about how wonderfully your dream car handles on coastal roads. Later that evening, you see a news report about a similar car being pulled from a canal. The universe has provided you with manifestational events that exactly match the muddled vibrational pattern of your desire. At the end of the day, the universe has actually helped you become even less clear of your desire. It has worked perfectly to match your desire's vibrational pattern. Your desire for the new car grows, as do your doubts and fears. This is the reason so many people have difficulty achieving their dreams.

II.

Thoughts of doubt and fear are just as valid in the eyes of the universe as thoughts of hope and joy. The universe responds to all thought in the same general way. This is a good thing. It is balance. It was designed this way. If you are predominantly thinking thoughts of fear, it is the intermittent yet persistent thoughts of hope that keep well-being flowing to you. It is right that the system works this way.

Throughout the history of humanity most people lived lives of struggle and hardship based on fear. They struggled against the elements and against their fellow man. Most thought was negative in nature. Over time, man gradually became hopeful. This hopefulness brought about great change. Many learned of the inner mechanism of self. Some spread the word. A small group of people learned that reality could be altered from within. The masses grew generally more hopeful in nature.

Hopefulness brought about feelings of security and love however brief they may have been. As feelings improved, so did life. As confidence grew, so did optimism. You now live in a world that is more optimistic than ever before. Many of you have come to believe that you have power over your own destiny. This is the tipping point for the future of humanity. You are living in the final days of general negativity and are seeing humanity as a mass consciousness becoming generally positive.

There are locations on your planet that are much more positive in nature than others. Due to your technological advances in communication, the more negative regions are gaining hope and becoming more positive as well. Mass consciousness must be led into being more positive; it cannot be forced. You may not intrude into the natural paths others must take. You can only lead by your example. They will follow at their own pace. You cannot assist them with either force or charity, only by your example.

This works on a personal level as well. You cannot teach through words alone. If you are living the life of your dreams, those close to you will notice and will either desire that for themselves or not. If they do, they will approach you. If not, they are not ready. You can only create in your experience and not in the experience of others. Advice usually does not assist others to an improved condition unless they are fully ready and asking for guidance. You want to help, but due to the nature of thought, they cannot hear you unless they are vibrationally prepared.

You cannot learn what you are not vibrationally ready to learn. You will not hear or understand the lessons until you are vibrationally ready for them. That is the purpose of manifestation events. They alter your vibration so you are ready for the next step.

Everything is a step forward. You cannot move backwards. Every step is a step in the right direction. You cannot make a mistake. You may have two choices and both are equally correct. This concept may be very challenging for you to accept given your perception of reality and your social conditioning, which asks you to make only the best choice available. But when you understand the nature of reality, you'll come to see that progression is just that. There is no regression.

If you trust in the mechanism of reality and know you are always moving toward your desire, whether you are moving swiftly or at a snail's pace, then you may be able to grasp our meaning here. Since there is no wrong anywhere in the universe, including your physical reality, including you as an individual in this time space reality, you cannot make a mistake. It's impossible.

No matter what choice you make, you move forward into an expanded version of you and into a new reality. If the new reality is pleasing to you,

you deem the decisions you made to be the correct ones. If, on the other hand, a decision appears to be a mistake (from your limited perception of reality and the larger overall picture), you believe the decision was wrong. However, both decisions were correct. One led you to the place you thought you wanted to go, and the other is leading to the place you want to go. Either decision will get you to a place that is a vibrational match for your desire; it's just that your limited perception of the big picture allows you to deem one decision right and the other one wrong.

When you look back at your life, you may have regrets about some of the decisions you have made and you may give thanks for other decisions. But due to your limited understanding of probabilities, you cannot trace the path that might have been. You cannot say that if you landed a particular job, then your life would have been better. You cannot know that if you had moved to a certain city, your life would have been better. The reality is, given your pervasive and persistent pattern of vibration, your life would have been incredibly similar no matter what choices you made. It's not the choices you make, but rather the vibration you offer that determines your life experience.

Perception is the key to understanding how decisions affect your life. The more open you are to an understanding of the nature of reality, the easier it will be to make decisions. If either decision is the correct one, then make the decision and follow through without having doubt about where that decision may lead you. It's doubt and fear that make the decision incorrect in your eyes.

The Law of Attraction is bringing you to your desire one way or the other. It does not care whether you take road A or road B. Both paths lead to the same place. However, if you take road A, go for it all the way and don't look back. Believe that road A is the best choice and never again wonder if road B would have gotten you there quicker. Quicker doesn't matter when you have all the time in the universe.

Most of your decisions are based on getting to your goals as fast as you can. Since the journey is the real prize, not the goal, relax about the time. There's no need to rush. Enjoy the trip. Have fun with either road you choose. By the way, time doesn't exist. It's an illusion.

It is fun to see yourself progressing toward your desire. Manifestation events prove that you're on the right path to your desire. Learn to pay attention to these manifestation events when they occur. Enjoy them whether they seem pleasurable, like a great coincidence or a wonderful conversation, or whether they seem painful like a stop light when you're in a hurry or like being fired from your job. All manifestation events are good because they let you know you're progressing toward your desire.

You cannot eliminate fear or doubt. It is a natural part of your consciousness. There is nothing inherently wrong with fear and doubt. Both let you know you are not yet ready for the manifestation of your desire. That is a good thing. You do not want your desire to manifest before you are ready for it because you will not fully appreciate it when it arrives. The object of your desire may leave you feeling worse. Therefore, a little resistance is a good thing.

Fear and doubt help you slow down the pace of your manifestation until you are ready. Once you are truly prepared, fear and doubt will become such a small part of the thoughts around your desire that you'll hardly notice them. Since you are ready for that which you desire and you now know it will come to you, fear and doubt enter your thoughts far less frequently and you will dismiss those thoughts as nonsense when they do appear.

Fear and doubt are like the brakes on your car. Sometimes they are necessary to keep the car on the road. However, when you're traveling on a straight road, you want to release the brakes so the trip is more efficient. You can reduce the effects of fear and doubt to a large degree and thereby remove your foot from the brakes. Remember, you're the one who is applying the brakes, so ease up when you're moving forward in a straight line.

There are tools you can use to lessen the resistant effects of fear and doubt. The first is to realize that there are no wrong decisions and that it's all good regardless of your perception. You can make any decision work for you if you trust that the universe is always working *for* you and never *against* you. You will get there if you simply ease up. This means do not take life so seriously. There is no rush. You have no one to impress. This world is built around and for you. You have control. You can choose to feel good in any moment regardless of the circumstances. *You* have that power.

If you have doubt, remind yourself that you're going in the right direction. Believe that the choices you've already made are the right ones. Never look back. Never play the "What if" game. You can't see the path not taken, so forget about it and embrace the one you're on. If you want to reach your desires and achieve your dreams, you must not indulge in the useless habit of looking back and imagining what might have been. Instead, imagine what is to come.

III.

Manifestation events shape and mold your vibration. These events cause you to react in a way that moves you toward the new reality that you seek. You can choose anything and if you stick to your desire without giving up along the way, it will come to you. You must persevere, not against all odds, but in the face of manifestation events that you perceive as damning. It's your perception of the unpleasant-feeling manifestation events that causes you to give up; it is not the event itself. If the event feels unpleasant, it is simply telling you that you must alter your perspective to reach your true desire. It is never a setback, but instead just an indication that you need to adjust your focus.

An unpleasant manifestation event, such as being fired from a job or the ending of a romantic relationship, can also mean you must adjust your mental picture of your desire. It does not mean you change your desire, because you cannot do that. It just means your vision of your desire might be different than the vibrational reality of your desire.

Let's say you have the desire to be unconditionally loved. Your life experience to this point has led you to wanting unconditional love and now you set out on your path toward it. The universe knows exactly how to bring you to your desire, but you do not. If you trust that the universe will bring you what you truly desire - unconditional love - and trust that all of the manifestation events along the way are leading you to unconditional love, then your journey will be one of joy and satisfaction. But since that might not be the way most people go about reaching their desire, let's see how this might play out in the real world.

Imagine you were raised in a family that used love as a carrot on a stick. If you behaved in a manner of which your parents approved, they supplied the love you wanted. If you behaved in a way that was not acceptable to them, they withheld the love you so needed. If you, as the freedom seeker you are, could no longer force yourself to conform to their arbitrary rules and so they withheld love in an intense fashion, you might be led to the desire for unconditional love.

You now look around the landscape that is your society for signs of unconditional love. You might believe that adoration is the same thing as unconditional love, so you seek to be adored. Fame seems to be the route to adoration, so you seek fame. You decide to become a movie star and move to Hollywood to begin your career. Because you seek adoration, believing that it's the same as unconditional love, many of the manifestation events you encounter lead you to painful circumstances. You force yourself to do things you really do not want to do.

You go on numerous auditions, only to face rejection, which reinforces your doubts and fears that unconditional love is not attainable. You support yourself by taking a job that is not fulfilling in order to give you the time you need to go to the auditions. You live in a dwelling that is far less than what you desire because you are paid less than you desire so you can go to auditions that bombard you with rejection. You meet some once successful members of the industry who were adored at one time and now are no longer the objects of affection. You realize that the whims of the masses are fickle and fleeting and that adoration does not last.

Eventually, after enough manifestation events, your idea of the desire you have held for so long is altered and you now understand that adoration is not the same as unconditional love. It was a belief you held that was flawed. You were never wrong, because your path led you to a new understanding of the nature of your desire. You now know fully the meaning of unconditional love and your mental picture of your original desire is altered in such a way that the universe can now deliver it to you in the most spectacular and elegant manner.

Let's look at the situation from another viewpoint. Through your life experiences to this point, you have come to a place where you desire freedom. You know that for you freedom is not only possible, but inevitable. You cannot live otherwise. You decide that the best way for you to be free is to follow your life's passions, no matter how ridiculous they seem to others. Your passion is to act. You are thrilled, exhilarated, and completely present when acting. As a child, you acted out spontaneous performances at family gatherings. In school, you were in every play you could commit to. During your summers away from school, you went to acting camps. All you want to do is act and now you are determined to follow your passion.

You are inspired to join the local theater company and they accept you with open arms. The audition process was easy and natural, and though you didn't immediately get the leading role, you were able to join the company and get started. You loved the rehearsals and took every aspect of the experience seriously. You felt a sense of growth even as you received criticism. You did not despair when things appeared to go wrong. You actually enjoyed the challenge and became more determined to do better.

A family friend gave you a job in an office so you could support yourself and have the time to go to rehearsals and performances. You found joy in the job, not because it was the greatest job in the world, but because you appreciated this position which allowed you the freedom to pursue your passion. In fact, you excelled at the job and found many things enjoyable about it including your co-workers.

You lived in a small apartment near the theater and you appreciated it, not because it was the home of your dreams, but because it allowed you to live within your means and pursue your interests and passions. You decorated it smartly and people commented on your sense of taste and style. It felt as cozy and warm as any place you had lived in before and you will remember the little apartment fondly.

Soon you achieved more success in the theater company by gaining larger roles and receiving more accolades. Your desire to pursue freedom is expanding and you have newer, larger desires. If you are able to keep up with your desires and pursue your interests and passions with purity of intent, you will reach new heights and your desires will expand further. This is the process of life and it never ends. You will always be led to the essence of your dreams. Sometimes you will be led easily and joyously and other times you will go kicking and screaming. It's your choice.

IV.

Your beliefs affect the manifestation of your desires. You have many beliefs of varying intensity. Beliefs can be helpful or not depending on your

A Perception of Reality

desire. Beliefs should be malleable. It is important to be open to new ideas and able to modify your beliefs.

It is our intention to shift your perspective on life to a new place. In order to accomplish this, you must be open to new ideas. If you hold on too tightly to certain beliefs, you will not be able to change your perspective and you won't fully understand much of what we have come to offer you.

Many humans hold onto religious beliefs that may not be appropriate for the times in which you currently live. Much of religion was written in the past in the language of the time. It had meaning for the people of that time. The essence of most ancient religions is not far from what we have to say; however, over the years, the message has been mostly distorted. If you hold on too tightly to beliefs about what has been written in religious texts, where the meaning may have been distorted over the years and through its translation, you will have more difficulty changing your perspective.

Beliefs are supported wholeheartedly by the Law of Attraction. What you believe will be reflected back to you every day of your life. Your beliefs are constantly being reinforced by the Law of Attraction. It matters not what you believe, because the Law of Attraction will prove your beliefs to be true. You will tend to gather around others who hold similar beliefs and they will help to reinforce your views. You will tend to read literature that supports your philosophies and see things in movies and on TV that also show them to be true. If you believe it, you will see evidence that reinforces your beliefs.

In order to gain new perspective and to change your life, you must relax many of your beliefs for they hold you in place. If you can modify your beliefs or leave them behind altogether, you will change your perception and alter the reality of your life.

Perception is the basis of all reality. What you perceive, you live - literally. It is not simply a different way of looking at life. It is a completely different experience of life. It is a different reality.

All is good; there is no bad. This may be counter to your beliefs. Most humans have spent much of their lives judging good from bad, virtuous from evil, right from wrong. There is no bad, there is no wrong, there is no evil. Are these statements counter to your beliefs? Can you think of things that are bad, wrong, and evil? If you can, you have a belief that is hindering your ability to gain a new, broader perspective of life. You are also allowing the Law of Attraction to provide you with ample evidence of those aspects you perceive as real.

Ultimately, there is no good or bad; there is only that which is preferred and that which is not preferred. You don't need to focus your attention on what you do not want. You need only to focus all of your attention on what *is* wanted. There is no evil, only good. If you judge something to be evil, it is only because your current perspective is narrow. We wish to broaden it. Anything that appears evil to you is misunderstood by you, your peers, and society in general. You need not eradicate evil; you need only to see the good that may be hidden within it.

If you can see the goodness, the rightness, and the worthiness of everything and leave behind the judgment of right or wrong, you can perceive the world in an entirely new way. This enlightened view of the world will literally raise your vibration, broaden your perspective, and change your reality so that you will be able to move toward that which you desire instead of away from that which you do not desire.

You do not have the ability to push anything unwanted away. You cannot eradicate anything by your attention to it. You will only draw it closer. In order for you to move toward your desires and not toward the unwanted, you must change your beliefs about the negative aspects of life. There are no negative aspects unless you, as an individual, deem them to be negative. You create the concept of negativity. You allow it to exist. It does not have to exist except in your perception. Now is the time to change your perception and therefore change your beliefs forever.

Manifestation events reveal your beliefs in great detail. If you believe the world is full of bad drivers, you will be provided with ample evidence. Bad drivers, car accidents, traffic jams, law enforcement, red lights, near misses, and many other examples of the existence of the perceived negative aspects of drivers will appear to you on a daily basis. The degree of intensity to which this belief is held will be the exact degree to which you will be exposed to your limiting belief. If the intensity of your belief is low, you will not observe many incidences of poor driving. You will hear fewer conversations about bad drivers, you will see infrequent examples of poor driving on the road, and you will see fewer news reports of accidents. If, however, the intensity of your belief is strong, you will see an intense amount of evidence that your belief is correct. Since there is no wrong in the universe, the Law of Attraction always makes you right.

If you understand that you have complete control over your beliefs, you will be able to modify them. As you lessen the intensity of any belief, you will reduce the number of manifestation events surrounding that belief. You will talk less about poor driving. You will turn the other cheek when you see a car accident. You will stop watching the evening news. Thus, you have lowered the intensity of your belief and while on occasion a poor driver will enter your experience as a manifestation event, it will be infrequent and inconsequential.

You can also heighten the intensity of those beliefs that support your preferred perception of life. If you believe you are safe, the universe will bring manifestation events to prove that you are safe. Maybe you wake up in the morning and realize you forgot to lock your doors. You realize that there was no break-in and you were safe.

Manifestation events are indicators of your beliefs. You can understand how your beliefs are affecting your reality by paying close attention to all manifestation events. Since almost everything is a manifestation event, it may be difficult for you to recognize them. If a co-worker is grumpy, you might assume he's having a bad day. But if that co-worker does anything that makes you feel something or stirs up an emotion inside you, that is a manifestation event and could be an excellent indication of a belief you are holding. If the experience is intense, such as an argument that leaves you feeling terrible in its aftermath, that is an indication of a high intensity belief that is not serving you. Remember; you are the center of the universe, so these events are **always** about you and not about the other person. You cannot perceive their vibration, their perception of life, or their belief system. Your only work is to understand your beliefs and how they affect your perception of reality.

If you have a high-intensity experience, or manifestation event, that is pleasurable and leaves you feeling wonderful, you have identified a belief that supports your positive perception of reality. This is a very beneficial belief and now that you've identified it you have the ability to intensify that belief even further. The higher the strength of positive beliefs the more intense the manifestation events will become and the more intense your positive belief will increase as a result. It is a spiraling upward cycle. Lower the intensity of beliefs that do not serve you and raise the intensity of beliefs that do.

Practice modifying your beliefs on a daily, moment-by-moment basis. This is the work that must be done in order to change your perspective and thereby change your life. You can identify every manifestation event for what it is and then reassess your belief based on the intensity of emotion held within the event. Don't dismiss anything for it might be a manifestation event. You must realize that everything, no matter how seemingly insignificant, has the potential to be a manifestation event and thereby a reflection of a currently held belief.

If you encounter a red traffic light and you experience an emotion, it's a manifestation event. The emotion, a good feeling or an unpleasant feeling, is the sign that you are experiencing a manifestation event. The emotion signals the event. If it is an emotion of low intensity, the intensity of the belief is low. If it is an emotion of high intensity, the intensity of the belief is high. The level of your emotion is the indicator of the strength of your belief. If no emotion was felt, there was no manifestation event.

Emotions range from high-frequency vibrations to low-frequency vibrations. Joy, exhilaration, and relief vibrate at a high frequency, while anger, despair and hopelessness vibrate at low frequencies. There are also intensities within these emotions. You may have a moment of low- intensity anger and it dissipates quickly. You might feel a sigh of relief at something that was not so important. And, of course, each emotion can present itself at a very high level of intensity.

When you are aware of manifestation events and you can identify the emotion surrounding the event and its intensity, you can identify the belief and its relative strength or weakness. This awareness is the key to expanding your perception, raising your vibration, and moving toward the life experiences you desire.

As you come to realize that manifestation events are happening all the time throughout your daily life, you can appreciate them for the guides they are. Manifestation events help you see your path more clearly. When you can see how your beliefs affect your desires you can modify your beliefs to create the outcomes you prefer.

Manifestation events have a role to play in your development. They help you align with your desires. They are an integral part of the process. Once you are aware that you are in a manifestation event, as it is happening, you can let it play out or you can modify the event itself. If you decide to let it play out, you can pay close attention to the signs that the event is bringing to you. You can observe your emotions and your actions. You can notice how the manifestation event is playing out for the other people involved. For this is not merely an event to spur your progress, but it is also an event for all of the other people involved. The event unfolds uniquely for each of the participants depending on their state within the process to alignment with their specific desires. The Law of Attraction has brought you all together knowing that the manifestation event will help each of you in the most efficient manner possible.

If you are aware that the manifestation event is occurring, you can change your behavior in the moment. If you are able to perceive the event as it unfolds, you can instantly modify your beliefs and behavior so that the outcome of the event is different for you. Many times this is difficult to accomplish because there has been momentum building to this point in time and the event must unfold as it was meant to. The understanding here is that you still have control even in the midst of an unfolding event.

Manifestation events occur to help you modify your beliefs so you can more easily align with your desires. They only modify your beliefs if you can understand the clues within the events themselves. If you do not realize that the events are revealing beliefs that either support your desire or hinder the progress toward your desire, you cannot benefit from the event. Manifestation events, left without the knowledge and understanding of their potential to guide you, tend to reinforce old belief patterns.

Manifestation events you deem positive work to strengthen your alignment with your desire. Those events which you consider negative reinforce belief patterns that hold you in place, away from that which you desire. If you want to move forward toward that which you desire, you must increase the intensity of those belief systems that support your journey toward your desire. You must also minimize the non-beneficial belief patterns so that they do not hold you back from attaining your desire.

V.

Manifestation events also carry lessons within them. If you can appreciate and understand the lesson, your vibrational pattern will be raised. As you raise your vibrational pattern, you are open to thoughts and ideas that were previously unavailable to you. Your level of vibration allows new thoughts and ideas to be revealed to you. When you reach certain higher levels of vibration, you become a match to thoughts and ideas that match that new, higher vibration. You become ready for bigger, brighter, higher vibrational thoughts.

As your belief patterns improve, you also improve your vibration. As your awareness of the laws of the universe becomes more profound, your vibration raises. The higher your vibration, the more access you gain to thoughts and ideas that also resonate at a higher vibration. As you become more aware of the lessons held within manifestation events and, as you gain understanding of the forces of the universe that are working to assist you, you'll start appreciating the manifestation events for what they can teach you. Your vibrational pattern will improve and you will have access to new levels of understanding.

Words don't teach. Life experience is the greatest teacher. You learn through manifestation events. If you have the ability to comprehend the lessons within each event, you will progress swiftly toward all of your desires and an enhanced life experience. This is the time of awakening and you are now regaining your awareness of your inner self and of the mechanism of the universe.

Your world is far less real than your current perception. Broaden your perception to include the nonphysical aspects of universal forces and you will open up a whole new level of understanding. Change your idea of reality and modify your belief system to include the inner world as an equal counterpart to the outer world and you can redefine your experience in both worlds. Live a balance between your physical senses and your nonphysical senses. Know that there is far more going on than you currently perceive, and in that knowing it will be revealed to you. Do not accept your reality at face value but understand the messages being sent to you all day, every day. Feel for guidance and guidance will be revealed to you.

A Perception of Reality

Withdraw your attention from the lives of others around you, for they are not vibrating at your level. Do not attempt to assist those who are not asking for assistance; it will only lower your vibration. Act in a manner that inspires others, but do not feel pity for them if they are unable to respond to your inspiration. They are in the process of creating their own life experience at their own level of consciousness and awareness.

You are here to create your life experience in any manner you choose. You've come this far and there's no turning back. You cannot unknow what you know. Your vibration is already gaining momentum toward an ever-growing, brighter and faster vibration. Your perception of the world is expanding and with it you are expanding as well. You have gained new awareness and are creating a richer life experience. Your troubles will begin to fade and your dreams will be coming into focus. You are just getting started and there's much more to discover. A new world awaits you and you feel exhilarated in anticipation.

Chapter Four

Intention

At this time in history, your planet is more diverse than it has ever been. There are great contrasts in the life experiences of those in this current space-time reality. The universe is one of expansion and your world is expanding as well. There is more wealth than ever before and, in the midst of this wealth, there is greater poverty than ever before. This contrast was intended. It is the perfect manifestation of a broader reality. For before your birth into this time period, you intended to explore certain aspects of this physical experience. You intended to live the life you are experiencing now.

You have lived many lives before, and in each of those experiences you chose to explore a certain aspect of reality. In one life, you may have chosen to explore the aspects of living in a large family and having many siblings and children yourself. In another existence, you may have chosen to explore solitude. In one existence, you may have chosen to experience great power and influence. In another life you may have chosen to experience servitude. You have been male and female. You have been many different ethnicities, have followed many different religions, and have experienced life in many different societies. All were intended by you prior to your birth.

From your limited perspective in this current life experience, you judge one experience to be preferable over another. You assume that a life of great privilege is preferable to a life of great poverty. You assume that the life experience of great power is somehow superior to a life of servitude. You may think it would even be preferable to be one sex over the other, or one race rather than another. But from the broader perspective of the nonphysical, and with the knowledge of the lives you have lived before, you chose your current life to explore a specific aspect of reality in order to learn more about that reality.

There are general intentions you made prior to coming into this physical existence and then there are more specific intentions. The general intentions are of well-being, joy, freedom, happiness, and love. All life experiences include these and other general intentions and no matter what your life experience is, you have the ability to live it in joy, happiness and well-being. You could choose to explore poverty **and** live a life of joy and well-being. You could live a life of servitude and be happier than your master. You could live a life of solitude and enjoy it more fully than any other life experience. These general intentions are at the basis of all life experience. No matter what the specific intentions may be, you have the ability to live the experience of joy, happiness, and well-being within any specific intention.

Your specific intention to explore an aspect of life may not be known to you at this present moment in time. It may be revealed to you in the future, when you're ready, or you may not understand it until you reemerge into the nonphysical. It is not necessary to understand your specific intention. You need not search for it as you will likely assume it's something other than what it really is.

You made your specific intention prior to emerging into physical reality. You knew your perception would be limited while living a physical existence. This is part of the fun and the adventure of being physical. You knew that once you were in your physical existence, you would be led to want certain things and you knew you had free will along the way. You understood that if you got off-track, you had guidance in place to help you traverse the path toward your intention. You knew that whatever the experience may be, it would be one of expansion. You knew there would be a positive outcome in any case.

We do not want to influence you in any way in regard to the life you are now living. If you knew your specific intention, you would try to take action to manifest its outcome. However, you cannot understand the full story that led you to choose your specific intention. The knowledge of the intention would be of no use to you now. Just know that your life is exactly as you intended it and that you are on the path to your specific intention. You cannot be wrong for there is no wrong anywhere in the universe. Therefore, you are doing extremely well, whether you think so or not.

Intention

If you are living your specific intention, then others on the planet are also living their specific intentions. If you are here to more fully understand the laws of the universe (as you must be if you are reading and understanding this book), then many others are here without the desire to understand the laws of the universe. They are here to understand poverty, fear, hunger, power, greed, despair, abundance, pleasure, freedom, success, failure, sickness, health, vitality, ignorance, etc., for every aspect of life has value.

The earth has never been a more perfect environment for the exploration of all aspects of physical reality. Your judgments about what's wrong and what's right lead you to improperly assume that some forms of life experience are better than others. From our broader, nonphysical perspective, all life experiences have great value. Therefore, it is not necessary to want others to conform to your idea of a better life experience.

You can only create in your reality. You can only change your life experience. You cannot create in the reality of others. They are living a unique experience, one that has never existed in history. You cannot assume that their experience is any less valid than your own.

If you are drawn by pure positive intention to assist another, take action only because you are inspired to because it will make *you* feel better. Do not take action to assist another because you think *they* need your help. They do not. Not ever. They are fully assisted by the universe and the Law of Attraction. They are receiving a perfect match to their vibration and, whether you see it or not, they are living a life they intended to live.

Attempting to help another when you are not inspired to do so only complicates their life experience. Help them if it makes you feel good, but do not expect your help to be appreciated or to receive accolades for your good deed. Do not do it for the material reward, the approval of others, or the prestige. Do it only if it it makes *you* feel good.

You are not here to fix the world because the world has never been more perfect than it is right now. There is nothing going wrong; it is all progressing as intended. There are intentions for your life, your community, your society, your country, as well as intentions for your planet. All is exactly where it is supposed to be. All is right.

When you place your attention on things you feel are wrong, you add them to your own vibration and they expand. It is not your place to outlaw drugs when there are those wishing to experience freedom. It is not your place to wipe out disease, hunger, poverty, abortion, homosexuality, autism, communism, socialism, or even capitalism when so many are here with the intention of exploring those aspects of reality.

Everyone living on this planet at this time came here because never before has the world seen the aspects of life experience that are now available to explore. There has never been more freedom to explore various realities. Any human born today will have the ability to travel to any part of the world and meet any other person alive on the planet. This has not been possible previously. There is so much potential for completely new life experience that was not previously possible. This is the reason so many are coming forward into physical existence now.

One could not experience poverty in previous times in the way one can now. In previous times, poverty was common. It was the norm of existence for many people. They did not understand the depth of their poverty because they did not know the height of wealth. It was not part of their experience. They were told stories, but they could not fully understand them. Today, you have great wealth living next to great poverty. The poor now understand the great disparity. They can see the homes, the airplanes, the boats, and the cars owned by the wealthy. They can watch TV and observe how the wealthy live in great detail. To experience hunger or starvation in a society where so much food goes uneaten is an experience that has never been before in all of history. There are those who have intended to experience this for themselves.

You cannot fathom why anyone would choose to experience poverty of this magnitude. We hope to expand your perception. The experience of great poverty (as is true with all life experience) is extremely beneficial. If you do not fully understand the depth of poverty or lack, you cannot fully understand the heights of wealth or abundance. If you have not experienced confinement, you cannot fully appreciate freedom. You cannot know joy fully until you know despair. All life experience is beneficial.

Now that you understand the benefits of each individual life experience to the one having the experience, you can leave them alone to fulfill their specific intention. They can find joy, happiness, and well-being on their own. They do not need you no matter how passionate their plea for help. All they are asking for is the guidance from within. They want alignment with their inner self. They are focusing too strongly on their outer reality. They cannot find inner guidance if you are the one guiding them.

Your unrequested advice is of little benefit. You do not know their vibration or their perception. Most often they will be unable to even hear or comprehend your words. They are not a vibrational match to the higher vibrational ideas you are conveying. They want to figure it out on their own. No matter how much you care for this person or how much you think they need your help, you cannot help them until you make the decision to leave them alone. Trust that they will eventually find the vibration that will lead them to the life experience they desire and have previously intended.

Without the burden of trying to help others, you are free to experience the life that excites you. Since all others are here to experience their own lives as they have intended, you need not care what they think of you. You are here to experience the life you intended. It may sound selfish, but this is the way of the universe.

Each and every organism on this planet is conscious and striving for an improved life experience. Your body is made up of cells, each one striving for improvement. Each point of consciousness that is experiencing a physical existence is primarily concerned with self. Your focus on the lives of others is a selfish one as well. If you think someone should be or do something differently than what they are currently being or doing, it is for one selfish reason. You think, by the alteration of their behavior, you will feel better. Your only intention in helping others is to feel better yourself.

If you embrace this selfishness, you will be of great assistance to those who are vibrationally in alignment with your assistance. Selfishness goes against the very fabric of your society, yet it is at the heart of the laws of the universe. This dichotomy will leave you unfocused and you will have trouble moving forward toward your desires unless you can comprehend this basic truth. You are the center of the universe and all that exists revolves around you. You have intended to live your life experiences without the guidance and influence of those who do not know your intention or vibrational pattern. You have intended to leave others to live their own life experience without your interference. You may influence through your example of alignment, but not through your advice or what you alone judge to be right.

It is good to be selfish and self-centered. You can only help others when you can be a shining example of alignment. You must strive to align with your inner self, align with your intentions, and align with your desires. You must feel your way to these things by focusing on your own feelings, thoughts, and emotions. The lives of others, when you judge them proper or improper, will only impede your progress. The life you are living now is your only concern in the present moment.

II.

There are those intentions you set prior to your physical arrival in this space-time reality. They set you along your path toward what you wanted to explore. Most of your intentions are general and some may be more specific, but they are only intentions and you have the ability to define your life based on the preferences you choose at this moment in time. If you had a specific intention to explore sickness for example, you may have been ill as a child and that illness caused you to desire health. That experience led you to form a desire. The desire is now burning within you and the Law of Attraction is bringing it to you.

Your specific intentions may lead you to new desires you did not hold in previous lives yet, in this life, you lived an experience that created a new desire. Your focus on that desire is what this life experience is all about. If you intended to explore aspects of poverty and in this life time you experienced poverty, that experience may have created a more powerful desire for abundance. This new desire for abundance may never have existed for you prior to this life experience and it now causes you to grow more powerfully than ever before.

The diversity that exists on earth today has never been more profound. This diversity has the ability and potential to create desires more powerful than have ever existed before. There are intentions being set that have never been made before. There are those coming into physical existence to explore ideas that are new. They are here to live with physical conditions and mental conditions in order to explore new ways of experiencing physical reality. Teachers are coming through at this moment in time to impart new levels of awareness and understanding.

More are being born into more contrast than ever before. This is all intentional. There are no accidents. There is nothing wrong. Whether one chooses a life experience that lasts a matter of minutes or a hundred years, it is all the same. Life experience is life experience. Time is irrelevant. It is no more valuable to live two years, twenty years, or a hundred years. All experience, no matter the time involved, was intended. It all unfolds as it should.

There are no wrong conditions. All conditions are intended. If a pregnancy is terminated by any means, it was intended and it is right. There is no need to experience grief or guilt. These feelings let you know that your inner self feels the opposite. All life experience, however brief, was intended to be that experience. You cannot see the intention from your perspective and this causes conflict within you. But if you can understand the power of intentions and that all life experience was intended, you can feel ease about the life experiences of others, including those of your own children.

If a child is born with a condition you consider a malady or disease, the child intended to come forth with this condition. There is no need to cure the child of autism. The child has come forth to experience life in a new way. He has come to teach unconditional love. He has come forth to create desires so powerful that none have ever been so powerful before. If you cure autism, you rob those of this experience, and new bodily conditions will evolve in its place.

If you can see and know that all is right, that all is intended, you can live free from fear and doubt. You need not worry that the lives of others will affect your life in a negative manner, for they are the creator of their life experience and you are the creator of yours. You can be inspired positively or negatively by the lives of others, but their only real affect is your attention to them. Withdraw your attention from the aspects of life you do not prefer and focus on your bliss, for this is your life to live fully and you have intended for it to be blissful.

III.

Intention is a powerful tool from your real-life perspective, as well. You can use intention to create your life as you would prefer it to be. Intention means focusing on an outcome you prefer. It can also be general in nature or more specific.

If you are going to dinner with friends, you can intend that the food be delicious and that you choose the right items from the menu. You can intend to have wonderful conversation and laughter. You can intend for the journey to be safe and easy. You can intend to connect with your friends on a deeper level.

Intentions can be made in the morning. You can intend for the day to be wonderful. You may intend to be productive at work, to be on time, to inspire co-workers, and to learn something new. You may intend to pay attention to manifestation events and to learn from them. You may intend to alter the course of a manifestation event even as it's happening.

An intention is the focus of your desire in the moment. It leads the universe to fulfill your expectations. When you intend, you expect. You expect that what you intend will be delivered. Your intentions are beliefs that things will work out in reality as you have worked them out in your mind. Intentions are thoughts that become reality before your eyes. When you know an intention will be fulfilled, then it will be. Knowing is the key to manifesting your intentions.

If you know things are always right, then they will be right. Since there is no wrong anywhere in the universe, everything is right. If you intend to eat today, and you know you will based on past experience, you will eat. You have no doubt that you will eat today and no fear that you won't eat. You intend to eat because it is the most obvious thing in the world. You eat every day and there's no reason this day should be different. You know you will eat and so you will.

If you intend to fly to the moon for lunch however, you might not make it. Is this because lunch on the moon is impossible? Hardly. It's simply because you doubt its possibility to such a strong degree that the doubt makes this intention highly unlikely. Therefore, intentions can only be made surrounding those things you deem probable, likely, and realistic. You can intend anything you want and if you can imagine it, it can be achieved. But if fear or doubt prevent belief and knowing, your intention has less power. You can intend to be on time for work. Because you believe it is possible more than you doubt it's possible, your intention has an excellent chance of coming to fruition. The stronger your belief, or knowing is over doubt and fear, the more likely your intention will actualize in your experience.

The very act of intending causes a momentum that has the power to materialize even in the face of your doubt. The chronic practice of intention, followed by your observation of manifestations, causes more positive momentum. The more you believe, the more evidence of your belief is revealed, and therefore the more you believe. Your belief transforms into knowing. The stronger you know something the more power you have. Confidence in your abilities adds to your power to allow the manifestation of your intentions.

Your intentions, once thought or stated out loud, must be followed through with clarity of focus. You must continue to believe that your intentions will manifest. You must keep your focus sharp in the period between intention and manifestation. Simply stating an intention is powerful in and of itself, but focusing on the intention gives it more momentum and more power to manifest in ways that will delight you. Your focus on the intention will enable you to see the full manifestation of the intention as it unfolds.

If you simply intend a safe drive to work and do not focus on your intention while you're driving, instead you're on the phone or listening to the radio, you may not notice how the universe is delivering safety to you. You don't notice how your foot eases off the accelerator just as the car in front of you hits the brakes. You might not realize that the traffic light has stopped you so that the traffic that would have been in your way has time to divert from your path. You arrive safely but were not aware of the mechanics involved in doing so. Had you seen the signs of the universe in action, you would have added momentum to your overall confidence and knowledge that you are a powerful creator.

Your intention gives you focus and focus brings you the manifestation of intention. Focus and intention are linked. Intention without doubt brings manifestation of intention. The absence of doubt creates alignment with your intention and gives the universe a clear signal of your vibrational pattern. The clearer the signal, the easier it is for the manifestation to unfold.

You can write your intentions, announce them out loud, discuss them with your mate, or simply think about them by yourself. Whatever feels best to you is the proper method. You can make intentions as often as you like on any subject in the world. When choosing a movie, you might intend that it be the best movie for you at the moment. You might intend that it be uplifting and no matter the subject matter, you will find something uplifting in the story that might be missed by others.

Practice intention in your daily life and you also practice focus and deliberate creation. You are here to create the life you prefer deliberately. The tool for deliberate creation is intention. In order to achieve movement toward anything you desire, you must intend to do so. The more intentions you make, the more deliberately you create.

General intentions create general experiences. Intend well-being, focus on observing well-being and it will be shown to you throughout your day. Intend to have pleasurable experiences and you will have them. Intend to see the best in people and they will show you their best. Intend to have fun and you will. Your general intentions carry less doubt making them easier to achieve. Make as many general intentions each day as you can. In fact, intend right now to make many general intentions each day when you awaken in the morning.

Specific intentions are more focused on specific outcomes and, by their very nature, carry more doubt and fear than general intentions. The more specific you are on any subject, the more likely you will have an idea in your mind of the outcome. Since you are unable to plan the outcome to match your vibrational signal exactly, you will feel the discord in vibration and this will manifest itself as fear and doubt. The universe understands your vibrational signal from a broader perspective and, if allowed, will bring you a perfect match to what you are offering. When you, from your more limited perspective, intend for a specific outcome and try to arrange it in detail without having an intimate knowledge of your vibration, you will be unable to visualize the outcome that specifically matches your vibration. You will feel discord in the form of fear and doubt.

All intentions must match the vibrational signal you are currently emitting for the outcome to manifest in your reality in the way that is most pleasing to you. If you intend to eat lunch today, the universe will plan for you an excellent lunch based on the vibrational signal you are emitting prior to lunch. The universe will take into account all of the other intentions and desires you have to provide you with the lunch experience that can accommodate many of your desires and intentions. If you have general intentions to have a certain body weight, to spend a certain amount of money each day, to improve a relationship with a co-worker and to be productive at work so you can get home early for dinner with your family, the universe will work out the perfect lunch that will best include all of those general intentions to which you are a vibrational match. The universe, through the Law of Attraction, will find you a lunch spot that is healthy, that is in keeping with your daily budget, and that will also be of interest to the co-worker you'll invite to lunch. All of your general intentions have little resistance and unfold easily and elegantly.

However, if you specifically intend to have pizza for lunch, the universe has to work this aspect into the equation and you may feel some vibrational discord. You might doubt that you can maintain a healthy body weight (which has nothing to do with the type of food you're eating), or you might worry that the place you like to go for pizza is too far from the office and it could take too long. You might worry that your co-worker had pizza for lunch yesterday and won't want it again today. You might have all sorts of doubts that arise from this more specific intention and thus your general intentions will face resistance and be less likely to manifest in the way that is most pleasing to you.

If you were able to make the specific intention for pizza and it was a vibrational match to your general intentions, there would be no fear or doubt. These elements arise through discord with your vibrational pattern. The more general you are in your intentions, the easier it is for the intentions to be a vibrational match to your overall set of desires without the presence of fear and doubt.

Intention is the path to deliberate creation. General intentions are easier, but specific intentions take a more direct route toward the manifestation of your desires. You can be as specific as possible until you feel the discord within the intention. If fear and doubt arise within you, you are being too specific in your intentions and you might try to be more general. You could step away from the specifics of your desire and understand that the universe will work out a better way for you to achieve that which you desire in a way that is most pleasing to you.

You can force a desire to manifest through sheer will, but it will not unfold elegantly and may not be as pleasing to you. You must allow the universe to do its job and let the desire unfold in ways you can't comprehend from your limited perception of reality. If you're getting too specific

A Perception of Reality

with an intention, you'll feel the discord and you'll know you're getting off-track. Your discord is your sign that the intention is too specific. The more intense your discord, the more off-track your intention is from your vibrational pattern. The universe knows what you want and how to bring you into alignment with your desires.

If you desire a promotion at your place of employment and you intend to get it, you can feel whether or not the intention matches your vibration. If it is vibrationally a match to your overall set of desires and beliefs, you will not feel discord. You will have very little doubt or fear. You will have confidence and know that you deserve the promotion and that it is a vibrational match to that which you truly desire. And the promotion will manifest perfectly and elegantly.

If, on the other hand, you are not a vibrational match to this promotion you think you want so badly, you will feel discord in the emotions of fear and doubt. Just thinking about the promotion causes you to mentally wander into the unknown. If you were vibrationally a match to this particular, specific promotion, your beliefs and thoughts surrounding the promotion would be clear. You would know that you're ready for the promotion. Even if the new promotion were to bring challenges, you would welcome them. All of your thoughts and beliefs about the new promotion would be clear and positive.

If you were not a vibrational match to the promotion, you might think thoughts that would bring on doubt and fear. You might worry that you're not ready for the promotion or that you don't really deserve it. You might think about how your family would react to the job change, either to the transfer to a new city or to the longer hours you might have to work. You want the promotion badly, yet every time you think about it, you experience thoughts of fear and doubt. Therefore, you are not yet a vibrational match to this specific desire.

You want the promotion because your overall set of desires includes within it the desire to be successful and to experience abundance. However, within your overall set of desires, you also include a desire for time with the family, the desire to remain in your city, the desire for freedom and many other desires. If this new promotion conflicts with those desires, it will not bring you what you really want. It will not fulfill your overall set of desires. In fact, if you were to receive this specific promotion, you would move away from that which you truly desire. This would still be alright since there is no wrong in the universe. The promotion, if you did get it, would cause such discord that you would alter your vibrational pattern so it would be even more focused on what you really wanted.

There are many facets of your vibrational pattern that you could not articulate if you tried. You cannot mentally see the big picture. You must trust that the universe and the Law of Attraction will work out the best path to your desire. When you allow the universe to take care of the how and when, you allow the manifestation of your dreams. Your intentions move the universe toward that which you desire and they are powerful tools, but you must be aware of any discord and adjust your intentions accordingly.

General intentions unfold in exactly the same way as specific intentions and actually carry as much power. You simply do not see the unfolding of a general intention as clearly as you do a specific intention. If you have the general intention to be happy, you might not be consciously aware of your happiness in any moment in time. But if you had the specific intention to receive $100, and you received it because you were perfectly aligned with it, you would feel exhilaration. You would see the complete and elegant way in which the universe brought you the $100 and you would assume that the specific intention was more powerful.

If you have the general intention for safety and you are safe every day, you cannot perceive just how that general intention manifests itself into your reality. If you were skydiving, however, and your intention was for the parachute to open, and it did, you would feel the exhilaration of relief. Your specific intention unfolded just as you knew it would. You might say that fear and doubt were fully involved in the skydiving analogy. One cannot jump out of an airplane without a modicum of fear and doubt. So how does one come to the sport of skydiving, especially the first jump?

In order to skydive, fear and doubt must be altered in such a way that they do not impede the desire from manifesting itself. What is the desire for skydiving? What is the emotional fabric of the event? Is it overcoming fear and doubt? Is it freedom and is the freedom one seeks the freedom from fear and doubt? Any activity so extreme is caused by the desire for freedom and that freedom is the freedom from fear and doubt. It is true freedom.

Fear and doubt hold you apart from that which you truly desire. When you can overcome the fearful and doubtful aspects of any intention, you remove their resistant qualities. How does one overcome fear and doubt when setting an intention or thinking about the manifestation of the intention? Let's play it out using the extreme analogy of skydiving.

If fear and doubt were strong within you, you would not skydive. Your thoughts about the act of skydiving would be so resistant in nature that you would never think about it again. If the subject was brought up, you would change it. You would have to allow for the possibility of a happy result which, at this time, you cannot.

If you could move desire forward and remove or lessen your attention from the fearful aspects of any endeavor, you could achieve the manifestation of your intent for any subject and you would be successful. If your first thought about skydiving was that it's a dangerous activity, your next thought would be of plummeting to the ground. If, however, you understood the value of the activity, you could create pleasing mental pictures of others skydiving. You could read reports that showed it was actually a relatively safe sport. If you could come to understand that the odds were stacked in your favor, you would reduce the resistance caused by fear and doubt and you would be one step closer to the manifestation of this desire.

Fear and doubt slow the progress to your desire depending on the strength of those thoughts. If they have a lot of energy within your thought process, they can stall the progress to your desire completely. If you can lessen their intensity, you'll move quickly toward your desire. If you're moving too fast toward your desire, don't worry; fear and doubt will intensify to slow your progress to a manageable speed. Do you see how the system works perfectly? There is a place for fear and doubt to exist within your thoughts. Fear and doubt are not to be extinguished; they are both useful and necessary components of the Law of Attraction.

You can reduce the effects of fear and doubt by changing your perspective. Roller coasters are designed to cause fear and doubt. You feel you are going too fast and fear and doubt enter your thoughts. This, ironically, is what makes roller coasters fun. You have fear and doubt and you are overcoming these sensations. Overcoming fear and doubt is exhilarating and you ride the roller coaster again. On your second ride, you experience less fear and doubt. Why is that? Because you've already engaged in the activity and you came out the other side unscathed. You now have more confidence, which means fear and doubt carry less energy. Your perspective has changed now that you've already experienced the ride and your belief has been altered.

You could have changed your perspective in advance of the first ride. Prior to the experience, you could have observed all of the people getting off the ride in front of you. They all survived. You see the quality of the safety systems involved and the quality of the structure itself. You realize the roller coaster is not going any faster than you drive in your car; it's just adding elements of speed, sound, wind and elevation changes that you are not accustomed to. While on the ride itself, you could want the roller coaster to move even faster and thereby eliminate the fear of speed. All of these things work to reduce the energy of fear and doubt and promote feelings of confidence. But what's the fun in that?

There is nothing to be feared from fear and doubt. They are simply tools to measure your alignment with your vibrational pattern. Be consciously aware of them and work to minimize their energy if you want. You have the capacity to live any experience you desire. Do not let fear and doubt hold you back, just learn to modify their effects and your outcomes will be wonderful.

Chapter Five

Emotions

Everything is right. Nothing is wrong. You are exactly where you intended to be at this moment in time. You are fine. If you could freeze this moment in time, you would realize that. However, time for you does not allow for the inspection of moments. You see time as a continuous flow of moment after moment. But in the moment, everything is right.

Your life is a series of moments that give you the illusion of time. It is like a film that is made up of many photos, and when played one after the other, you receive the impression of movement and an unfolding story. But in each moment, everything is fine. You are well, abundant, and fulfilled in each moment. It's the illusion of time that creates discord within.

If you could stop time and examine a moment, you would change your perception of your reality. When you are able to change your perception, you actually change your reality. Let's examine this moment right now. Let's pretend you can stop time. What do you see? What do you notice? What do you feel?

Are you, in this moment, sitting in a chair or lying in your bed? Are you alive? If so, you are fine. If not, you are also fine and everything is still right. Are you breathing? Is your heart beating? Do you have an abundance of air to breathe and an abundance of blood to flow through your heart? Have you had enough food to eat or are you starving? Have you had enough water to drink or are you dying from thirst? Do you have an abundance of light? Is the temperature right or are you freezing in this moment? Are you focusing on all that is right or is your focus elsewhere? Where is your focus as we ask these questions regarding the present moment in time?

You see that all is right. You have an abundance of air to breathe into your lungs and blood to flow through your heart. You have enough food to eat and water to drink. You have an abundance of light. You are warm in this moment. You are still alive. Nothing is wrong.

Let's broaden the picture and explore the moment. The world outside your window is all right as well. The sun is shining on your planet. The trees are growing, the birds are chirping, the animals are alive. The people of the world, in this moment, are flooded with well-being. In this moment, as time has been eliminated and there are no more moments, everything is fine.

The illusion of anything being less than right is the focus of your attention away from the well-being that is and toward a condition that has not manifested. The discord you feel within is due to your focus away from all that is right. You are either focused on unwanted things or you are focused on the lack of something you desire. Otherwise all would be fine in the moment.

It's your focus that causes the discord within. You have the choice at any moment in time to focus on the well-being that exists or on something else. It is your choice. If you focus on the well-being that is inherent in any moment, you will not feel discord; you will feel ease and comfort. Your focus away from the well-being that is within any moment causes a variety of unpleasant emotions. These unpleasant emotions, whether they are anger, frustration, envy, jealousy, resentment, despair, depression, worry, etc., are your indication that you are not focused on the well-being of the moment.

Pleasant-feeling emotions indicate that you are aware of the well-being of the moment. Your focus is on the positive aspects of any situation, whether it is the present, past, or future. You could conjure a memory of the past and experience a pleasant emotion. You could focus your attention on the dog sitting at your feet and feel a pleasant emotion. You could think about an event that is to happen in the future, maybe Christmas morning, and feel positive thoughts.

So what are the differences between pleasant-feeling emotions and unpleasant-feeling emotions? They are indicators of your current, in-the-moment focus. If you are focused on anything you perceive as wrong or bad, you experience unpleasant emotion. If you are focused on anything you perceive as right or good, you experience pleasant emotion. Therefore, emotions are simply an indication of your current focus.

The more pleasant or unpleasant the emotion, the more you perceive the object of your attention as good or bad, right or wrong. If you feel hatred, something has captured your attention that you feel strongly about as being bad or wrong. If you are in love with something then you feel strongly that it's good or right. Since there is no wrong in the universe, your unpleasant emotions let you know that you're off-track regarding this subject. Your perspective is not allowing you to see that whatever it is has positive aspects that you cannot or choose not to see.

Since everything in the universe is right the way it is, when you love something, you are seeing the full, complete rightness of whatever you are focusing on. When you witness a birth, you might experience joy. You see the full wonder of life and the possibilities for the baby to explore a world that is new and fresh. When you witness a death, you might feel grief as you perceive it as a loss. In the case of death, your focus is on the negative aspects of the situation and not the positive aspects.

What are the positive aspects of death? When you witness a death you could see that life experience was lived, however brief, and that all life experience is good. You could choose to understand there is no death, only life after life. You could realize that there is no loss or separation. You could know that there is only love and an even deeper connection, just on another level of reality. It is how you choose to perceive any situation that causes positive or negative emotion. You can choose to see the positive in everything or you can choose to see the negative in anything. Your emotion lets you know where your focus lies.

Given the choice, would you prefer to feel positive emotion or negative emotion? You would surely choose positive emotion. What does that mean? Does it mean you are physically meant to feel positive emotion over negative emotion? Is this the way physical reality was designed from the start? If the universe was trying to tell you something, to guide you in one direction over the other, could it pick a better method?

If you knew that emotion is just an indicator of your focus, and you realized that positive emotion and negative emotion are simply choices you make in the moment, then you could change your perspective on any situation. When you change your perception, you actually change your life. It's that simple.

II.

Emotions, as indicators of focus, are valuable tools in delivering the manifested reality of your dreams. Emotions are to be felt fully in the moment and not suppressed. Highly-emotional people have a head start toward understanding the process compared with those who show or feel little emotion. If you are lucky enough to be blessed with an abundance of emotion within you, rejoice, for it is a wonderful gift. If you feel little emotion in your day-to-day life, try to go deeper and be more analytical regarding your feelings of emotion at any point in time. Always try to increase your awareness of the emotions as they happen.

Manifestation events often bring out great rushes of emotion. If you observe a manifestation event and feel great joy, success, understanding, interest, pride, love, relief, etc., your focus is on the positive aspects of that event. If you feel anger, frustration, uneasiness, apathy, or indignation as a result of a manifestation event, you are focused on the negative aspects of the event and you are resisting the message within it. It's your choice either way. It has nothing to do with the event itself. It has only to do with your focus. You can choose to see the positive aspects of anything or the negative aspects of anything. You are blessed with free will.

If positive emotions feel good and negative emotions feel bad, why would you ever dwell on the negative aspects of anything and incur the wrath of a bad-feeling emotion? It's because you have forgotten that this guidance system was in place when you were born. However, it's a thrill to remember it now.

As you have progressed in your life experience thus far, you have had many good-feeling emotions and many bad-feeling emotions. Hopefully you've had more good than bad. Either way, due to your observance of others and your society, you've never pondered why good-feeling emotions feel better than bad-feeling emotions. You may never have considered that it's your perspective on a subject that initiates the good or bad-feeling emotion.

It's really as simple as that. Your perspective on a subject initiates an emotion within and that emotion is the indication of the focus, either positive or negative and the strength of that focus. If you are observing an event

A Perception of Reality

and you feel bored, that is an indication that you perceive the event in a mildly negative way. If you perceive the same event with some interest, it means you are seeing some positive aspects of the event. If you are observing an event and you feel rage, you are intensely focused on the most negative possible aspects of the event. If you are focused on an event and you feel sheer joy, then you are focused solely on the most positive aspects of the event. You are in total control of your focus, always, no matter what the event. You can choose to see the positive or negative side of anything.

Some events seem to be intrinsically more likely to inspire positive emotions over negative emotions. This too is an illusion because, due to your current perception point (which includes your current state of emotional being), you have the ability to choose to see the negative or positive aspects of any event.

Let's say the event is your daughter's wedding. You can choose to focus on the joyful aspects of the event or the painful aspects of the event. And you can choose to focus on both positive and negative aspects simultaneously. As the parent, you may focus on the negative aspects of the wedding. You are losing your child to another man. You are sharing her with another family. She is moving out of your house. You will see less of her. Her attention is now removed from you and placed on another. Each of these aspects of your focus initiates a negative emotion of some sort and intensity.

Now let's focus on the positive aspects of the wedding. You are gaining a son and new members of your family. Your daughter is starting a wonderful new life. You feel proud of her. You look forward to turning her room into your den. You anticipate the happiness that will come when she gives birth to your first grandchild. Good-feeling emotions accompany each of these thoughts.

Your emotional guidance system was designed to help you see the positive aspects of everything and remove your attention to the negative aspects of those same things. When you focus negatively on any subject, you add it to your vibration. When you focus positively on anything, you add the positive aspects to your vibration. Since you are here to create the life of your dreams, you want to experience the good in life and to lessen the experience of anything that is unwanted. Therefore, the more good you can see, the more good you will receive. The more unwanted you notice, the more unwanted you will receive. It makes sense, doesn't it?

Just for further clarification, let's take the example of an event that seems to be predisposed to one's focus on the negative aspects. You might recall seeing images of the civil rights demonstrations in the United States during the 1960's. Black and white Americans were marching for equality of the races. In certain areas of the country at the time, black Americans were treated differently than other races. During these marches, those in power would try to disperse the marchers with fire hoses, attack dogs, and clubs. As you watched the events, either in person or on television, you could focus on many aspects of the event. You could see the people being brutalized and feel anger, despair, or pity - all unpleasant-feeling emotions that indicate your focus of attention is squarely centered on the negative aspects of the event. Or, you could see the people fighting for their rights and be inspired, which is a pleasant-feeling emotion. You could see how they are moving the world forward toward peace and harmony and feel gratitude for their efforts. You could look into the future and see a time when the color of skin had nothing to do with the individual and that these brave people were paving the way toward a future where a black man would be elected president.

The events themselves are neither negative nor positive. It's the focus of your perception that matters. Your emotions are indicators of your focus. Your focus attracts and adds to your vibrational signal. The Law of Attraction responds to your vibrational signal and your life unfolds as a result of that signal. Focus your attention more on the positive aspects of every event and you will create a more positive life experience. Focus your attention more on the negative aspects of any event and you will include those negative aspects in your vibration and the Law of Attraction will show you more aspects of life that you deem negative. It's your choice.

III.

Your emotional state of being has an impact on your focus on the negative or positive aspects of any event. If you are currently in a lower emotional state, such as depression, you will likely find a match to your state of being in whatever event you are observing. If you are in a high emotional state such as passion or happiness, you will likely be a match to the positive

A Perception of Reality

aspects of any event. Your emotional state attracts like vibration and, as always, you have control over your emotional state of being.

You are always in a varying emotional state of being. You are often in the emotional state of contentment and well-being. Sometimes you dip into the emotional state of anger and sometimes you rise to the emotional state of exhilaration. Emotional states are similar to moods and can change as easily and as often as your mood alters. You could be in the emotional state of well-being but as you observe something unwanted, you might dip into an emotional state of frustration. As you observe something that you perceive as pleasing, you raise your emotional state once again. As you remain unaware of your control over your own emotional states, you allow them to rise and fall as a result of your observation.

You have control over your emotional state of being at any time. However, you must practice your way into higher emotional states for longer durations. It must be your conscious decision and focus to bring yourself to these higher vibrating states of emotion. Your state of emotion determines your access to thoughts and therefore it's at the basis of that which you attract.

At lower emotional states of being, such as rage or jealousy, you have access mostly to lower vibrating thoughts that match your present emotional state. If you are in an emotional state of jealousy, for instance, the thoughts you attract are not those of compassion, love, and peace. They are most likely those of fear and doubt, injustice and revenge. Your state of being limits or expands access to thoughts.

You might think you create your own thoughts in your mind. This is not completely accurate since all thoughts that have ever existed still exist and are still available. You attract thoughts. The type and quality of thoughts you attract is dependent on your vibration at the time you summon the thought. If you are in a high emotional state, you are vibrating at a high level and you will attract thoughts that match your high vibration. You have gained access, through your higher vibration, to thoughts that exist and are only available at this level.

When you find yourself in a lower vibrational state of emotional being, such as anger, the first thought that might come to you at this lower level is of an act of violence. You might have the thought of punching the object of your anger, whether it's another person or something inanimate, such as your computer. This thought, given your lower emotional state of being, might appear to be a good idea at the time. You might be inspired to act out this idea. Given your lower emotional state of being, the idea of striking someone or something may feel good to you. But lower vibrating thoughts bring an even lower vibration when acted on or just dwelled upon.

When you feel the higher emotional state of interest in something or passion for what you're doing, you will have access to thoughts that vibrate at a higher level. When you act upon these thoughts, which also make you feel better, you raise your emotional state even more. You begin attracting at an even higher level. Higher emotional states of being give you access to higher vibrating thoughts which increase your attracting power to even higher emotional states of being. The cycle spirals upwards. Lower emotional states of being bring lower vibrating thoughts, which feel just as valid but result only in lower emotional states of being.

When you're in the lower emotional state of anger and you receive the inspiration to strike your computer, the result is a broken computer, a fractured hand, or both. As a result of your ruined computer you feel even worse. Your computer must be fixed and you're going to have to explain how this occurred. Your emotional state of being now dips even further.

Since you have total control over every aspect of your life, as you are the sole creator of your experience, you have control over your emotional state of being. Any chronic state of being, whether it's joy or depression, is simply the result of a consistent level of thought. If you chronically attract higher vibrational thoughts through your focus of attention, you tend to live in higher emotional states of being. If you are consistently seeing the negative aspects of events, your emotional state of being will tend toward and may even be based in a lower emotional state of being such as depression. Any given state of being is the result of consistent focus on either positive or negative aspects of one's life.

Generally, happy people focus on aspects of life that are more positive in nature and pleasing to them when they turn their attention to them. Similarly, unhappy or depressed people tend to focus on the aspects of life that are more negative in their perception. They focus more on the unwanted things or the current lack of wanted things and they experience bad-feeling emotions. The bad-feeling emotions drive their emotional state of being toward a lower level and they receive more unpleasant-feeling thoughts.

Their emotions are chronically bad-feeling and they lose the ability, from this perspective, to gain a high vibrational state of being. They are unaware of their power over their state of being and fall into a trap of delusion. Since they have access only to lower-level thoughts, from their limited perspective it seems like they have no control over their situation. They may not regain control until they transition into nonphysical, where they will have full access to higher-vibrating thoughts and much higher levels of being.

You must be consistently aware of your current state of being. If you are in a high-vibrating emotional state, you will have access to high-vibrating thoughts. When you act on these thoughts you can be assured that they will lead to higher vibrating emotional states of being. These thoughts, at this level, can be trusted. If you make a decision in a high emotional state, it is the right decision. You must be fully aware of your emotional state before acting on any thought that comes while in that emotional state. Awareness of your emotional state of being is the key.

Once you have made a decision in a high emotional state, you might reconsider the decision at a lower vibrational state. The decision does not appear to be as sound from a lower state of being. It is not because the decision or the events surrounding it have changed; it's because you have changed perspective. Your perspective, from your lower emotional state of being, has shifted from one of a generally positive nature to one of a more generally negative nature. You see the world, and this particular decision, in a new light. It's a more negative light and the thoughts that come to you as you ponder this decision are of a negative nature and make the decision appear to be negative. However, this is an illusion.

You have control over your emotional state of being as long as you are aware of this control. For most of your life, you may have been under the assumption that your state of being was caused by conditions that were out of your control. Because you now realize that you are the creator of your reality and thus you cause the conditions, you now know you have the power to be in a state of alignment under any set of conditions. We understand the difficulty involved in reaching and maintaining alignment when you are not used to practicing thoughts that bring you into alignment with your inner self, with your desires, or with an improved state of being. But you *can* come into alignment if you learn how and if you practice it often.

Emotional states of being are similar to moods with varying degrees of intensity. Moods are generally either good or bad. You're in a good mood one moment, a bad mood the next, and a good mood again later. Emotional states of being are more variable in intensity and range from a very low vibrational state of being to a moderately low vibrational state of being to a moderately high vibrational state of being to a very high vibrational state of being. The lower your vibration at any moment in time, the lower your emotional state of being. The higher your vibration, the higher your emotional state of being.

All emotional states of being have specific and unique vibrational frequencies. Rage is different from anger in vibrational terms and has variations of intensity within it. We could get very specific in describing the vibrational patterns of every aspect of every possible emotion. Attraction is specific to your overall vibrational pattern at each moment in time and brings to you that to which you are a match based on your overall vibrational pattern. As you can imagine, your vibrational pattern is not static but is in a constant state of flux. In the long term, your life will unfold based on your overall vibrational pattern. In the short term, you will attract manifestation events that reflect your vibrational pattern in the moment or, we could say, during the short term.

An awareness of your emotional state of being allows you to realize what you are attracting during the day. This is of great importance given the nature of momentum. If you are in the lower emotional state of worry, for instance, you'll attract thoughts of worry that will manifest into events that reflect your worrisome thoughts back to you in the form of a physically unfolding manifestation event. The event confirms your worry and you tend to become even more worried.

However, if you understand that the event is just indicating the nature of your emotional state of being and has no other significance in and of itself, you can see the event simply as the physical manifestation of your state of being. It works like a mirror reflecting back to you the image of your state of being. You can now stop and realize that it was your worrisome thoughts that led to the event. Once you change your state of being and thus change the predominance of your thoughts, you will change the type of manifestation events that occur.

The key to changing your state of being in the moment is to understand in more detail the mechanism of emotional states of being. Most humans react to the conditions they see around them. They want the conditions to be different before they allow themselves to feel differently. If they hear some bad news, they might internalize it and start to feel badly. If they hear some good news, they react in a positive manner. However, if you realize that others, including the news, society at large, and all other people, have no ability to create in your reality, then you do not need to react to outside conditions. You make the conditions. It is time for you to understand this fact and realize that you can change your own conditions.

You cannot alter conditions by reacting negatively to the conditions in the moment. You must change the conditions over time, through thought alone. Action, in the moment of an unwanted condition, will generally worsen your feelings regarding the condition. Any condition that exists in your life, either wanted or unwanted, was previously created by your predominance of thought. This is a very specific concept regarding the process of deliberate creation but it is important to understand that even in your ignorance of the process, you created the conditions that currently exist in your life.

You must understand this key concept before you can change or improve any single aspect of your life. You created the job or lack of job you now have. You created all of the relationships in your life whether they bring you joy or its opposite. You created the things in your possession whether you appreciate them or find them burdensome. You have created it all in your mind before it ever existed in your reality. Your state of being, over time, played a part in what you've created. If you have a happy life, you've been mostly living in higher states of being. If you are unhappy with the present conditions of your life, you have been more often in lower vibrational states of being.

Each aspect of your life is reflected in your predominant emotional state of being. If you are happy at home with your family but unhappy at work, you have different emotional states of being as a direct observance of these different environments. Change your state of being at work and you will change that aspect of your life.

How can you change your emotional state of being while at work when you hate your job? First, you must realize it was your thoughts that created your job, which in turn created the aspects of your job you do not like. If you were in a low emotional state of being when you took the job, then your focus was on the negative aspects of the job. If you were in the emotional state of being described as unworthiness, you took a job that fit perfectly with your emotional state and reflected that state back to you. With this knowledge, should you now quit your job to remove yourself from the condition? You could, but only if you were sure you could find a higher state of being prior to finding a new job.

However, a far more productive course of action would be to understand the role your emotional state of being plays in any condition, including your present work environment. The job itself is neither positive nor negative in nature. It's your focus of attention that creates the illusion of positivity or negativity within you. Your perspective creates a job that is either hated or loved. Your perception is the only thing that matters.

As you change your perception of the job you once hated to a perception of the same job you now appreciate, your job will actually change. You have all the power. So, instead of quitting that job, try focusing on all the positive aspects and removing your attention from the negative aspects. Like a large ship with you in control of the rudder, your attention to the positive will slowly begin to turn the ship in the direction you prefer. Over time, with consistent attention to the positive aspects of the job, you will come to either love this job, be promoted to a position you love, or be inspired to find a completely new job. However, the job will not change until you consciously realize you have control and start to think better thoughts.

You improve your emotional state of being by deliberately improving your thoughts. Since your emotional state of being is predisposed to thoughts that vibrate at that level, you must consciously and consistently reach for better-feeling thoughts. You may not achieve thoughts of joy from a state of depression, but you can reach for general thoughts of well-being which will lead to thoughts of hopefulness. In a state of depression, you must focus your attention on the positive aspects of your present condition. You must stay general in nature. You must realize that, in the present moment, you are fine and everything is fine. Slowly, with more deliberate thoughts of well-being, you will bring yourself to an improved emotional state of being which will bring you to better-feeling thoughts. The better you feel, the more good-feeling thoughts will arrive naturally.

A Perception of Reality

Your emotional state of being is usually based on your perception of the present conditions of your life. You thought your way into these conditions and you will have to think your way to conditions you prefer. You must think more positive thoughts about your present condition. You cannot change your present condition by wishing it was different. That only holds you in place because you're focused on what's wrong with the present condition.

Since there is no wrong anywhere in the universe, the universe believes that because you're focused on the present conditions you do not like, you actually prefer the negative aspects of your present condition. Therefore, through the Law of Attraction, the universe brings you more of what you do not want., Due to your attention to the negative aspects of your present condition, the universe assumes that these are the aspects you prefer. The universe assumes you would only focus your attention on the aspects you want, not on the aspects you dislike. Thus, you get more of whatever you focus your attention on.

If you want a better house, you must focus your attention on the aspects of your present house that you like or even love. The more you focus your attention on the aspects you like, the more you will like your house and the easier it will be for you to move toward ever-improving living conditions. If you come to love your house, you will be inspired to an improved condition regarding your home. This may lead to someone wanting to buy it, or the inspiration for you to put it on the market, or maybe to remodel it. Focus on the positive aspects you already appreciate and those aspects must become more and better. It is the law of the universe. Focus on the aspects you perceive as negative and those aspects must become more and worse. This too, is the law of the universe.

By focusing on the positive aspects of any present condition, you improve your emotional state of being, which will begin to improve your present condition. There is always the lag of time in physical reality. Your present emotional state of being affects how your life unfolds over time. Your new, improved state of being will also begin to affect how your life unfolds over time.

Momentum has brought you to this place, so your ship turns slowly toward the new direction. Give it time and, with consistently improved thoughts and improved emotional states of being, you will move in the direction of what is desired rather than what is not desired.

Chapter Six

Inspiration, Motivation, and Action

Your action will cause manifestation, but not the fully realized manifestation of your dreams. Your vibrational pattern contains within it the full, all-encompassing version of that which you truly desire. Your conscious mind can only perceive a small and limited version of your desire. You might envision the result of your desire, but you cannot envision the journey that must take place for the fullness of your desire to manifest.

Right now you could get a shovel, go to your backyard, dig a hole, and fill it with water. This hole is a manifestation, but it is not the swimming pool of your dreams. You can cause manifestation through action, and often the manifestation seems to match closely to your idea of the dream you've been thinking about. But action alone will only create only a mere shadow of the full realization of your dream. When you align with that which you desire, you will feel inspiration prior to action.

Inspiration is a key aspect to creating the full version of your desires. You must be led to action, not forced into it. Inspiration leads you willingly into an action that you want to do because you feel it is right. Motivation may cause action, but it is forced action. The inspired action comes from within and it is what you want to do right now.

If you are not inspired to act, don't act. Your society is based on action and any inaction is viewed with a sense of contempt. You might be called lazy or labeled a procrastinator. Yet uninspired action always leads to less desirable results and often to complete failure. It is through uninspired action that you come to learn failure at an early age.

Inspired action comes when the universe has lined up the components necessary to complete the full version of your desire. The universe can only bring you what matches your vibration. Through your life experience, you have come to create powerful desires from within. You may not know the fullness of your desires due to your limited perception at this point in your development, but your vibration pulsates with the complete version of everything you want.

You might have heard others say they can't believe they were able to achieve their dream to the extent to which it manifested. They use the term "beyond my wildest dreams." This comes, not because the manifestation is greater than what they had asked for, but because it was exactly what they asked for. It was simply that they were unable to perceive the fullest, most wonderful version of the dream from the reality they were living at the time.

You, as you are in this moment, are not ready for the physical manifestation of any desire that has not yet been fulfilled or has not yet manifested in your reality. If the desire came to you now, you would not appreciate it and you might lose it relatively quickly. Your perception must be altered to allow the desire to manifest. **You** must change in order to be ready to receive the physical manifestation of that which you truly desire.

Let's say you desire a loving relationship with a mate. The three most common desires of humans are better relationships, more money, and an enhanced bodily condition. So it is easy to talk about the subject of relationships since most people can identify with the desire to create a loving, long-term relationship with a mate. Through your life experience thus far, you have added thoughts about what you prefer in a mate to your vibration. As a child, you witnessed the behavior of your parents and added what you perceived as preferable to your vibration, as well as the knowledge of what you did not like. You have seen countless movies about relationships and you added those idealized aspects of scripted relationships to your vibration. As you grew older and experienced relationships of your own and those of your friends, you added pieces of these relationships to your vibration. You did this all in the moment without conscious awareness of what you were doing.

You may not be consciously aware of every piece you have added to your vibration, but your vibration has kept a vigilant account of every single aspect of your desire. Your vibration pulsates with the knowledge of the fullness of your every desire. Every time you experience something you don't want in a relationship, your desire is modified to reflect what you do want. Your desire grows sharper and clearer with each new experience. However, you have a path to travel to reach the fullness of what you desire.

You have to be molded into the version of you that will be ready each step of the way. You will be physically, emotionally, and perceptually changed into a version of you that is vibrationally ready to receive the fullness of your desire. When it finally arrives, you'll exclaim, "This relationship is beyond my wildest dreams!"

II.

On your path toward the fulfillment of your dreams, action will be necessary. While the universe is lining up all components needed for you to realize your dream, it will inspire you do to something at the exact point in time when the other components have lined up as well. As we continue with the analogy of your ideal relationship, we will look at a very common tactic used by the universe to mold you into a state of being that is required to bring you the full manifestation of your desire.

Think of yourself as you are now, prior to having the relationship of your dreams, as a solid block of granite. The version of you that has the relationship of your dreams is the finished work of art. Somehow the universe must chip away the unnecessary pieces of granite to reveal the sculpture. Each time you take action, a chip falls off. If you take uninspired action, only a small chip of granite is removed and it might even be the wrong chip. In fact, the uninspired action might cause a crack in the entire block of granite and the universe will have to start over from the beginning. If, however, you only take action when action is inspired, the right pieces of granite will be chipped away easily and soon the magnificent sculpture will be complete.

The universe sets you up to experience certain manifestation events that will lead you to your desire. With each manifestation event you gain more clarity. The event may cause you to learn or realize something new. The event may cause you to alter your belief system in a way that allows you to become more aligned with your desire.

You carry patterns of beliefs that you have developed since childhood. These beliefs, or prejudices, often block the path to the fullness of that which you desire. The universe must chip away at these beliefs in order to create a version of you that will be ready for the fullness of your desire.

Imagine that you were once bullied in school by a person with red hair. Since childhood you have always held a negative association with red-haired people. You hold this belief, or prejudice, unconsciously. When introduced to anyone with red hair you feel uneasy. You may not even know why this happens to you or even remember the bully, but it's a part of your vibration. Now imagine that the person who will eventually fulfill your desire for a relationship beyond your wildest dreams just happens to have red hair. If you were to meet this person today, given your current prejudice, you would never be able to get the relationship started. You would think, "This can't be the one." So the universe must remove your prejudice before you are allowed to meet.

This is common to all manifestations. You must be cleared of any hindering beliefs, prejudices, or thought patterns so you will be ready for the full manifestation of your desire. The universe will use a never-ending series of manifestation events to mold you into alignment. If you are a willing participant in the manifestation event, you will quickly become ready. If you hold onto your limiting belief patterns, it will take longer. If you can see the manifestation event for what it offers, even if it's unpleasant, you will grow quickly. If you resent the manifestation event and dig in deeper to your limiting beliefs, you will stay where you are and might never find the relationship of your dreams.

If you harbor this prejudice against red-haired people and must change your beliefs in order to fulfill your dreams, the universe will provide you with manifestation events that will slowly change your belief system if you allow the change to take place. You might be inspired to read a book you have come to love and then, to your astonishment, find that the book was written by a red-haired person. Your belief has been altered to an extent. If as a result of this manifestation event, you release your red-haired prejudice to a high enough degree, the universe will understand that you are now ready to meet your red-haired mate and will inspire you to take the next step.

If you have released a portion of your prejudice but not to the extent needed, the universe might inspire your best friend to change her hair color to red. You love your best friend and are quite surprised to see that she looks great with red hair. Your prejudice is reduced even more. Then you're inspired to turn on the news and see a story of a child saved from a burning building. As the reporter interviews the brave fireman, he takes off his helmet to reveal his bright red hair. Your prejudice has now been reduced to the extent necessary and you are ready for the fullness of your desire to manifest into your reality.

In the example above, the person was led through inspiration to take certain actions that led to manifestation events. These events chipped away at their prejudice. Without following the inspiration, the manifestation events would not have occurred. It is important to understand the role inspiration has as it leads you to your dreams. If the person had taken any action that was not inspired, it would not have had any positive effect on the realization of the dream because the removal of the prejudice was necessary before the dream could fully manifest. If this part of the journey was left out, like a bridge over a wide river, the destination could not be reached.

This is an over-simplification of the process because there is much more involved. The universe is constantly lining up rendezvous and manifestation events to help you create new and beneficial belief patterns while simultaneously reducing the prevalence of hindering belief patterns. If you can become aware of the mechanism and understand the value of each and every manifestation event, you can expand quickly and be ready for dream after dream after dream.

When you are inspired to take action, whether you understand the source of the inspiration or not, it feels right. You enjoy the action no matter what the action entails. Action as a result of inspiration is often fun. Action through inspiration blurs your sense of time. You get involved in what you're doing and then look up at the clock and realize that hours have passed in what seems like minutes.

Inspiration often occurs when you are aligned with your desire and your hindering belief patterns have faded into the background. You feel a passion for what you are doing. You care less about eating and sleeping. You are more focused on the moment and less concerned about the outcome. You feel excited in anticipation of what may come, yet what you are doing in the present moment is just as exciting.

When you are working on something you're passionate about and are inspired to take action, you might be immediately successful or, more often, you'll face what appears to be failure. When pursuing your dream through inspired action, failure is an illusion. You have never failed unless you have given up on your true dream. You will face necessary obstacles on the journey to your dream. These obstacles occur in the form of manifestation events.

As you have already learned, manifestation events are an integral part of the process that will mold you into the version of you that is ready for your dream to fully manifest. The limited, narrow version of the dream you carry in your mind is different from the fullest version of the dream that will unfold in your reality. Manifestation events that seem like failure are working to shape your version of the dream so that it more closely coincides with the fullest manifestation of your dream. You can see only a very limited aspect of the dream, while the universe, because it completely understands your vibration, knows the fullest, richest possible version of your dream.

Failure points out your specific resistance to your desire. Failure is always a manifestation event that often carries a lesson. You must realize the lesson contained within the event, adjust your belief pattern, and then try again. If you come upon a similar manifestation event that carries a similar lesson, you have not learned the lesson. The feeling of failure will again present itself. You must adjust. Usually the thing you must change is a certain limiting belief. The most common hindering belief is that of unworthiness. Every human, no matter what their position in your society, has experienced the feeling of unworthiness. We will discuss this topic in more detail because it is so pervasive in your society. However, as you realize that the feeling of unworthiness is likely to arise, you must reduce the intensity of that hindering belief.

When you are inspired to take action, and you take it without fear or doubt, that action will lead you directly to the manifestation of your desire. When you take inspired action with a hindering belief present, it is the hindering belief that brings fear and doubt and the action must bring up a manifestation event. Manifestation events present themselves to add clarity to your desire. They contain lessons to help you understand how your belief patterns may be hindering the progress to your desire. Once the hindering belief pattern has been removed or reduced, you feel less fear and doubt and you're on your way to the physical manifestation of your desire.

III.

Uninspired action will create physical manifestation. However, the result will always be unrewarding and unfulfilling. Uninspired action never leads to the fullest manifestation of your desire. WHEN YOU TAKE ACTION WHEN YOU ARE NOT YET INSPIRED TO DO SO, YOU TAKE THE ACTION FROM THE LIMITED PERSPECTIVE OF YOUR EGO.

Your ego is a mechanism of your personality and is responsible for the version of reality you now experience. It sees the outer world and organizes it, through your beliefs, in the way in which you now perceive your world. Your ego helps you believe that what you perceive as real *is* real. It defends reality and fights the idea of the inner world. Your ego has been trained over time to defend your belief systems. Your ego makes you take action even when not inspired to do so.

If left alone, free to explore the world without the influence of others or your society, you would take only inspired action. Your ego would support you in your belief that only inspired action was necessary. Instead, through the socialization you've undergone, your ego supports your belief that in order to get something done, you must take action immediately. Action is the only thing that matters. Inspired action is nice, but you can't just sit around waiting for it to happen. Your ego wants you to act now.

Uninspired action feels less exhilarating than inspired action. In fact, it often feels like work, whereas inspired action feels more like fun. You have been taught that hard work is the key to success. But if hard work was inspired it would never be hard; it would be easy. Easy work is the key to success.

You believe in the phrase "No pain, no gain." That is uninspired action. That is motivation. Motivation urges action. Motivation is necessary to force action when one is not inspired to the action. Motivation is the illusion of inspired action. Motivation may be effective in the short term, but it will produce only scanty results. Motivation can lead, through the manifestation event of failure, to inspired action, but motivation is only a tool used to force uninspired action.

Guilt works like motivation. It often forces you to do things you do not want to do. Since guilt has a low vibrational pattern, the resulting action will most likely be of a similarly low vibration. The action taken through guilt will not move you toward your desire, but will most likely lead you further from your desire.

Anything that motivates you to act does so at a lower vibration than inspiration and will result in a less than desirable condition. Action through inspiration will always lead you on the path toward the physical manifestation of your desire. You may experience manifestation events along the way that feel like failures or setbacks, but once you realize the lessons contained in them, you will be inspired to act again.

When a manifestation event occurs as the result of uninspired action, the feeling of failure also carries a lesson. However, the feeling of failure is far more intense as a result of uninspired action as compared to inspired action. When a manifestation event of failure occurs after inspired action, you will soon have the strong urge to try again. You must try again. You will do it differently this time, but you're going to do it. You're never going to quit.

When the manifestation event of failure arises as a result of uninspired action, you feel deep despair. You feel despondent. You do not want to try again. You want to give up altogether. It does not feel right. The lesson contained is unlikely to be understood. You want to try something entirely different.

Uninspired action is generally the result of not understanding your true desire. You think you want one thing when actually you want something else. You take action toward the goal, but that goal was never your true desire. All action toward this goal will be uninspired. You feel you must do it and you take the uninspired action which must lead to a painful manifestation event.

Unless you are on the path to that strong and true desire that vibrates forth from you to the universe, you will not receive the inspiration to act. You will force yourself to take action you deem a struggle. You will talk yourself into action before you are ready. You will move in the wrong direction until, after many painful manifestation events, you start to turn in the direction of your true desire.

Your attention to the lives of others often causes you to want things you do not truly desire. You can only observe the shallow surface when you turn your attention to the lives of others. You do not see the depth beneath the surface. You cannot perceive what their life is really like. You are fooled by the illusion of their facade, but you cannot see their full vibrational pattern.

You must withdraw your attention from the lives of others and turn to your life inside. You are here to explore certain aspects of physical reality. Your path is unique to you and is one of joy. It may seem lesser than the paths of others, but it is not. Your path, which you will know through the feelings of passion, excitement, happiness, exhilaration, and joy, is exactly as profound as the path of those you admire. You are predetermined to feel good when you're on your path and uneasy on any other path. This is how the system was designed.

When you're off your path, the universe will provide manifestation events that let you know it. When you're on your path, the universe will bring you manifestation events that let you know that as well. If you understand the value of all of the manifestation events you encounter, you can move quickly along your path to reach even further joy and expansion. You are here to expand joyously. Inspired action will get you to wherever you want to go.

IV.

You were born into this physical reality to explore certain aspects of life. You came with general intentions and more specific intentions. Those intentions set you on a path in this life experience. When you align with your true desires, your path unfolds naturally. When you are influenced by others to a desire that is not your true desire, you step off your path. Action toward the goal of attaining a desire that is not a true desire will often feel like struggle.

When you find yourself doing something you do not want to do, when the action is not pleasurable, you are off your intended path. However, you need not be concerned because you can easily return to your path at any time. Often, action in the course of following the path toward a desire that is not true will help you find your true desire. You may want something very specific and be willing to do anything to get it. If it is your true desire, one in which you came here to explore, you will find joy in the journey. The action will be inspired. The journey will be fun. You will encounter manifestation events along the way that will guide you. You might face a few setbacks but never failure.

If the thing that is so badly wanted is not your true desire, but one you picked up due to the influences of others or one you feel will validate your existence, you will find struggle and hardship in the pursuit of this false dream. You are worthy beyond measure. The universe is designed specifically to bring you joy and fulfillment. You do not have to prove your worth to others. They would not see it anyway.

You must ask yourself often what you truly desire. If you were free from the influence of others and your materialistic society, what would you truly want? If you believed you could have, be, or do anything, what would it be? If you believed you were as worthy as anyone else, what path would you take? If you can imagine it, you can achieve it. But your desire must be your true desire.

Action toward a true desire, when inspired, has the leverage of the universe behind it. If you were aligned, you could work as little as a few minutes a day and achieve great wealth. The value of your action is not measured in time, but in productivity. You do not need to work hard to earn great sums of money. In fact, the harder one works, the more likely it is that money will not flow to him or her easily.

Action has no correlation to income in and of itself. Inspired action has leverage and one can, if open to the flow, achieve great sums of money in very short periods of time. Action without inspiration is relatively unproductive and the income generated by uninspired action is mostly limited in nature.

If you are on your path and are aligned with a true dream, income will flow easily into your physical reality to the degree you allow it to. If your work is your passion, you will have lined up the leverage of the universe to assist you and your inspired action can produce great sums of money if that is what you want. In this case, your work will be so filled with joy and ease that you would do it for no income. The work is what gives you joy and the money flows to you as a result of the joy, not the work.

If your joy is to paint and your art is inspired, you will enjoy the flow of money and fame, if that is also what you desire. However, you could be a great painter, producing masterpiece after masterpiece, while earning no recognition or money in your lifetime. Once you have died, your work is found, the resistance you held against earning money and fame has also died with you and your art sells for great sums of money.

You can take inspired action and feel joy in your work and still earn little income. If you have resistance against income, money will not flow easily to you. You can be passionate about your work, enjoying the action that is inspired and leveraging the power of the universe to be incredibly productive and produce fine work, yet the resistance around the subject of money stops the flow of money into your life.

At the base of most resistance to money is the feeling of unworthiness. If you truly felt you deserved the money, it would flow easily into your life. But if you lack the confidence to attract money, it will come exactly in the amount you allow and no more. In every profession there are masters who make very little while there are many who are less skilled earning far greater sums of money. It has nothing to do with skill, for money flows to those who allow it to. It's as simple as that.

Your passion for your work does not have to involve money. We will explain how to allow money to flow later. For now we want your perspective to be modified regarding the subject of action. Inspired action leads to joy and passion. Uninspired action leads to struggle and frustration. Your true desire will create the urge to pursue inspired action. Your false desire will motivate you toward uninspired action.

Your true desire has an attractive effect in your life. You are drawn, through many manifestation events, to that which you truly desire. You can pursue your true desire as a full-time profession or as a part-time hobby. It makes no difference. If you pursue your true desire, the one you came here to explore, you can make it a full-time profession and earn as much money as a result as you will allow. It does not matter what your true desire is; you can turn it into something that will earn money.

If you believe your true passion cannot earn money, then due to your belief system, it cannot. If you believe it can earn money, then it will and you can turn it into a profession. The benefit of turning the pursuit of your true desire into a profession is that you can earn your living from focusing on your passion. Your profession is fun and exhilarating because you're following your dream passionately.

On the other hand, if you believe you cannot earn enough money to support yourself or your family though the pursuit of your dream, then you will have to earn your income by doing work that is not inspired. You can find joy in anything you do and can have fun and satisfaction in any form of work, but without the alignment of inspired action, you omit the leverage of the universe and the results of your labor are less than what they might have been had you taken inspired action.

You are in total control of your life at every moment. You had a set of intentions you made before your birth. These intentions will call to you, but you have the choice to ignore them and choose a new set of desires based on your experience in this lifetime. You can justify any action as a result of your life experience. You can stick to the path you're on and see where it goes. You are free to choose any path and you have the ability to experience joy along any path. But if your action is forced rather than inspired, you are simply making things more difficult than they need to be.

If you can understand the concept of inspired action over required action, your life will improve immeasurably. If you realize you can take action but do not need to take any action that is not inspired, your life will change for the better immediately.

Fear often causes much action that is not inspired. If you fear the consequences of not acting, you will force yourself to take uninspired action. This may alleviate your fear, and that might be a positive outcome, but the fear was never real in the first place. If you are aligned and only take inspired action, you will be inspired to act when necessary to achieve your dream. You never have to force action.

The difficulty lies in your habit of action. You have lived your life to this point taking mostly uninspired action to reach your goals. You will have to change your perception regarding action slowly over time. We are not asking you to stop all uninspired action immediately, but simply to focus on the action and observe whether it is born of inspiration or not.

You may get the inspiration to buy your mate a gift. The inspiration might take you shopping which you normally do not enjoy. However, due to the inspiration, you find shopping strangely pleasurable. If aligned fully with the desire to buy the perfect gift, you will be drawn to it through more inspiration. You will overhear a conversation or notice someone wearing something that catches your eye. A memory might enter your thoughts and you'll think of the perfect gift. You will be led into the store that has the item and the staff will even suggest it to you. If you follow the inspiration, it will lead you to your true desire - in this case, the perfect gift for your mate.

You may hold the desire of a clean, well-organized home free from clutter. You may take inspired action, when fully aligned with your desire, to clean your home or hire someone to do the task for you. If, however, you feel that others in your household should also hold your desire as their own, you might expect them to do their share. You cannot expect others to share the desire you hold as your own for each person holds their own desires that are unique to them. If you expect your mate or children to share your desire to the intensity to which you hold yours, you will find conflict. Others will never hold the same desire as you to the same degree. Your desires are unique to you and their desires are unique to them.

Your child, for instance, does not mind a messy house for he or she holds desires for fun, ease, love, and activity. A clean and organized home does not bring them the same feeling of joy it brings to you. They find joy in the pursuit of desires that are much different than yours. They are inspired to action that aligns with their true desire, not your true desire. And, while they can be forced or coerced to clean their room, for instance, they are not inspired to do so. This does not mean they should not share in the duties of the household; it simply means that you should not expect them to perform their duties with glee. Instead, you could accept their forced action for what it is and praise them for being active participants in the household whenever possible. If you see a sock on the floor, stop and realize that your desire does not coincide with their desire. Your desire is just as valid, not more so, than their desires. Do not blame them for not aligning with your desire to the degree to which you hold that desire for it is not possible for them to do so. Pick up the sock if you want, but release your belief that they should know better.

If you resent someone for not aligning with your desire they will, by the laws of the universe, move further away from your desire. If you resent them for not desiring a clean and organized home and you antagonize them because they do not align with your specific desire, they will cause disharmony in the home and lead you away from what you truly desire. You must understand their desires and align with those desires as closely as you can. If you can see their desire, you can enjoy harmony.

For example, you may hold the strong desire for a clean and organized home, while your children hold the desire for a loving relationship with you. Instead of withholding your affection when they don't align with your desire, praise them when they do. Support their desire for love and attention and align with it as much as you can and you praise them when they align with your desire. Eventually, they will be inspired to align with your desire more often and they will be inspired to action in a way that aligns with your desire. Your attention and alignment to the desires of others actually causes others to align with your desire. It is simply a function of the laws of the universe and nothing more.

When you focus your attention on something unwanted, or in this case, something annoying, you bring more of it into your physical experience. The Law of Attraction is universal. If it works for one thing it works for everything. You may argue that the Law of Attraction is not responsible for your child leaving socks on the floor, but by your attention to the sock on the floor, you activate the Law of Attraction and you find more socks on the floor. It is not your child who is responsible, it is actually you.

If you can understand this concept you can change your perspective and reduce the frequency of the things you find annoying. The first step is to understand that anything you place your attention on grows more and more. If it is unwanted, you will feel negative emotion when thinking about the subject. The unwanted sock on the floor causes you to attract unpleasant thoughts. You might think that if they loved you they would pick up their socks. You might attract the thought that they are irresponsible. All of these thoughts, however, are contrary to your true beliefs about your child.

You love your child and normally think wonderful thoughts about them. You believe your child loves you as well. You know your child is good. If you are able to change your perspective when you find a sock on the floor and think thoughts that align with your true beliefs, you will reduce whatever is unwanted in your life. When thinking thoughts that feel good, you'll feel positive emotion. This indicates that the thoughts align with your true desire.

You would not send your child away so that he is no longer able to leave socks around the house. So when you see a sock on the floor, or anything else you find annoying, change your perspective from one of negative thoughts to more positive thoughts. Realize that a sock on the floor means you have a child and a family. Think the best thoughts you can of the child. Remember how much you love your child. Be grateful for the sock on the floor and realize that soon your child will grow and leave your home and there will no longer be socks on the floor. All you're doing is changing your perspective which helps you focus on wanted rather than unwanted conditions.

V.

All action has its own vibrational signature. The action vibrates at high or low levels depending on its alignment with your specific individual and unique set of desires. Inspired action vibrates at a much higher frequency than uninspired action. Action taken out of fear vibrates at a low frequency. You can feel the vibration of any action. High-frequency actions feel good as you are performing the action, while low frequency actions do not feel good.

When taking action that is vibrating at a high level, you attract thoughts that feel good to you. You feel positive emotion. The feelings of fun, joy, interest, passion, exhilaration, productivity, etc. all feel good in the moment. You know this action is inspired.

When taking action that is uninspired or forced, you attract thoughts that vibrate at a low frequency. You know the action is uninspired because the thoughts you attract feel unpleasant. The emotion that surrounds the action feels like boredom, struggle, fear, doubt, uneasiness, etc. You are forcing yourself to take the action because you believe the action will lead you to the manifestation of a desire. It may, in fact, lead you to a manifestation, but that manifestation will be of a false desire and will not be truly satisfying or fulfilling.

Only the manifestation of true desires feels fulfilling and rewarding when it actually manifests in your physical reality. If you're on a path to your true desire, the action needed to manifest the desire will feel good. It will be accompanied by good-feeling thoughts and good-feeling emotions. You may experience setbacks that, at the time, do not feel good. But that is only because your limited perspective does not allow you to see the full picture. If you understood that the perceived setback was just a small part of the enjoyable journey, you would not experience negative emotion as a result of a setback.

Allow your emotions and thoughts to guide you to your true desire. If you are feeling positive thoughts and emotions while taking action, it is an inspired action and you know you're on the path to a true desire. If you are feeling mostly negative thoughts and emotions around an action, you might realize that the action is not inspired and is therefore not leading you to a true desire. Pay attention to your thoughts and emotions surrounding any action and you can start to align with true desires. This is the guidance system you were born with and it works to make life more fulfilling, expansive, and joyous.

Chapter Seven

Parenting, Education, and Intelligence

You are in control of your life experience and you are the creator of you. Everyone else, including your children and your mate, is the creator of their life experiences. You cannot create in their life experience and they cannot create in yours. Parents and teachers have influence over children. This influence can often be misguided and even detrimental.

You were born into this physical reality with a unique set of intentions. Your desires are also unique to you. What is right for you may not be right for another, including your child. You came here to explore a certain aspect of life and your child also came to explore a certain aspect of life. What you are here to explore is different than what your child is here to explore. You came with certain general and specific intentions. While you and your child may share many of the same general intentions, you likely have very different specific intentions.

As you were born into the world, the earth environment vibrated at a certain frequency. Your vibration was a match to the earth's vibration at that time, on the day of your birth, and hence you were born. Since everything, through the Law of Expansion, grows more, the earth is now vibrating at a higher frequency than it was on the day of your birth. You could say the world was a very different place on the day of your birth compared to the day of your child's birth.

Your child was born into this time because he or she is a vibrational match to the earth as it is now. Your child was born at a higher frequency than you were at your birth. Your child comes to this physical existence in an advanced state compared to your vibrational frequency on the day you were born. You could say your child is better equipped to explore the earth of today than you are.

Like you, your child has a guidance system. He knows what action to take based on his emotions, thoughts, and feelings. When left uninfluenced by you or others, he will make the proper choices that align with his true desires. Your influence and the influence of others cause him to lose trust in his guidance system. You do this out of a false sense of concern or fear. If you would allow your child to use his guidance system without interference from you or others, he would be flooded with well-being and not subject to your random set of fears.

As you love your child, the feeling you get is one of true alignment with your inner self and your own true desires. You use your child as your reason for alignment and assume that your love for your child is what causes the good-feeling emotions. You fear that if anything should happen to your child you will lose those good-feeling emotions. So you act to protect your child from the perceived dangers of the world. This protection, enacted out of fear and doubt, actually hinders your child's ability to find his own guidance system. He learns to accept the authority of others over his own inner resource.

Your child was born with a set of intentions. Manifestation events must occur to guide your child to her path. If you are on guard against any manifestation event you deem painful from your limited perspective, you stall your child's progress to that which she is here to explore. In time, your child will eventually face those same manifestation events when you are not around to interfere. This might happen when she leaves home and goes out on her own. She will face many manifestation events that will guide her to her path. Unfortunately, they are likely to be significantly more intense due to her age, entrenched belief patterns, and life experience at that time.

It is the misunderstanding of most parents that they should make life seemingly easier for their child. If you clear the path of any obstacles your child may face, you make it more difficult for them to find their path. As a parent, you want your child to find passion and joy in life. But, ironically, you are the one, through your attempts to protect your child, who makes it more difficult for your child to align with their true desires.

The universe will provide your child with many manifestation events throughout their childhood. Some of the manifestation events will be pleasant and others may appear painful. But, like the manifestation events you face as you pursue your true desires, they are necessary to mold your child into the version needed for life to unfold in a way that is most joyous and expansive.

Your child was born with a level of understanding of the laws of the universe that is far beyond your comprehension. Many that are born in this time are here to discover, or we should say, reinterpret the laws of the universe from a physical perspective. As you are reading these pages, you are coming to a more enlightened understanding of universal laws. Your child was born with an even greater understanding and may be here to explore those laws even further.

Your perspective that you are the parent, have experienced more of life, and assume to know what's better for your child than he does is flawed. Your life experience has often led you away from the general well-being that is pervasive. Your attention to much that is unwanted is a condition you have practiced and one your child need not practice. You will notice that your interest in the news on television and in newspapers is not shared by your child. Your child is naturally focused on wanted things and has little interest in anything unwanted.

Your child has come here with pure vibration. As he experiences life, he adds to his vibration. We talk about the child not because you are a parent and we want you to be a better parent. We want your perspective to be modified on the subject of life in general. As you gain new perspective on the process of physical reality and we take you to the beginning of any life experience, your perspective can be modified. We hope to show you what happens when you add the vibration of something wanted as well as what happens when you add the vibration of something unwanted to your overall vibrational pattern.

We also want to show you the benefit of finding your path. If you could find your path at an early age, you would experience the joys of life for more of your life experience and this would enable you to explore more of that which you are here to explore. However, it matters not whether you learn your path early in life or late in life because there is no end to life and there is no end to exploration.

If we talk about the pure vibration one is born with, you might be able to envision a white pulsating light. We will use this image to represent the early vibrational pattern in a visual manner. This white light will change its shape and intensity as new desires are added. It also changes shape and intensity as fear and doubt are added. At your birth, the vibration has within it the set of desires that were intended by you, your inner self, from the non-physical realm. When left unaltered by fear, doubt, and attention to things unwanted, the vibration will attract manifestation events that will lead to the general and specific intentions that were determined prior to your birth into physical reality.

Without the influences of others, your child will find his true path naturally. He will be led by the Law of Attraction to that which he truly desires through many manifestation events. He will be given the knowledge he needs at the time he needs it. It is a process of leading him to a vibrational pattern in which he is ready for each and every step in his journey. The process would unfold elegantly and perfectly when left without undue influence from the world outside.

The child's guidance system will alert him through inspiration to action. He will feel when something is right and he will also feel when something is not right for him. He will not push against that which is uncomfortable, but focus on what holds his interest. When left unadulterated, his vibration will be modified and expand and life will unfold as intended.

You, your child, and all others who have come to play in this space-time reality understood prior to your birth the tremendous vibrational variety that now exists on earth. This variety is intensely exciting and makes for higher levels of life experience and diversity. Many new things are possible in this period in time and your child understood that it was unlikely to live in this environment without the influences of others. One intention that is most common is the intention to experience the diversity that presently exists.

Since there is no wrong anywhere in the universe, it is not possible to make mistakes in parenting your child. You are often the center of many of your child's manifestation events and they work to mold your vibration in much the same way they work to mold the vibration of your child. You and your child are co-creators in this environment. Your child specifically chose to be born from you. You chose your child and your child chose you, specifically.

When you act out of inspiration, you are called to do so by the alignment with your true desire. When you act out of fear, you are not aligned with your true desire. Your true desire is for the well-being of your child. You need not carry the burden for that well-being alone. The universe supplies well-being in immeasurable abundance to your child and to you as well. Your child naturally allows all of the well-being to flow to him. You can allow it to flow to you also. You have the power of the universe to support you as you raise your child. It is not necessary or even preferable to try to do it all on your own.

Your fears and the fears of others often appear well-intentioned. You feel that being safe involves the pushing against, the standing guard against, the protection from, all things unwanted. As you are now fully aware, there is no pushing against in the universe. It is all attraction. You want to strive for a feeling of security, peace, and love and not fear danger, threats, or annihilation. For there is no danger, just the fear of danger that becomes your reality.

As a parent, you live with the love of your child and worry over the well-being of your child. The love feels good and the worry feels unpleasant. There is no need to worry, for it brings unpleasant thoughts that bring unpleasant emotion. You are guided to your true desire by your emotions and you now understand that pleasant emotions indicate that you're on your true path to that which you desire and unpleasant emotions indicate you are momentarily off your path. Worry indicates that you are off your path.

Your child must learn to trust her emotions, as well. Her emotional guidance system is pure. She should not be encouraged to suppress her emotions. At an early age, her guidance system is lean and uncomplicated. She either feels good or bad. When feeling good she is calm, happy, interested, and filled with joy. When feeling bad she cries, screams, or expresses rage. Children express emotions purely and are tuned to feeling good. They do not accept bad feelings easily and they express their emotions vividly. Asking them to alter their bad feelings is asking them to suppress their guidance system.

You are meant to feel good and to know when you are not feeling good. You are designed to return to feeling good often and easily. When you do not feel good, your emotions are there to indicate that fact to you. If you had the emotional guidance system in the pure state you once had as a child, you would throw fits of rage, have temper tantrums, and scream out loud whenever you did not feel good. However, you've modified those basic emotions to conform to societal norms and the emotions have become more specific. Instead of simply feeling bad you now call it guilt, despair, apathy, envy, etc. You have many more terms for feeling bad, but they're all indicators that you are not on your path or in alignment with your desire.

If your child is allowed to freely express his emotions, without being forced to conform to the pressures of society, he will come to understand his guidance system earlier in life. He will know when something feels right and when something feels off. He will learn to work his way through the world based on how he feels inside and not by the influence of others. He will know when something does not align with his true desires. He will not push against it, he will simply turn his attention back to what is wanted. Emotions, especially in the early years, must be allowed to develop naturally without the influence of what others perceive as right or wrong. It is simply the design of this physical reality and is an integral part of the process.

As you look back on your own childhood, you might remember all the times when you were told to suppress your emotions. You may have felt joy when others were experiencing sadness and, due to their influence, have been told to suppress your joy. You might have cried when you felt sad and you were told this type of emotion was not acceptable. You may have been told to show no emotion at all. The modification of emotion in childhood is common among most humans and is responsible for many of the difficulties faced later in life. If you lose the ability to use the emotional guidance system given to you at birth, you lose a valuable tool for uncovering your true desire and the more specific intentions you made prior to your emergence into physical reality.

If you have lost some or all of your emotional guidance system, do not worry. We will show you how to regain full control later. For now, understand how as a child you initially had full control of your guidance system, how it may have been suppressed, and how your children use their guidance systems. When you allow your children to express their emotions, good or bad, you allow them access to their natural and fundamental guidance. Observe how they move through life guided by their emotions without fear for any discomfort they may experience, and you'll regain the understanding of your own guidance system.

II.

You are here to joyously expand. The path to all expansion is through many manifestation events. You encounter manifestation events on a daily basis that help you to progress on your path to your true desires. Your children face manifestation events as well. In your efforts to smooth out their path you might unintentionally alter the manifestation events that are meant to occur in your child's life.

We'll give you a fun example. Your child was given the gift of a bicycle several years ago. He has always loved this bicycle and has taken loving care of it. Lately, however, he seems to be leaving it around the yard instead of carefully putting it away as he once did.

One day you notice he has left his bicycle in the neighbor's driveway. He is friends with the boy who lives next door and they often play together. But you feel it's odd that he left his bicycle in their driveway, so you pick it up and put it away. Later, you plan to talk to him about being more responsible for his belongings.

However, the Law of Attraction was working for your child to fulfill his true desire. We'll see how the story might have developed had you not removed the bicycle from the neighbor's driveway.

Your child has always loved his bicycle, but lately he has come to realize that he has outgrown it, since it was originally intended for a much smaller child. His friends all have new bikes. He has seen the bike he now wants in the bike shop and he's dreaming of it. His mind is full of visions of riding his new bike with his friends. His old bicycle is making its way out of your child's reality so that the new bike may enter.

Your child finds himself leaving his bicycle on the neighbor's driveway. He was playing all afternoon with his friend in the house next door. As he leaves the home, he completely forgets about his bicycle even though he walks right past it. Looking back, he will think it odd that he left it there. Later that evening your neighbor comes home and runs over the bike with his car.

Now, there are several ways this manifestation event could play out and they all have to do with the vibration of each of the participants. If each of

Parenting, Education, and Intelligence

the players in this event were fully aligned with their true desires, the following scenario is most likely.

Your neighbor comes to your front door with the broken bike in his arms. Since he is aligned with his desire for safety and the well-being of children in the neighborhood, he is truly sorry for running over the bike, but he is relieved your child was not on the bike at the time. He expresses his apologies and offers to pay for whatever new bike your son wants.

Being aligned with your true desire for peace and harmony with your neighbor and the love of your son, you are also grateful that no one was harmed. You do not blame the neighbor for running over the bike and you do not blame your son for leaving his bike in the driveway. You also do not blame yourself for not picking it up in the first place.

You understand that this is simply a manifestation event and you trust that the universe is working to fulfill the desires of all involved. Your son does not blame the neighbor for running over his bike as he was ready for the bike to leave his experience and for a new one to enter. According to the laws of the universe, since all were aligned with their desires, this was the path of least resistance for the old bike to go and the new bike to enter your son's experience. It was elegant in its manifestation.

Now, would you like to explore some of the ways this scenario could have ended differently?

First of all, imagine that you removed the bike from the driveway yourself, taking action not out of inspiration but out of fear or concern for what your neighbor might think of you as a parent. You took action that was not inspired but was taken out of fear. You felt negative emotion, which was your indicator that something in your action was off, and you canceled the manifestation event completely. The universe will have to create another scenario in which your son loses his bicycle, and this new scenario may turn out to be less elegant.

Let's say you are the one who is fully aligned in this scenario and you see that a manifestation event is about to unfold so you are inspired to leave the bike where it is. In your alignment, you are not bothered by what your neighbor might think of you and you feel no need to teach your son any specific lesson regarding caring for his property. You know he wants a new bike and you can see that this bike is making its way out of his experience. You decide to step back and see what happens.

A Perception of Reality

Your neighbor comes home from a long day at work. While normally he is aligned with the safety and the well-being of the children in the neighborhood, he has let the conditions of the day determine his emotional state, which is now vibrating at a lower level. He turns into his driveway and crashes into the bike. At first, he is shocked and jumps out of the car to see what happened. He feels great relief that no one was hurt, but due to the momentum of his lower emotional state of being, he is flooded with the emotions of anger and guilt. He picks up the bike and storms over to your front door. When you open the door you can see his rage. You see the broken bike in his arms and piece together what must have happened.

You can see how aligned you must be in order to keep calm in this situation. If you are not aligned in the moment, you will easily fall into a lower emotional state yourself. You might feel guilty for leaving the bike there in the first place. You might second guess your decision as you did not foresee the anger that would rise up in your neighbor. You might feel anger toward your child and blame him for leaving the bike in the driveway. But imagine if you could keep your alignment solid and instead of being defensive you flowed love to your neighbor in spite of his emotional state and you tried to soothe him. That's the power of the universe.

If you could keep your alignment with your true desires strong through this manifestation event, you would also act differently toward your son. If you understood the true purpose of the manifestation event, which is to demonstrate to your son that the Law of Attraction supports his every desire, you would do wonders for your son's expansion as well. His observation of your alignment, especially in times when conditions are not easy, will be the greatest gift he could ever receive from you.

When you come to understand how the universe works to bring all of you exactly what you truly desire as long as you allow it to flow to you, you can stand firm in your alignment. When you can remain aligned with your true desires even in times where the conditions challenging, you will be a purely positive example to others, including your children.

Imagine your son as he walks down the stairs from his room after hearing the angry voice of the neighbor next door and asks you what happened. You turn to him and say, "Let's go get that new bike you want." We imagine you would both be filled with joy.

Parenting, Education, and Intelligence

There is no wrong anywhere in the universe. Your current educational system, as unproductive and misguided as it is, is not wrong either. It is simply the stimulus for great change that is coming in the near future. Before you destroy old systems and replace them with new ones, you usually go through a period when deep desire is created. Your frustration with the current system will lead you to a true desire for a better system. The new educational system will only come after the concept of vibration and the laws of the universe are understood at a broader level.

You assume that humans are born with varying degrees of intelligence. This is a misconception. You all have access to infinite intelligence. You have the ability to access all the intelligence in the universe right now. For one reason or another, you allow only a limited amount of intelligence to flow to you.

Intelligence is nothing more than interest in a specific subject. When you find interest, you attract intelligence. The more you focus on any subject with passion, the more knowledge naturally flows to you. As you gain confidence in your knowledge, you remove fear and doubt from the subject. When confidence is present and fear and doubt are not acknowledged, you will gain access to higher and higher vibrational thoughts and ideas. It's as simple as that.

However, you learn to cut yourself off from this flow and make up many reasons for this. We do not want to minimize the emphasis you give to certain conditions you describe as learning disabilities, but we want to enlighten you to another perspective. Once you gain the broader perspective of the universe and understand how the system really works, you might be able to see the flaws in your beliefs about education.

You are a vibrational being. The universe literally revolves around you. You create your own reality. Your beliefs are mirrored back to you by the life experiences that unfold daily. You are born with a pure vibration. You have made a set of general and specific intentions before your birth into this physical reality. You were a vibrational match to the earth on the day you were born and you were meant to experience life and explore this time.

You were given everything you needed to fulfill your intention. Your intelligence was not predetermined, but your access to intelligence was.

Intelligence does not come from within your mind. You do not create thoughts and ideas from within; you access the intelligence of the universe. You have control over how much access you have at any moment in time. As you get better at accessing intelligence, you gain confidence, and the access improves. Your access to intelligence expands with confidence. As fear and doubt enter your vibration, your confidence is diminished and you begin to limit your access to intelligence. As you limit your access at an early age, you attract labels that reinforce your inability to access intelligence. These labels are false. It is not that you have a fundamental, incontrovertible disability; you are simply not allowing the access to intelligence to flow as much to you as it seems to flow to others.

Most of the conditions that foster learning disabilities stem from a misunderstanding of how learning evolves differently for each individual. It all starts with interest. You do not have the ability to learn something you are not ready to learn. If you have no interest in a subject, you will not learn it. You might be able to remember certain aspects of the subject as long as needed to take a test, but that is not learning. You are accessing the intelligence of the universe in a very limited and short-term way only because it is required. Once the test is over, the vast majority of the information will be lost to you.

Learning requires interest. Interest requires desire. Desire impacts the timing of that which is to be learned.

If you consider yourself good at math, it is simply because you were fortunate enough to be in a place of readiness when you were being taught the subject. You were vibrationally within the general vicinity of readiness when the lessons were taught, and you gained confidence in that subject.

If you consider yourself a poor math student, it is simply due to the fact that you were not vibrationally ready when the lessons first began. Had you had time to develop a desire to learn about mathematics, you would have been in the vibrational vicinity of the subject and it would have made sense to you.

Dyslexia is the easiest and most clear example of vibrational readiness. Many humans are vibrationally ready to read at a certain age. However, since you are all completely unique individuals with completely unique vibrations, intentions, and desires, you align with your true desires differently. If you find yourself with the label of dyslexia, it simply means that you were not vibrationally ready to learn to read when the lesson was presented to you. In fact, you were not ready to stop exploring nature at the time. You were enjoying the physical aspects of life. Your eyes were tuned specifically to see the physical beauty of nature and the world around you. Words on a page could not yet be vibrationally translated by your eyes. You were in a different state of expansion.

Because you translate all vibrations into reality through your senses, you all have different levels of experience of sight, sound, taste, touch, smell, and feeling. You only know what you feel, see, hear, taste, and smell but you have no idea what other people are experiencing. You assume it's the same for everyone, but it is not. Even the sense of time is completely different from one person to another. How you expand is different than how another expands. Everything in life is viewed from a completely unique perspective. It is not possible or even conceivable for all humans to be taught in the same manner.

Since each child has a path that unfolds at a different pace, each child learns at a different rate. You must first realize that intelligence is not the aspect to be measured, but one's access to intelligence is what actually defines intelligence. Each child uncovers his birthright to access intelligence at a different rate. If given confidence in the ability to access intelligence, it will flow naturally to the child for the duration of his life.

However, if doubt and fear are introduced to the child regarding his ability to access intelligence, the child will limit this access to the degree to which the fear and doubt exist. Varying levels of confidence (or fear and doubt) even exist around certain subjects. This is the reason some do well in math while others do well in reading, for example.

Access to intelligence is always preceded by interest. Interest and passion for any subject will open the flow of access to intelligence. True interest is the awareness and curiosity one would have for a given subject if left free from the influence of others. A false interest is one where the person is influenced to study the subject because others are interested in that subject. The access to intelligence that stems from true interest is far greater than the access that comes as a result of a false interest.

You can see that it is easy to influence your child to be interested in a subject you believe is best for them. Your child is eager to please you in order to receive your love and attention. When you praise your child for excelling in a subject you deem worthy, your child gains confidence in that subject and allows access to more intelligence. However, it may be false interest, in which case the access to intelligence will be relatively limited.

If you as a parent allowed your child to follow a true interest, you would do your child a great service. Your child's interests may not coincide with your own interests or even those you deem respectable or worthy. However, your child is here to explore and travel along a path that is unique to him. If you trust in the laws of the universe and the mechanism that guides each of you to your own true desire along your own true path, you must have trust that the universe is supporting your child along his path.

When a true interest presents itself based on a true desire, your child will be inspired to learn. This inspiration will open access to intelligence regarding the specific subject of his interest. However, access to other intelligence unrelated to this subject will remain closed. If in his pursuit of an interest or passion your child desires access to further knowledge and understanding, it will be fully open to him at that time, but not before.

You do not have access to specific intelligence when there is no interest or need for that intelligence. Like everything else in the universe, intelligence is attracted. It cannot be forced. You cannot force intelligence on someone who has no desire for the specific knowledge. Desire precedes interest, and interest opens access to knowledge. This is how intelligence works.

Much of your current school system forces education on its students in a similar manner. Each student receives similar education at predetermined stages, regardless of their individual readiness to receive the information. In many cases they are able to retain the information because they have the desire to please parents, teachers, and others by receiving positive marks in school. These good grades may increase confidence in some children; however, the negative marks they receive will offset their gain in confidence.

Other children, those who refuse to play the game and understand that there must be interest and vibrational readiness before there can be access to intelligence, are deemed unintelligent or are burdened by the label of a learning disability. They receive low marks, are placed in special programs, and are called slow learners and therefore experience fear and doubt when it comes to intelligence. They have reduced their own access to the infinite intelligence of the universe due to the label they have received from others.

A child who becomes a "good" student early in life often desires good marks on tests only to please others. Since the focus is on the desire to please others and not oneself, it is not a true desire. While action in this case will produce results, it is not inspired action because it is not a true desire. Instead of enjoying the process of aligning with true desire, the child finds struggle and pain in achieving good grades. The child might be stuck in a cycle that prevents her from finding her true passion. The child is so concerned with the approval of others that she forces herself to get better and better grades at school. This cycle will continue to lead her on a path toward a false desire until something happens to interrupt the cycle and awaken her to a true desire.

A child who does not perform well in school at an early age might encounter negative feedback from parents, teachers, and even friends. This will lead to doubt and fear which will limit access to intelligence. If the child is labeled with a disability of some kind, the doubt and fear will persist. If the child desires approval from others, the child will follow a false desire that will allow access to intelligence for the sole purpose of receiving improved scores on tests. This child will also struggle through school in order to receive good grades and the approval of others.

However, all of these children, without the influence of others, if allowed to pursue their interests whatever they may be, will have full and open access to the specific intelligence they desire. As they reach for more understanding on a certain subject, they will receive higher levels of understanding and intelligence will flow at even higher levels regarding the subject at hand. If the desire for intelligence is at a very high level and the intelligence is allowed to flow at full capacity with great confidence and little doubt or fear, the label of genius is given. Genius is simply one's ability to access intelligence at a very high level for a specific subject. It comes from intense desire, not from any special gift. It is available to all, not just a chosen few.

When left without the influences of others, negative or positive, a child will develop access to intelligence as they find interest in specific subjects. They will allow their life to unfold easily and naturally according to the intentions they set prior to their birth. They will not only gain confidence in their ability to access intelligence, but will also learn the laws of the universe through their life experiences. When not labeled or compared to others or to social norms, they will access intelligence at their own rate. Since everyone on the planet is unique, with their own set of intentions and desires, intelligence is accessed at different rates. There is no one rate of learning or level of access that is preferable. It is all made perfect given the unique path of each individual.

When we talk about intelligence, we are talking about most humans who have come here to explore life experience in a mostly general manner. There are those, however, who come to have experiences in a very specific range. These people are born with completely different access to intelligence. They have come to help you understand many things such as unconditional love, freedom, and individuality. They have also come to help you understand more clearly the nature of intelligence. You cannot change these people with your educational system, your social norms, or your expectations of right and wrong for they will not change to please you. They come here so you might change your perspective thus changing your limiting belief patterns.

You will soon come to learn the true nature of intelligence and will change your belief systems as well as your educational systems. You will no longer force your ideas of what should be learned on those you consider to be lacking knowledge. Your children come here in a much higher state of vibration. This is the time of awakening. They are prepared for the changes that will come. We want you to understand the way intelligence works so you can be ready for the change as well.

IV.

Your access to intelligence is granted to you through desire. Desire sparks interest, which allows intelligence to flow. True desire allows access as well as false desire. But true desire causes inspiration to act and the journey is one filled with joy, fun, interest, and passion. When you find your passion, you open access to intelligence. Your access is limited in some degree by any doubt or fear that may be present. If you think you are not smart, you limit your access to intelligence. If you consider yourself brilliant, you have access to the free flow of intelligence. The Law of Attraction supports your belief in either case.

We have come to tell you that no matter what your past experience has been, you now stand in a new place of understanding. You may now look back and see how your educational system failed you as a child. If left to pursue your interests you would have confidence in your ability to access the intelligence you wanted. There would be no difference between you and anyone else who was following their passion.

We are here to ask you to find something you're interested in and see for yourself how intelligence flows. You can observe examples of this everywhere in your society. Doctors complete impressive levels of education. They are considered brilliant practitioners, yet they may not know how to do simple tasks such as fixing a leaky faucet or balancing a checkbook. They have access to intelligence in one area but because they have little interest in household repairs or accounting they have little access to those specific areas of intelligence.

Most people have a general interest in many things and therefore have some level of access to intelligence regarding these matters. For instance, you might not be particularly interested in math, but when you are out shopping you can roughly calculate in your head the savings when an item is marked 25 percent off.

You know as many words as you need to know based on your interests. You can read and write at levels that work for your day-to-day life. If you have a job that deals with a specific category, such as law, you know words that pertain to this specialty and you have access to the intelligence you need for the job. You have access to legal terms which come easily to you because the access to intelligence around the subject is open. But, in your legal profession, you do not have access to the intelligence a florist might possess. You could gain access to the intelligence associated with a florist and the florist has the ability to gain full access to intelligence surrounding the subject of law. The thing that keeps you separated from any specific subject is interest.

Interest is the key to intelligence. If one is not interested in a subject, one has no access to the intelligence of that subject. You might be able to pique one's interest, but if it is not born from a true desire, the interest will be forced and no great knowledge will come as a result.

As you sit in your chair reading this book, you have access to all the intelligence needed regarding anything you find of interest. It matters not whether you were an excellent student in school or were labeled with a learning disability. In this moment, you have full access to infinite intelligence in the amount you allow. Find something to be passionate about and the intelligence will flow. You will see that it works and you will gain confidence. There is no such thing as smart or stupid; you have simply been misled regarding the true mechanism of intelligence.

At this moment in time, you have the ability, through your access to infinite intelligence, to do anything you truly desire. If you find interest in a subject, you'll be inspired to read new books faster than you ever thought you could. You'll think thoughts at higher levels. You'll put more time into what you're passionate about, and the time will seem to go very quickly. You'll be inspired to talk to people you may have been afraid to talk to before. As you gain more confidence, your access to intelligence will be opened even wider. There is no limit to the genius you already are.

V.

Your current emotional state determines the type and level of intelligence you have access to at any moment in time. If you are in the emotional state of interest or passion, you have access to the fullest and broadest levels of intelligence. However, if your emotional state at the moment of learning is vibrating at a low level, you will have access only to intelligence that matches it. If you are in a state of boredom or apathy, you have almost no access to intelligence. Your emotional state itself will not allow you access to intelligence. If you are in the emotional state of anger, you have access only to the intelligence that will support this emotional state. You will receive ideas that help you navigate the world depending on the state you're in. Access to intelligence will support whatever state you're in, be it high or low. Like the Law of Attraction itself, intelligence will match the frequency of your vibration.

If you have been a victim and you desire revenge, you will have access to intelligence that supports your desire. You can plan your revenge easily. You could learn how to build bombs, or handle weapons like a master. You would be inspired to learn to fight and to kill. You would rendezvous with other people who are also inspired to vengeance. Although revenge is a lower emotional state of being in vibrational terms, the Law of Attraction, as well as access to intelligence, responds equally.

There are many people in your world today who, due to their life experiences, are seeking to feel better through revenge. Though you could say they are vibrating at low levels, the Law of Attraction is responding to their desires. They are gaining access to intelligence that reflects their desires. They may even seem intelligent based on the levels of sophistication of their revenge tactics. However, they are simply accessing intelligence that matches their desire for revenge and nothing more.

If their emotional state of being changed from revenge to love, their vibration would alter, their desires would shift, and their access to intelligence regarding revenge would be closed. Their new vibrational state of being would give them access to new intelligence. The moment they lost interest in revenge, they no longer had access to that specific type of intelligence or even those types of thoughts.

If you have a desire to learn something, you can only do so if your emotional state of being allows it. If you are interested in success but at the moment you feel unsuccessful, you could be in a room full of successful people and learn nothing. You must be in the right emotional state to receive the information you want.

If you desire to improve your ability to access information you must first practice being in higher emotional states. You must do whatever it takes to feel better on a moment-to-moment basis. You cannot access the intelligence you desire unless your emotional state matches that which you desire.

If you just ended a relationship with a boyfriend or girlfriend and you feel miserable, it might be a good idea to skip school that day. You would only have access to thoughts and intelligence that match your emotional state. You would not have interest in the subjects you normally find fascinating. You would only notice things that make you feel even worse.

Before learning anything, your child must be in the proper emotional state. If your child is angry, bored, or upset while at school, he will not have access to intelligence at the level needed to learn. He will miss whatever is being taught that day. If he is in a lower emotional state over a period of time, he will be unable to learn while at school even if he was vibrationally ready to learn. His emotional state of being predetermines his ability to receive information. He may have been labeled with a learning disability when, in fact, it was his prolonged emotional state that did not allow learning to occur. If your child was in a higher vibrational state of being more often, he would be receptive to learning more often.

Children (and all humans) must be in a positive emotional state of being prior to learning. Their emotional state indicates their access to intelligence and therefore their ability to receive information. If you can raise the emotional state of the student, you can increase their access to intelligence. The higher one's emotional state of being, the easier it is for them to access broader intelligence and receive information at greater levels.

Consider your emotional state of being each time you sit down to read. The better your emotional state at the time you read each page, the higher level of understanding you'll receive. You might read through this entire book once and then in a year you'll read it again. If your emotional state of being is different the next time you read this book, you'll receive new and different information. If your emotional state has improved, you'll gain new insights and improved understanding.

This is especially true if certain areas of your life have greatly improved. If your finances have improved, you'll gain new insights into the topic of abundance. If your physical body has improved, you'll understand more about the nature of reality and how it affects your body. If you have a new relationship and a new person to love, you'll understand how you attracted that person into your life and you'll have access to more of the information given on the topic of relationships.

If you are going to write something, you must be in the highest emotional state possible prior to typing out the words. If you are in a low vibrational state of being, don't write anything that day. You will have access to the words you need to convey your ideas only if you are in the proper emotional state. At lower emotional states you will simply muddle your thoughts and lessen the impact of your words and ideas.

If you are going to teach something, make sure that you are not only in the proper emotional state, but that your students are as well. If your students are in low vibrational states of being while you give your presentation, your words will be lost on them. You must help them raise their vibration in order for them to gain access to the intelligence needed to hear and comprehend what you are conveying.

If you could practice meditation each day, you could raise your emotional state of being. If you could reach for better-feeling thoughts, you could raise your emotional state and access broader intelligence. If you could appreciate what you have and how you live your life, you would raise your emotional state of being. If you will expect to feel better and consciously intend to raise your own emotional state of being, your vibration will increase. As you raise your emotional state of being, you allow greater access to the intelligence of the universe.

If you can help your students raise their emotional state you will give them greater access to intelligence. If you can give them words to help them feel better they will hear you better. If you can expect their emotional states of being to increase and you intend for them to feel better, their emotional states of being will increase as well.

You have control of your emotional state of being at any time as long as you are consciously aware of your abilities. You can increase your vibration by thinking better-feeling thoughts. You can meditate each day which will help to raise your emotional state of being. You can live in the moment and see that in each moment everything is fine. You can release worry, doubt, and fear from your life and know true freedom. The only thing that matters is your alignment with your true desires and your inner self. Everything else will take care of itself.

Chapter Eight

The Flow of Life

There is a rhythm to life. The earth has its own vibrational pattern. There are cycles in everything. Life is always moving. The universe is working to bring you the full and elegant manifestation of your desires. This is called "the flow of life."

It is a term you are well aware of, but you may not have understood the truth behind it. You are familiar with the phrase "go with the flow." You understand what that means to some extent. It means take it easy, everything is working out, there is nothing to worry about, the conditions are right, everything is perfect.

The flow is the way things are. It's the conditions you face in this moment. There has been momentum that has led to this point in time and everything is the way it is meant to be. If you are in the flow, you accept the conditions for what they are. You do not try to change the conditions in the moment. You do not argue against the conditions. You might prefer things to be otherwise, but in this moment you accept everything as it is, as it is perfect, as it should be. You understand that your preferences and desires will improve the conditions over time, but not in this moment.

Going with the flow, allowing things to be exactly as they are, is ease. Ease is to be reached for in every moment. Ease is the grand goal of life. Everything should be easy, and nothing should be difficult. Ease is accepting the conditions, as they exist in the present moment, fully and completely.

Struggle is resisting the conditions as they exist in the moment. Fighting against the way things are causes tension or dis-ease. There is no fighting against anything in the universe and the present moment is no exception. In order to live a life of ease, you must accept that things are unfolding in the perfect manner at the perfect time even though you cannot see it. Your perception, from your limited point of view, may sometimes cause you to misunderstand the conditions of the moment. You might see that something is happening that you do not like and you react to it negatively. This is fighting against the conditions.

The universe is working to bring you a match to all of your desires. In order to fulfill your desires, you must be transformed from the person you are now to the person who is ready for the desire you seek. In order for this transformation to take place, the universe must move you and your environment to a new place. There is change that must take place for the transformation to occur. If you resist anything in your environment that may be appearing to change, you slow the momentum of your transformation and you slow the manifestation of your desires.

If you recognize that you and your environment must literally change in order for you to become the version of you that is in vibrational harmony with your desires, you must understand that the universe is creating the conditions for your transformation. If you resist the change, you cause tension. The universe will continue to move in the direction of your desires, but as long as you resist you will feel disharmony and tension within your life.

Tension causes dis-ease, which may lead to disease. All disease is caused by resistance to the transformation that must occur for you to receive the manifested reality of your desires. If you had no desires there would be (almost) no transformation and therefore you would feel at ease. You would not become ill. There would be no disease.

Desire causes transformation. The extent of the desire causes the extent of the transformation and the speed of the flow. Big desires cause big transformations and the flow is fast. Small desires cause small transformations and the speed of the flow is slower. It is easier to transform to a vibrational alignment with a desire you do not consider too big. There is little resistance to the change and the small desire manifests easily.

In the case of small desires, your belief systems are already in line with what you desire. You expect the small desire to manifest soon. You have experience that this type of desire has manifested before and are confident that it will manifest again. You believe you are worthy of the small desire, so you do not resist the small transformation needed to achieve the desire. And the desire manifests exactly as you knew it would.

A Perception of Reality

It is the big desires that cause dis-ease because the flow seems too fast. You feel a great divide between where you are now in your life and where you need to be to experience the manifestation of your desire. You cannot perceive from your current state of being how you will get to where you want to be. You do not see all the subtle changes the universe will make to transform you into the vibrational being who will eventually be ready to receive that which you desire.

Your perspective is limited, so you make up stories in your mind that seem like the path to your desires. When real life does not match up with what you have imagined, you feel tension, dis-ease, and disharmony with the flow. Whenever you feel that something is not going your way, it is because reality conflicts with the story you've set forth in your imagination. You want to change reality in the moment so it matches up with your version of how things should be. Ultimately, you have no faith in the universe to do its job. You feel dis-ease.

If your feeling of dis-ease continues, it will, through the Law of Attraction, manifest into your physical reality in the form of pain, irritation, sickness, and actual disease. Depending on the specifics of the resistance, you will encounter specific diseases. You can even trace the root cause of each disease to a specific type of resistance. It matters not what disease you acquire; it only matters that you understand that resistance to the flow causes dis-ease.

The reverse is also true. If there is little or no resistance to the way things are happening in the moment then there can be no disease, only well-being. If you can come to trust that the universe is working on your behalf to bring you all of that which you desire, you can relax and let the flow of life bring you to wherever you want to go. It is trust in the universe that will give you peace. You have nothing to fear but your own untrained imagination.

II.

You have the ability through your senses to comprehend your environment. If you look out your window you can see the sky, clouds, birds, trees, the street, power lines, your lawn, flowers, etc. You can focus broadly or you can focus on minute detail. You have a choice. What seems like a full

The Flow of Life

spectrum of reality in this moment is mostly background that is filled in. You think you are seeing everything at once but you are really only experiencing a tiny fragment of the world around you and the detail is being automatically filled in by your mind.

If you examine an expressionist painting from a distance, it appears to have great detail. Once you move closer, you see that it is nothing but a series of differently colored, well-placed dots on canvas. Your televisions and computers work this way as well. You see an image on your screen that appears to be moving, but it is simply a vast array of pixels all changing colors in a certain pattern. As you broaden your view, you see an image that appears to be highly detailed.

Life works this way, too. You see the broad image. You combine all of your senses to experience your reality. However, you only see the image presented to you from your perspective. But there are tiny, unseen particles that hold matter together that cause vibration and react to your awareness. In other words, from your perspective, you see the image, not the mechanism.

If you can understand that your perspective is limited and trust that there are universal forces at work striving to bring you to your dreams, you can feel ease in the way life unfolds. If something does not match with your imagination of how it "should" be, abandon your version of how it should be and embrace what is.

If anything seems like it's not working out for you, it is only from your limited perception that you come to this conclusion. You cannot see behind the scenes. You cannot see how your path will unfold. It is beyond your comprehension. It would be better if you had no rigid mental picture about the exact path to your desire, but only held to the feeling of that which you desire. When you imagine in specific detail how you will achieve your desire, you will be more resistant to the transformation.

Because you hold many desires simultaneously, the universe is transforming you and your environment to reach all of your desires in the most elegant way possible. While you hold the manifested image of one of your desires in your imagination, the universe might be working on another desire in the moment. When you encounter a manifestation event that is preparing you for your dream job, you might be focused on your desire for a relationship. As the manifestation event plays out, it is actually moving you toward the job you really want. But, if you are focused on a future relationship, you see the manifestation event as a failure because it did not move you closer to your lover.

You resisted the manifestation event and have lost the transformational benefit of it. The universe will now have to create another event to move you in the direction of your dream job. That's okay though, because the universe never gives up no matter how hard you resist. If you keep resisting, the universe will keep working. Eventually you will give up resistance and go with the flow. This can happen while you are alive or after you have died. It really doesn't matter. Once you die, you give up all resistance.

There is no point in resisting life. You came here to explore and to expand and to have fun and joy along the way. If you are not getting what you want, it's simply because your idealized, imagined version of how things "should be" does not match how they really are. You cannot see everything that is going on to help you in your transformation toward the vibrational version of you that is ready to receive your dreams. You must simply trust the power of the universe.

If you have trust in the power of the universe you will be given plenty of signs along the way. If you offer no resistance and hold no preconceived conceptions about the way in which your dreams manifest, you will receive the indicators that you are on your path. These signs come in the form of coincidence, positive emotions, goose bumps, chills down your spine, chance encounters, and many other indicators. As you recognize the signs along the way you will gain more confidence that the universe is working toward the physical manifestation of your desires.

If you perceive that things either **are** or **are not** working out for you, the Law of Attraction will prove it to you either way. Since that is really up to your control you might as well believe that everything is working out for you. If you think it and believe it, the Law of Attraction will prove it to you. You can choose to believe anything. Some beliefs are helpful and others are not. Release beliefs that resist the manifestation of your desires and you will live a life of ease. Hold onto the beliefs that do not support you and you will live a life filled with dis-ease. It's your choice.

If you desire abundance, a loving relationship, and a healthy body but believe you are unworthy of one or all of these things, you will resist the transformation that must be made in order to bring you the realization of your desires. If you hold onto the completely inaccurate belief that you are unworthy in any way, you cannot make the change necessary to bring you that which you desire. You will resist and the universe will work harder. You will then have to resist even more and the universe will work even harder.

If you continue to resist change you will manifest physical disease or some other equally unpleasant condition. The universe will show you what you feel in the form of manifestation. If you feel love, you will receive love. If you feel dis-ease, you will receive disease. The more you resist, the longer you feel the tension, the greater the disease will be in its physical manifestation in your reality. The sooner you realize you are truly worthy, the easier your life will become.

III.

Fear and doubt are signs of resistance. Worry is a sign of resistance. Any negative emotion is a sign that you are not, in this moment, going with the flow of your life. Your emotions are your guidance system. When you feel negative emotion in the moment, you are feeling resistance or tension or disharmony with the flow. Release resistance and your dreams will begin to flow into your life.

Fear is your projection of a negative outcome through the mechanism of your imagination. You can use your imagination in either a positive or a negative manner. There is no conscious reason to imagine any outcome that is not preferable. It is of no benefit in the manifestation of that which you desire. Fear, doubt, and worry are the result of habitual patterns of thought that do not serve you. They are the result of a flawed belief system. You are free to experience fear, doubt, and worry if you wish. Just understand that they may bring unwanted experiences into your life. If it does not feel good when you think it, then it is an indication of resistance to your true desire. It is an indication that you are moving away from what you truly want instead of toward what you truly want.

Joy, happiness, ease, harmony, passion, interest, and fun are all signs that there is no resistance around the subject in the moment. The conditions feel right. You are appreciating life in the moment and feeling good. In this state your true desires are flowing to you in a perfectly unfolding manner. You are going with the flow.

If in the moment of a manifestation event you can feel any discord, you have the conscious ability to realize you are offering resistance to whatever is happening in the moment. You are not seeing the manifestation event for what it is. You are imagining that the conditions are wrong when in fact everything is always working to bring you closer to your desires. This is simply a transformational event, and if you accept it for what it is, you will move one step closer to your desire.

If you are sitting alone in your home staring vacantly out the window without much thought being offered on any particular topic, you are not experiencing a manifestation event. Nothing is really happening that you need to concern yourself with in that moment. But if your phone rings and you are inspired to answer it, it may be a manifestation event. If you find yourself in an argument with the person on the other line, then it is most definitely a manifestation event. The event signals something that must be changed in your belief system for you to realize a certain desire. If you can consciously identify the basis for the conflict within, you can modify your beliefs in such a way that it will bring you one step further along your path.

If you feel negative emotion as a result of the argument, you are feeling resistance to the transformation that must take place. If you can understand the message in the event, even after some time has passed, you have received the benefit of the manifestation event and will experience positive emotion. This positive emotion is your sign that you're going with the flow. You're on your path.

The flow presents itself in each and every moment. When you stop to think about how you are feeling, you can discover whether or not you are in the flow. Your goal is to be in the flow as much as you can. Are you in the flow now? Are you focused on what you are reading, or is your mind elsewhere? Being in the flow means being aware of this present moment.

The flow, like a river, always takes the easy route of least resistance. Imagine a small stream as it winds its way to the sea. If it meets a rock in its path, it does not wish to destroy the rock, it simply moves easily around it. The little stream meanders along its path of least resistance until it eventually meets the sea.

Your life within the flow works in the same manner as the small stream. You gently move with ease through your day, moving around all obstacles. You do not fight against anything you do not want; you simply withdraw your attention from the unwanted and move with the flow toward the wanted. The flow is easy and your decisions in the moment will be the ones that give you the greatest sense of ease. As you are in the flow, you strive for the feeling of ease. Ease and flow, ease and flow, ease and flow - this is your mantra.

The flow is always the path of least resistance. In the flow everything is right. The conditions are always right when you're in the flow. There is no argument. There is no wanting things to be different. You accept the conditions as they are. Everything is fine in the flow. You need not change anything in the moment. The right choices are being presented to you even if you don't think they are right. If you go with the flow everything will turn out as it was intended. You'll eventually arrive at the sea. You'll eventually arrive at the physical manifestation of your dream. If you simply go with the flow, you'll get to where you want to be.

Being in the moment is flowing. Realizing that everything in this moment is fine is the act of flowing. Flowing is always easy and gentle, and never abrupt. Flowing is peace, love, understanding, patience, willingness, and ease. Flowing is knowing that the conditions are right even if they seem wrong from your perspective. Flowing is trust in the universe, acceptance of the Law of Attraction, confidence in your abilities, and knowing you are worthy.

You cannot flow fully until you understand your true level of worthiness. You are worthy. There is no one who lives now or has ever existed that is more worthy than you are as you stand in this present moment in time. You must come to know your worthiness if you are to flow with the rhythm of life. The only thing that blocks you from flowing is your flawed belief that you must challenge the events in your life. If you felt worthy, you would not react to the conditions. You would not fight against the current of the flow.

The flow moves whether you go with it or fight against it. There is a flow to life whether you believe it or not. There is a rhythm to the earth, to nature, to the animals, to all humans, to all cells in your body, and there is rhythm within you as well. When you tune into this rhythm, you tune into the flow. It is time for you to accept the flow of life, to feel your worthiness, to stop your habit of resistance, and to simply ease up on yourself and go with the flow.

You spend much of your current life wanting the conditions that exist in your everyday, moment-by-moment life to be different than they are. You want your traffic to be less congested. You want there to be no line at the coffee shop. You want people to get out of your way. You want your children to pick up their socks. You want more money, more time, and more love. You feel lack at every turn. You are constantly fighting the flow of life.

Your perspective is focused on lack rather than abundance. You feel a lack of time because, from your perspective, you think there are things you must do. In the universe as it really exists, from the broader perspective, there is never anything you must get done because you can never get it done. From the broader perspective, time is an illusion. Your belief that time exists, your sense of time, your belief that time is finite - these are all flawed premises. Time is simply a matter of perspective. If you focus on the lack of time, you choose a perspective that goes against the flow. You make your life more difficult simply due to your limited perspective on the subject.

When you realize that there is nothing you need accomplish in this life, you gain more time. When you understand that life unfolds wonderfully when you are working with the flow rather than against it, time loses meaning. When you come to understand that life is lived in the moment and there are an abundance of moments, you gain a better perspective on the definition of time. When you realize there is no death and time is simply a construct of physical reality, you come to realize that the aspect of time as a component of physical reality is here to make life more interesting.

When you focus your attention on what is right in this moment rather than what is wrong with the present conditions, you are in the flow of life. When you focus your attention on the abundance that surrounds you, such as the abundance of air, sunshine, water, food, people, energy, and well-being, you are in the flow. The more you're in the flow, the faster the flow will go and the sooner you will realize the physical manifestation of that which you so desire.

IV.

The flow affects everything in life. The flow is a current in which the entire physical realm rides. All of nature is tuned to the flow. You can see

The Flow of Life

it in your seasons and you can see it in the animals. All wild creatures are tuned to the flow of life and do not resist it as humans do. The physical world is comprised of points of consciousness. All of the blades of grass are conscious as are all of the cells that make up each blade of grass. Each point of consciousness is seeking and finding well-being. Well-being is within the flow.

Each and every cell in your body is a point of consciousness. These cells are seeking and finding well-being as they live within the flow. All of your cells experience life in physical reality. Their lives allow you to live your life. While each cell does not focus itself in physical reality for the same duration of time you do, they are living points of consciousness focused in physical reality for as long as they choose to be focused here.

You are not your body; you are simply its captain. You are not consciously aware of the moment-by-moment functioning of your body, only the mechanism by which it works. You do not make your heart pump or your liver process; you allow your organs to function independent of your conscious command. So it is with every cell in your body. You trust that each cell knows what to do and does its job accordingly. You do not dictate commands to your organs or to the cells of your body, you simply inspire them.

You inspire each cell of your body to perform its function through your thoughts. When you are in the flow, so are the cells of your body. When you resist the flow, you cause tension and inspire the cells of your body to resist the flow as well. When you resist the flow, you momentarily remove yourself from the well-being that is being offered by the universe and you may temporarily remove your cells from that well-being as well.

However, you do not live in a constant state of resistance and you are never completely cut off from well-being. Your cells tap into the flow quite easily and freely whenever you choose to give up resistance and go with the flow. We do want to point out that when you are resistant to the natural flow of life, your cells may become resistant as well. If you resist long and hard enough, your cells may choose to leave physical reality because they strive for well-being and they are influenced by your resistance to well-being. Some of the cells in your body may die or simply function in a way that was not intended.

Do not worry about anything that may have happened in the past. All of your power is in this moment. You can decide that you are worthy, that all of your desires are being fulfilled, that the conditions are right, and you can choose right now to go with the flow of life. You can drop all resentments, forgive yourself and everyone else, and accept that your life has unfolded in the perfect manner to bring you to where you are today. From this point on, as you consciously choose to allow the flow of life to carry you toward your desire, you can give up resistance. Nothing is wrong; everything is right.

When you reach for thoughts of appreciation, you turn with the flow of life toward your desire. When you complain about anything, you resist the flow of life. You can change the condition of your life with thoughts of appreciation for what you already have. You create more abundance by focusing on the abundance you already have. You cannot change the conditions that exist in the moment by wanting them to be different than they are. You change the conditions over time by thinking thoughts of the best aspects of your current condition.

You can always choose to see the positive aspects of anything, anyone, and any condition. You can also choose to see the negative aspects of anything. It is your choice. When you choose to see the negative in any moment, you resist the flow of life. If you choose to see the positive, you join the flow of life. Complaining is resisting the flow, and appreciating is allowing yourself to go with the flow.

When you complain about something to another person through verbal or written communication, you resist the flow in a very strong manner. You not only make it more difficult for yourself to go with the flow, but you also make it more difficult for the other person to find the flow of their own life. When someone has lived a life experience focused on the negative aspect of any condition, they may never understand the reality of the flow of life. Children who are exposed to a parent who is in constant struggle against the flow may find it more difficult to discover the flow in their own lives. If you love and care about another person in your life, be very careful when speaking to them or writing to them. You do not want to influence those you love in a manner that may cause them to be resistant to the flow.

When someone you love comes to you with a complaint about the conditions of life, you may have an unconscious desire to soothe them. It will not benefit them or you to engage or agree with their complaint. It may not be possible to have them see the positive in the situation due to the momentum that has been created. If you are able to see the positive aspect of any situation, it may not benefit the other person immediately, but it will benefit you. As you habitually look for the good in everything, everything will become good.

When faced with a complaint from another person, you must think about the flow prior to taking any action. Try not to react to the complaint or solve it. Do not argue against the complaint for that too goes against the flow. Soothe the other person as best you can. You can try to help them understand the situation from a broader perspective, but if that does not work, it might be best to simply remove yourself from the situation entirely.

People who complain go first to those who will help to intensify their problem. If they find a willing ear, they will bend it. Do not be the one who allows the complaints of others to be voiced in your presence. Help them see the positive if you can or try to change the subject. Remove yourself from the conversation if you cannot change their perspective. You are responsible for yourself and you must not allow yourself to be pulled out of the flow by your attention to or participation in the complaints of others.

V.

You live in a society that is preoccupied with the notion of ambition. Ambition is the desire for and pursuit of success. You strive for success and are driven toward it. In essence, you are motivated toward the possession of the dreams of your society which are false dreams. In order to live in the flow of life, you must discover your true dreams and your own true path.

You are a highly successful being as you are now in this moment in time. You live in a space- time reality that has never been more than it is now. You have come to explore the vast array of potential experiences in a landscape that has never before existed. To be born into this environment at this time means you are truly successful.

Once you delve into the inner most part of you and for a moment withdraw your focus from the world outside, you will discover the success you are. You are worthy beyond words and you are a master creator. Your creation is you and it is a masterpiece, whether you realize that fact or not.

The reason you may not realize the mastery of the creation that is you comes from the outward perception of your world and your comparison to others. You believe you do not measure up to the others you see as symbols of excellence in your society. You see someone who has gained fame and recognition and you feel less than, in comparison to, that other person. Your comparison is based on a flawed premise.

You do not know the path of the person you hold in high regard. You do not know what they have come here to explore. You see the appearance of their alignment and envy that alignment. But you have the same power and ability to align with your inner self, your true dreams, and your own intended path. If you see the alignment of others, let it inspire you to your own alignment and do not focus on any lack of alignment you notice in comparison.

You cannot see the true vibrational patterns of others. You see what simply appears on the surface. You do not see the depth of their alignment. While they may be aligned with the subject of abundance, they may not be aligned with the subjects of physical well-being or relationships. Do not compare yourself with others, for the comparison will never be accurate. Focus on your own alignment and see yourself as the successful and worthy person you are. Maintain a balance between your focus and attention to your outer self in equal proportion to your focus and attention on your inner self.

You are a creator, and your creation is you. You have the tools, ability, and power to create whatever you want. But you must draw your inspiration from the inside and not from your observation or the influence of your outer world. Only you will ever know what truly pleases you. Others may offer advice, but they cannot see your set of intentions or your current vibrational pattern.

Living in the flow of life means allowing the inspiration for your dreams and passions to come from within. In the flow of life you are not concerned with the opinions and activities of others. You allow them to be or do whatever they please, but you do not allow yourself to be influenced away from what pleases you. Being in the flow of life means you do not react to the influences of others. Instead, you move like a small stream around others and toward your own true desires.

There is no outer success without inner success. Unless you come to know yourself for the worthy and creative person you already are, you cannot live fully in the flow of life. Success means alignment with your inner self, who understands who you really are. You must learn to please yourself first and worry less about pleasing others. It is not possible for you to maintain another person's alignment. Align to the real you and allow them to align with their real selves, or not. It is not your concern.

You cannot allow yourself to be swept up in the lives and dramas of those around you. You are not here to save them. They are here to find their true path and align with their inner selves. You can inspire them through your own alignment, but you cannot motivate or otherwise help them. Your attention to their cries for help only activates a greater sense of lack and causes them to reach out for more help rather than to find inner alignment themselves.

Being in the flow of life means that you are sticking to your own true path. You might step off the path occasionally to explore and poke around the landscape, but it is always easy to return to your path. You know you are in the flow of life when you are experiencing positive emotion and things are working out for you. You know when you are going against the flow of life when you experience struggle, difficulty, and negative emotion. Your guidance system lets you know when you're going with the flow or against it.

There is nothing that must be achieved in this lifetime. Success is not measured by the attainment of accolades, prestige, or wealth. Success is measured by your alignment with your true desires. Success is the only possible outcome because you are now and will always be a work in progress. You can only fail when you fail to live up to the illusion you've created in your mind.

Take your life less seriously and it will improve dramatically. You cannot strive for outward signs of success without noticing the lack of success in the present moment. You must view yourself as already successful, already worthy, already capable, to create the manifestation of those feelings in your physical reality. You are a powerful creator, as powerful as any who have ever lived. Once you give up judgment, self-criticism, and the awkward and unrealistic comparisons to others, you'll see yourself as the magnificent being you already are.

The feeling of tension in your solar plexus, the feeling of uneasiness you can taste in your mouth, comes from the divide you feel between the person you think you are now and the person you want to become or wish you could become. If you ease up on yourself just a little and relax that feeling of tension, you'll see you're on the way to where you want to go. If you have faith that the universe will work its magic and transform you into the version of you that you so want, you'll ease your way there. There is no amount of struggle or sacrifice that will get you there any faster. You will be transformed, if you allow it, in the time that is meant for you and not before.

You create yourself through your desires. As you align with your true desires, the universe will mold you into the vibrational version of you that is ready for what you desire. You birth a desire, the universe responds, you go with the flow of life, you are transformed into the version of you that is ready for your desire, and it is then realized in your physical reality as a manifestation. The flow of life is an essential part of the process. When you allow yourself to travel with the flow, you move in the direction of your desires. When you fight against the flow, you stall the physical manifestation of your desires.

You have complete freedom to do whatever you want. If you enjoy the drama within the lives of others, you are free to participate in and ramp up their dramas even further. If you want to fight against injustice and thereby add it to your vibration, you are free to do so. If you would like to complain about the way things are in the present moment rather than focus on the positive aspects of any moment, that is your choice, too.

However, if you want to expand and explore in the manner you intended prior to your birth, you must go with the flow of life. If you want to live a life of passion and fulfill dream after dream, you must go with the flow of life. If you want to experience the joys of life and be in true alignment so that you can inspire others to do the same, you must simply and easily go with the flow.

Chapter Nine

Focus

Before your birth, you were not primarily focused in physical reality. Once you were born, you were fully focused in this physical reality. When you once again transition to the nonphysical, you will not be primarily focused in physical reality. Therefore, focus is a key component of physical reality.

Focus is your attention to something. For our purposes we will define focus more specifically as the attention paid to what is wanted in any moment in time. Of course, you could just as easily be focused on something unwanted at any given moment. However, when we talk about focus, we are talking about your ability to concentrate your powers in the pursuit of deliberate creation.

Most humans go through their day with very little focus. They are not typically summoning thoughts about the things they desire. Their minds wander from one observation to another. They think about what they prefer and what they do not like as one thought flows haphazardly to the next. They let the occurrences of the day distract them from deliberate creation. They understand neither the power nor the utility of the mind. Their thoughts are mostly random and their lives are a mix of the wanted and the unwanted. Without focus there, is no control.

Focus is the steering wheel of the mind. It allows you to summon thoughts that are of a certain vibrational nature. You have the ability to summon thoughts that feel good or thoughts that feel bad. Your emotions tell you the difference. Now that you are aware of the power of your thoughts and that you are a deliberate creator, you can use focus to summon thoughts of that which is wanted.

A Perception of Reality

Deliberate creation not only demands that you direct your focus of attention to what is wanted, it also requires that you do not dwell on anything unwanted. Focus is the attention to the thoughts you are summoning in the moment. It is the awareness of how you are feeling in the moment. Focus is the ability to discern your better-feeling thoughts from those that do not feel as good. Focus is constantly reaching for better-feeling thoughts.

You use focus to align with your desires and to manifest your desires into physical reality. You do not use action; you utilize the power of your thoughts through focus. As you become more aware of what you are thinking and how you are feeling, your life will become clearer, your path will unfold easier, you will go with the flow of life, and you'll achieve dream after dream. Focus is what separates a life of clarity and purpose from a life of chaos and uncertainty.

As a child you were focused. Your thoughts were general and easy. You lived in the moment. You gave your attention to your mother, your toys, nature, and the world around you. You felt good when you received the well-being that was your birthright and occasionally, when you could not express your desires, you felt bad and cried. Your parents tried to soothe you as best they could and you easily returned to your normal state of feeling good.

As you grew, your attention was slowly taken from well-being to that which was influenced by your parents, teachers, peers, and to a lesser extent, society in general. Fear, doubt, and worry entered your thoughts as you were told what to do and why it was so important that you conform to the whims and wishes of others. You were expected to become a conforming member of whatever society you were born into. You had to go to school, you had to eat your vegetables, you had to do your chores, and you had to behave in a certain way so you would not embarrass yourself or those around you. Soon you lost the focus you intended before your birth.

As fear, doubt, and worry entered your experience, your mind was left to summon random thoughts. While much of your youth was spent dreaming about your future and your desires, much of it was spent fearing your own individuality. You believed you had to conform to society in order to fit in and become an upstanding member. You feared being shunned or becoming an outcast.

The influence of others may have led you away from your natural ability to focus on what you desired and soon you learned to focus on what was unwanted with the same fervor. As you simultaneously focused on the wanted and unwanted, you lost the knowledge that you are the creator of your life. You assumed, due to your lack of focus on the wanted, that life simply unfolded in a random, haphazard manner. It was your equal attention given to the wanted and the unwanted that caused your life to bring to you examples of both.

Had you retained your natural ability and understanding that focus was to be applied only to what was wanted, your life would have unfolded in a way that was much more aligned with your desires. You would have gained confidence in your ability to focus. Like everything else in the universe, the more you practice focus, the better you become at focusing on that which you want.

When you are working on something with passion, you are focused on what is wanted. Time loses meaning. You are enjoying each moment and the journey itself. You are less concerned with the outcome. Since you are focused on what is wanted, your vibration is raised as a result. In this state, your desires manifest easily.

The exact same properties are involved when your attention is focused on anything unwanted. The difference is that in the case of focusing on that which is wanted, your emotions are pleasant and you know your attention is focused on the positive. When you are focused on what is unwanted, your unpleasant-feeling emotions indicate you are focused on the negative. Your focus is just as powerful either way and when you focus on anything unwanted, you bring more of it into your experience.

If you feel there has been an injustice in the world and you rally to fight this injustice, you are focused on the negative aspect of the subject. You are focused on the unwanted part of it. And, through your focus, you bring more of it into your experience. When you write about it, talk about it, or summon thoughts about that which is unwanted, you focus your powerful being on the subject and bring more of it into your experience.

You cannot realize the solution while focused on the problem. You can only solve a problem by being focused in a positive manner on the solution. You cannot eradicate war by eradicating the enemy. You can only achieve peace by focusing on peace, wanting peace, and loving your enemy. You

A Perception of Reality

must see the positive in everything and your reality will be reflected back to you with the positive of everything. If you see only the negative, you will get more negative and thus spiral downwards. If you see the positive, you will get more positive and spiral upwards. Again, it's your choice; it's your point of focus.

Determination is different than focus. Focus is not action; it's deliberate thought. As you set your intention to what you desire, it's your focus on your desire that summons thought. As you feel pleasant emotion in response to the thoughts you are receiving, you recognize that your focus is on the path toward your desire. When you focus on what you want, thoughts about the subject flow to you. If the thoughts feel good, your focus is accurate. If doubt or fear enters your thoughts, your focus must be redirected. It is this constant fine tuning of those thoughts which bring pleasant emotion that is the sole purpose of your focus.

With focus, you can achieve anything. You can summon good-feeling thoughts, your actions will be inspired, you will simply go with the flow of life, focusing every step of the way, and your desires will manifest into your physical experience. That's deliberate creation.

Without focus you do not have the ability to deliberately create your life. Without the power of focus the thoughts that come to you are random. Your mind wanders from one subject to the next seemingly unrelated subject. Without a steering wheel you cannot drive your car. Your life would meander without meaning, only to be guided by the unreliable influence of others and by events occurring in your experience.

II.

No matter what your life experience has been up to this point, you have the power to regain your focus. It is an ability you were born with. If you have made it, through the Law of Attraction, to this book, then you have a greater ability to focus than you may currently know. The key is to realize you have control of your thoughts. It will take practice to regain focus and thus full control of your thoughts. But in time, with the proper training, your thoughts will be summoned according to your desires and not as a reaction to random occurrences.

You must first become aware of the value of focused thought. You must understand that all thoughts carry vibration and send signals out to the universe that attract similar thoughts. You must become aware of the power of your thoughts and words, whether spoken or written. Thoughts make the difference between a deliberate life and a chaotic life. It's the thoughts you consciously summon that matter. In fact, thoughts precede all matter. That's how powerful thoughts are.

If you do not have the ability to control your thoughts, you do not have the ability to control your life. If you do not believe thoughts are powerful, you cannot understand the need for focus. For only with the full understanding of the magnificent quality that thoughts bring to reality can you know the value of focus. A focused thought is the most powerful element in the universe.

Your thoughts are not something you create out of nowhere; they are summoned by your desires, influences, feelings, and attention to anything. Focus controls the mechanism that summons all thought. If a thought is summoned that is unpleasant, you need not dwell on it, because doing so will only attract similar thoughts. When you become aware of an unpleasant thought, use the power of your focus to summon a new thought that is pleasant. You do not eradicate the unpleasant thought. Instead, you turn your focus toward a pleasant one and summon more and more pleasant-feeling thoughts. When you reach a level on that subject where fear or doubt enters, you again refocus your attention and reach for another new, better-feeling thought.

You are not required to constantly and only think thoughts of joy, love, happiness, glee, prosperity, freedom, abundance, fun, happiness, interest, etc. You will at times come across thoughts that feel terrible to you. At these times simply focus on any thought that feels better. One better-feeling thought than the last is what focus is all about. Sometimes you cannot feel joy in the midst of sorrow, but you can reach for feelings of hope or forgiveness, which feel better.

Your practice is to be aware of your thoughts in the moment and reach for ones that feel just as good or even better. You want to see the positive in everything. This will attract more good-feeling thoughts. If the thoughts feel good, you will gain confidence in your ability to focus. This is a game with no score to keep. You have lived a life feeling comfortable in the random manner of your mind. It will take focus to consciously become aware of your thoughts and to attract higher-quality thoughts. You have patterns of habit that can be broken over time. Take it easy and have fun. Notice your thoughts and how they feel. Reach for better-feeling thoughts if you can. Soon you'll regain your focus and with that comes clarity of mind.

III.

There are tools for regaining your focus. The first tool is meditation, which helps you stop thought or at least reduce the frequency of thoughts. In meditation you can separate yourself, the thinker, from the thoughts you summon.

Have you ever taken the time to analyze a single thought? Have you ever observed a thought and wondered, "Where did that thought come from?" You are thinking a thought in the middle of another one. This concept makes you think about the nature of thoughts in general. Why do you think thoughts at all? What is the purpose of thought in physical reality? Is a thought a point of consciousness in and of itself? Where do these thoughts come from?

Thoughts are points of consciousness that exist in your physical reality. All thoughts are vibration and they act as signals to the universe. Thoughts are the building blocks of physical reality. Without thought, there would be no physical reality.

You are a receiver of thought. You attract thought as one consciousness to another. You can perceive thought and the thought perceives you. You can attract multiple thoughts at once or you can attract them in an orderly manner. Without focus, the thoughts you attract are random based on your feelings in the moment. If you observe something unwanted, immediately thoughts of that unwanted thing rush to you like waves on a beach. If your feeling persists, without focus, similar thoughts will keep coming. You are the attractor of your thoughts and the thoughts are attracted to you based on your feelings.

If you feel good, you will attract good-feeling thoughts. If you feel bad, you will attract bad-feeling thoughts. Your focus can direct the thoughts you attract like a nozzle on a hose. Your focus can tighten the nozzle so that a fine stream of good-feeling thoughts flows to you and from you. Your lack of focus opens the nozzle so a wider array of thoughts are received in a less organized or controlled manner.

The ability to feel good at any moment allows your focusing capacity to greatly increase. The fact that you feel good makes focusing so much easier. When feeling good, good-feeling thoughts come easily and naturally. Your ability to focus is enhanced.

If you are in a bad mood, you will naturally attract bad-feeling thoughts. Your ability to focus will be compromised. You will have to work very hard to attract better-feeling thoughts. Unpleasant thoughts will rush to you and reinforce your mood. It will be difficult to focus your attention on what is wanted. When you are feeling despair, similar thoughts are attracted. When you feel like a victim, similar thoughts are attracted. When you feel lack, thoughts of lack are attracted. If you have practiced focus, you have the ability to slowly improve the quality of your thoughts. You may not be able to attract thoughts of joy, but you can attract better-feeling thoughts and in time you can rise to a higher emotional state of being.

Meditation enhances your focus by turning your attention inwards. As you meditate, you slow or stop thought. You are in control of the thought receiver that is you. Through meditation, you can turn the spigot of your mind so that the thoughts flow more slowly and may eventually stop altogether. The goal of meditation is to increase your ability to focus. As you are able to slow the flow of thought into your consciousness, you increase the power of your focus.

Meditation can be practiced by any means you find desirable. You only need to meditate for a few minutes a day to begin focus for that day. Each day starts off new and with a morning meditation you can begin to focus throughout the day. The practice of meditation is the practice of focus.

Meditation takes practice. Most will not be able to stop or even slow the flow of thought when they begin meditating. It may take weeks or months for you to achieve a level of focus through meditation where you have the ability to slow or stop thought. If practiced daily, meditation will work on its own. There is nothing you need to do but meditate.

When you meditate, you move your focus inward. As you move inward, you connect with your inner self on a new and higher level. Your inner self

A Perception of Reality

is always fully aware of you and is completely connected to you. Through meditation, however, it is you who becomes more aware of and connected to your inner self.

Your inner self will adjust your vibration and tune your focus if you allow it to. When you meditate and slow down your thoughts, the thoughts that do come are delivered by your inner self. This part of you is aware of your desires and is always focused on the dreams you have for your life. Your inner self is able to maintain this focus even when you cannot. After a period of time and with practice, the thoughts you receive as a result of meditation will be communication from your inner self.

When you achieve focus, you create a stronger connection with your inner self. As you align with your dreams and desires, you also align with your inner self. As you walk your path toward the physical manifestation of your desires, you walk your path alongside your inner self. If you veer from your path, your inner self will maintain the course and help guide you back to your true path. It's the connection you now know, through meditation, that will allow you to easily return to your path with assistance from your inner self.

You are much more than the flesh and bones of your body. You are a vibrational being who experiences physical reality through the senses of your body. But your body is only half of the story. Your inner self is the other half. Through focus, you are really connecting with the larger part of you that is your inner self.

More of your life, on a day-to-day basis, is guided by your inner self than you know. For example, when you begin a sentence in a conversation, it is your inner self who flows the thoughts to you, which you then translate into words. Before you begin to speak, you do not plan each word that will flow forth from your mouth. It happens spontaneously. You might never have thought of this before, but what is happening is a partnership between you and your inner self.

The extent to which you are aligned with your inner self is the level of focus you have achieved. Sometimes, when you're feeling good, you have a strong connection and feel your best. Words, actions, and clarity come forth from you easily. You might be amazed at your eloquence or wit at these times. You have the ability to remember details, spur on the conversation, inspire others, and engage. All of these abilities come from your inner self to the degree to which you find alignment.

You may also notice that, during times when you are not in a good mood, you have less capacity to engage others, your clarity is not as sharp, and your wit is duller. Your memory is foggy and you might even enter into an argument. At these times your alignment with your inner self is a bit off. Your inner self is fully connected with you, but due to your misalignment, you're not receiving the message.

Focus allows you to be more aligned more of the time and to receive the best your inner self has to offer. There is much more to tell on the subject of your inner self, but for now simply be aware that your inner self has the ability to work with you toward your desires to the degree of your focus and alignment.

IV.

Focus allows you to maintain progress toward your dreams and desires. With the proper focus, you can handle any situation that may arise. You understand that obstacles are meant to form you into a higher vibrational version of you so that you will be ready when your desire manifests. If you can maintain your focus through each manifestation event, you will move toward your desire faster. Focus is the understanding that whatever happens is a result of your vibrational pattern. The extent to which you can see the positive aspects of any situation is the extent of your focus.

When you are able to pick out the positive aspects of anything you turn your attention to, you increase your focus. If you are seeing mostly negative aspects of situations, you are losing your focus on what you really want and you are tuning your focus to what is unwanted. Focus is powerful when applied in either direction, positive or negative. The more focused you are, the more powerful you are. Now that you understand that positive focus will bring you toward that which you desire and negative focus will bring unwanted experiences into your life, you will automatically be focused in a more positive manner.

Positive focus is all we care about. In the nonphysical we are only ever focused on the positive aspects of anything. We do not see or draw our attention to anything unwanted or to the negative aspects of any situation. If you decide to tune your focus more positively, you will be more aligned with us and with your inner self. We will, as you say, be on the same page.

The universe does not see or understand the concept of negative. The universe only gives you more of what you give your attention to. If you want freedom and abundance and you are focused more on the freedom and abundance you currently enjoy in your life, you will get more freedom and more abundance. If you want freedom and abundance but are focused on the current lack of it in your life, you will be given more lack of freedom and abundance.

You now have everything you want. Focus on what you have now that you like and it will grow. Focus on the apparent lack of what you have, as you compare it to what others have, and the sense of lack will grow deeper. When you compare your life to others, you sense the divide. When you focus on the positive aspects of your life, without comparing yourself to others, the gap shrinks. It is only in your comparison that you notice any difference.

When you focus on the positive aspects of your life in its current state, others will see the same positive aspects and compliment you. The influence of others will have a positive effect on you. If you focus on the lack you notice in your life, others will notice it as well and they will reflect it back to you by giving you advice or otherwise influencing you in a negative manner.

If someone offers you advice, they are focused on an apparent lack in your life. They only see the lack because you see the lack. The advice is a mirror to how you are feeling about your life. Unsolicited advice has no other purpose, because others cannot see your vibration and therefore cannot know what's right for you.

If someone offers you a compliment, it's because you are focused in a positive manner on something in your life. A compliment is a mirror to your positive focus, while unsolicited advice is a mirror to your negative focus. When you hear more compliments, you will know that you are becoming more positively focused.

Focus is simply a tool of deliberate creation. What you focus on grows, be it positive or negative. The more you like what you get, the more of it you will be given. The more you dislike what you get, the more of that you will be given as well. Focus on what you like and do not think or speak of anything that you do not like. Could this be any simpler?

Chapter Ten

The Power of Abundance

You exist in an abundant universe and live in an abundant world. You have everything you need to fulfill your wildest dreams. It is all located here on earth at this present time. You are not running out of resources and you never will. You are simply using the resources in different ways and creating new resources as you go. Your world has the capacity to supply you with everything you'll ever need. There is no lack in the universe unless you create the feeling of lack within yourself.

Feelings, thoughts, and emotions are your tools for navigating your reality. If you want something, you must feel for it. It is this feeling part of you that brings what you want to your physical experience. You can feel for anything, wanted or unwanted, and the universe will bring you to whatever it is. There is nothing more commonly desired among humans than more money, or, in our words, abundance.

Abundance is money and more. Abundance means freedom, ease, and security. In your mind, if you had more money, you would be secure, you would have more freedom to do what you want, and your life would be easier. This is not really true, but it's what most humans believe and so the thirst for more money is prevalent in your society.

You should be aware that your life is currently, in its present state, completely abundant. You simply take the abundance you have for granted. What you seek is more abundance and you feel the lack of money, the lack of time, and the lack of freedom rather than the true abundance you now experience.

Let's examine the abundance that is present in your life right now. As we speak for the general population reading this material, we speak in general terms. You have an abundance of air to breathe. You are not worried about your next breath. You have all the air you'll ever need to live the rest of your life without having to worry that you'll run out of air. This is a very general statement of abundance and yet, as you read those words, many of you are thinking thoughts about lacking air. When confronted with idea of an abundance of air, which you know is true, your mind places you in situations where there is a lack of air. How many of you pictured yourself underwater when reading that you have an abundance of air? How many of you thought of a future where air was in limited supply? This is a normal reaction when confronted by the obvious positive side of any concept. You see the positive and the negative. It is your habit of unfocused thinking.

When you think thoughts of what you want, you often have thoughts about the opposite of what you want. The degree to which the positive or negative side of each topic appears in your mind is an indicator of how you feel about the subject. While all of you feel an abundance of air and are generally not worried about the lack of it, you still receive small thoughts of this lack. Thoughts of lack lie within the nature of the mind and are practiced when you hear stories of those who have run out of air. Your fears and doubts bring thoughts of lack that does not exist in your reality.

You must remember that your reality is created entirely by you. You are not going to run out of air or anything else. You see lack in others and bring their lack onto yourself. You project the lack you see around you into your existence. This should not be the standard by which you create reality. If you can understand the basic and simple premise that others create their reality and you create your reality, you can let them be as they are and focus on what is important to you.

II.

The first step in creating abundance in your life is recognizing your personal abundance and appreciating all that you have. It may seem as though some have more abundance than others, but abundance is subject to your perspective. What you might think of as wealthy is different from almost everyone else's perspective. You think that a certain amount of money in the bank is abundant while, another might think that sum extravagant beyond their wildest imagination and another may consider the figure paltry.

Abundance is an individual concept, so it is best not to compare. What you consider abundant now will completely change once you reach a new, higher level of abundance. No matter how abundant your life is, you will always seek more. This is woven into the fabric of existence. There is always more to be had, more to give, and more to receive. Life, in both the physical and nonphysical realms, is always the seeking of more. Once you get used to that idea, you can begin to see existence from a new perspective.

What is abundant in your life now? Start with the general concepts, such as an abundance of water and air. Do you have an abundance of food to eat? We know you do. Do you have access to all the tools and knowledge you need to bring more abundance into your life? The answer for all of you is yes. Are you on your way to far greater levels of abundance in your physical reality? Yes, absolutely and definitely. Are you being shaped by the universe so that you are ready to receive all the abundance you are asking for? Yes, absolutely and definitely.

Do you feel, in this present moment, that you have an abundance of time? For most of you reading this material right now, the answer is no. You might even be having difficulty finding the time to read these pages. Yet time is also based on your perspective. For some, there is too much time and they must find ways to pass it. For others, there is never enough time in the day. Time is a subjective reference determined by one's perspective on the matter. Let us first tell you that since time does not really exist, you have an abundance of it. Did that help? No? Okay, let's delve a little deeper.

The feeling of time is just that: a feeling. It is dependent on your perspective. If you feel you have enough time, you literally have more time than if you feel time is scarce. If you sat and did nothing but watch the clock on the wall as the seconds ticked by, an hour would feel like an eternity. If you spent that same hour doing something you are passionate about, the hour would feel like just a few minutes. Time is a matter of perspective and you have all experienced this enough to understand the basic idea that time is fluid.

If you have ever watched a sport in which the game is timed, you have experienced the varying perspective of time. If in the final minutes of the game your team is winning, those last few minutes seem like a long time as you pull for your team to keep its lead to the end. When the other team has the ball, the clock seems to go in slow motion and you just can't wait for the final seconds to tick away. Conversely, if your team is behind in the game, it seems like they won't have enough time to catch up. The seconds keep ticking faster and faster.

As you can see, through the use of examples like these, time is relative. It's both static and fluid and it depends on the perspective of the observer. Time, like money and nearly everything else in physical reality, is completely determined by the perspective of each individual. Abundance is the same.

You can look at your life in every area and see abundance or lack. Do you have an abundance of love or a lack of love? You have either depending on what you're focused on. Do you have an abundance of security or a lack of security? Do you have an abundance of freedom or a lack of freedom? It all depends on your perspective and your point of focus.

Because you are always wanting more, lack seems like an appropriate measure to use when determining what it is you want. If you lack enough food in the house to make dinner, you might want to go to the grocery store. You understand the lack of what you now have and make a plan to eradicate that lack by purchasing groceries. This makes perfect sense; however, it is a false premise. When you notice that you lack food in your pantry, you are really realizing that you have an abundant supply of food. You know the grocery store is just down the road and is open for business. You know you can always get what you need. You absolutely know there is an abundance of food in your life and the grocery store is your source of that abundance, not your pantry.

However, when you notice a lack in your bank account, you do not feel the same abundance. There is no store where you can simply walk in and pick money off the shelves. But this too is an illusion. The universe is constantly supplying you with as much money as you will accept - in fact, with the exact amount you can handle and no more. It all depends on your perspective and how you see either the abundance or the scarcity of money from your point of perspective. The universe is your money store and you can take as much as you like. It's always open and the shelves are fully stocked at all times. You just have to get yourself to the store.

III.

You believe that "money does not grow on trees." This is a false premise. Money is everywhere, but if you're not tuned to it, you cannot see it. It is easier for most to tune into abundance rather than money because you are experiencing more abundance in your life in areas apart from money. If you can appreciate the abundance that exists in the other areas of your life, you will attract money in abundance as well. It is a fundamental construct of the universe. Therefore, feeling abundant will bring an abundance of all things, including money.

The easiest way to experience the flow of money into your life is to reach for the feeling of abundance. You have an abundance of sunshine and on sunny days you can simply step outside and feel the sun. It beams its rays on everything. The sun never turns off. It radiates outward from itself and lands on everything it touches, bringing with it the energy of life. There is an abundance of rain and water. The clouds fill with vapor in the air and turn it into rain, which brings life to every blade of grass it touches.

How would it feel to have more abundance in your life? What would you do? How would life be better? How would your physical experience feel richer and more intense? How would an abundance of money affect your perception of time and freedom? If you can focus on the positive aspects of these questions and stay as general as possible while always reaching for the feeling of abundance, remarkable things will begin to happen.

As you reach for the feeling of abundance you will attract thoughts of abundance. When you experience good-feeling emotions in connection with your thoughts of abundance, you know you are feeling the positive aspects of abundance. If you are experiencing fear and doubt and the associated negative emotions in connection to your thoughts of abundance, you are thinking thoughts beyond your vibrational readiness. You are still focused on the lack of abundance.

The manifestation of money into your life is a process. You start from wherever you now stand. It matters not what your previous experience has been to this date. From this date forward you are starting from a completely new vibrational level. If you have read the preceding pages on the subject of abundance, your perspective on physical reality has shifted to a new place.

You are a new person as a result of reading and absorbing this material. You have risen to a new level of understanding, a new point of perspective, and a completely new, higher vibration exudes from your being. You are now ready to receive more abundance and with it, more money.

The process is simple, but it takes focus and practice. You must become aware of your limiting beliefs. You must pay close attention to the manifestation events that occur along your path, for they will indicate any unhelpful belief systems you might hold to. If you overhear a conversation about money, pay close attention to how it makes you feel. If you feel positive emotion, you're on the path and this manifestation event is moving you in the right direction. If you feel negative emotion as you overhear the conversation, you must recognize that you are holding onto beliefs that do not serve you.

If you are receiving advice from others on the subject of money, recognize that there is something you are considering that you do not feel ready for. Those offering unsolicited advice are noticing your lack of confidence. You must be aware that what they are saying is a reflection of what you are feeling. If others give you a compliment regarding the subject of money, this is a reflection of your newfound confidence on the subject. You are now well on your way.

IV.

In order to attract money into your life, you must adopt a new perspective on the subject. Start to see money as energy. Money, like energy, flows. It works best when the flow in and out is easy. While you can store energy, as in a battery, stored energy is not as powerful as when it is allowed to flow freely. Money should be allowed to flow in and flow out without blockage. If you fear that money will stop flowing in, so you decide to limit the flow out, it will not flow in. If you allow it to flow freely out, you allow it to flow freely in.

Money, like time, does not exist in and of itself. It is a concept you simply agree on among yourselves. These agreements do not matter in your reality to the extent you think. Your beliefs about money, however, have tremendous impact. If you believe money is the result of hard work (or work at all, for that matter), you will have to work hard to get it. If you find your passion in life and now your work is your play, you will greatly enjoy your work. If, however, you still believe hard work is needed to bring money and you no longer work hard now that you've found your passion, your passion will not bring money. Your belief system is blocking the money from flowing even though you are passionate about your work.

Money is created through thought, just like everything else. Ideas create money, thoughts create money, and inspired action creates money. Hard work earns small amounts of money, but hard work does not create money. You can create a fortune without participating in any activity you consider work. When we say you, we mean the you who is reading these words right now. *You* can create great wealth without doing anything you consider to be work. Money is energy and is created with the power of feelings, thoughts, and emotions.

Many of the wealthiest people in the world have created their vast fortunes without doing any of the work that created the money. The work was done by people who had a more limited concept of money and belief systems to match. The wealthy understand how to use the leverage of the universe to create wealth and their beliefs do not stand in their way.

Very few of those considered the wealthiest among you considered the collection and amassing of great wealth to be their primary objective. Almost all of them followed the path of their true desire and found their passion in life. They did what excited them and their belief system did not restrict the flow of money. They allowed money to flow because they understood their worthiness and easily accepted the money. The money was simply an exhilarating byproduct of their passion.

Passion for money does not normally bring wealth unless you are passionate about the subject of finance. Most people who go into the field of finance believe that being around money will bring more money and as long as they are not focused on the lack of money, this belief is a helpful one. If they compare their situation with others and notice the lack, they can be in the middle of this arena where money is flowing to everyone else but still be unable to create the flow of money into their life.

It is much more likely for you to naturally allow money to flow into your personal experience when you find your passion. As ease flows into your life, money will follow. When you struggle through your work only because it brings money, more money will not easily flow. It is blocked by your own struggle. You allow money to flow to you through ease. The flow of money must be easy. Struggle and sacrifice restrict the natural flow of money.

Until you find your passion, however, you must accept your present conditions and strive to see the positive aspects of everything around you. If you are in a work environment you do not love, you must find a way to appreciate the positive aspects of the work and the job. You must strive to see the best in the people. If you can recognize the best qualities of your employer, co-workers, supervisors, customers, and others you interact with on a daily basis, you will discover a love for your current work. As you begin to appreciate and enjoy whatever it is you are now involved with, your work experience will improve dramatically and you will be led to your passion. It is only by accepting what is that you can move on to a better experience.

If you are constantly focused on the negative aspects of your current work environment, it is unlikely that you will be able to move in the direction of what you prefer. Since you are focused on unwanted aspects of your work life, you will be given more examples of what you don't want. Even if you were to quit your job and find a new one, you would encounter the same negative aspects of your old job. They would simply be packaged within the wrapping of a new job.

If you switched jobs or careers as a way of escaping what you do not like about your present job, you would not be moving forward along your path. You would not be achieving a higher vibration and your work life, after a period of adjustment, would remain very similar from an emotional point of view.

If you switched jobs or careers, initially your vibration would gain a little momentum because you find the change exciting. At first, you would focus on the positive aspects of the new job as compared with your last job. You would notice how all of the people seem to be nicer to you. You would notice how the job has new appeal. But soon, as your vibration settled into it's previous pattern, you would start to see the negatives of your new job. You would end up in a very similar position. You would dislike your new job as much as you disliked your old one, if not more.

You must achieve a higher vibration if you are to expand. Obviously, the higher the vibration, the more expansion you can achieve, both physically and nonphysically. As you expand in your physical reality, your inner self expands as well. The way to a higher vibration is through the searching for and finding that which pleases you in your current situation, no matter the condition. As you habitually look for the positive aspects in your current condition, your vibration will raise. As you constantly appreciate the good in what you have now, your vibration rises. As your vibration rises, you expand. The only way to move forward toward your desires is through expansion. The only way to expand is to see the positive aspects in all areas of your life.

V.

You were destined to be successful and prosperous. You did not come here to explore poverty; you came here to explore abundance. If you are experiencing poverty now, it is to give you a better understanding of abundance. If you have experienced poverty or lack in your past, it was only to make the abundance you feel now that much richer. You are never stuck in poverty. Poverty is a state of mind. Wealth is also a state of mind.

Poverty is simply a result of the feeling of unworthiness. You cannot feel worthy and experience poverty at the same time. Wealth is the feeling of worthiness. Abundance comes with your complete understanding of your worthiness. You are worthy and therefore you are destined for abundance.

The extent of the money you allow to flow into your life is the direct result of the level of worthiness you feel. If you feel truly worthy, money will flow. If you feel a bit unworthy in the realm of your work environment, money will be blocked to a degree. When you release doubts about your own worthiness, the blockage will be released and money will flow into your physical reality. Since your birthright is worthiness, why not accept it and allow money to flow into your life?

Your state of worthiness is a result of your beliefs. These beliefs of unworthiness are not accurate or helpful. They were created by your feelings of being less in comparison to others. The belief in unworthiness may have arisen as a result of the influence you allowed from others. You thought your parents, teachers, employers, or peers knew better than you and you accepted their influence. The negative aspects others saw in you were simply the reflection of how you were feeling at the time and you accepted them as the truth.

The truth is that you were born into this world just as you intended prior to your birth. You chose the time and place of your birth. You chose your parents. You knew the vibration of the environment at the time of your birth and you knew that you would have certain defining experiences in childhood that would help you find your path and get you started on your intended exploration of certain aspects of life. You never intended to feel anything but absolutely worthy. In fact, it never even occurred to you that you might feel unworthy as a result of conditions in your childhood.

The environment you were born into was newer and vibrated at a higher level than had ever existed previously. The conditions at the time of your birth had never existed before. It was a considerably faster-moving vibration than had ever existed on earth previously. All of the human inhabitants on the planet were coping in the fast-moving environment as best they could. There were a lot of things they did not know and they relied on the methods used by previous generations to cope with life. These methods were now, in this new environment, obsolete. When you were a child, living in the home of your parents, you were very different from them. You vibrated at a much higher level. The generation gap is the gap in vibration and it had never been wider than at the time of your birth. You came into this space-time reality knowing that gap was going to be vast due to this time we refer to as the time of awakening.

The conditions you faced in childhood may have led you to your false beliefs in anything less than your complete worthiness. But now you must release these beliefs and recognize that they were constructed at a time that was confusing to many. There is no one to blame. Simply know that you now have a better understanding of reality and just release all unhelpful beliefs.

If you have ever felt inferior in any way, these feelings were amplified by the Law of Attraction through the influence of others. When you accepted this simple system of feedback, you thought it to be truth rather than a mirror to your own feelings. If you were treated poorly by your parents, teachers, or anyone else and felt negative emotion as a result, you gained momentum and began to notice the negative aspects of yourself through the eyes of others. If you were unable to discover the truth of your worthiness as a child, your beliefs became hardened and solidified the feelings of unworthiness. The Law of Attraction has simply amplified these feelings over time by showing you more of what you are feeling.

If you have been led to this material, you are already becoming aware of your own innate and complete worthiness. You are a worthy being above which no one has ever been more worthy. Your beliefs are simply the result of feelings of inferiority you may have adopted as a child. Because the Law of Attraction is here to mirror your feelings, you saw more evidence of your inferiority. However, had you felt feelings of well-being and worthiness as a child, the Law of Attraction would have provided evidence of your worthiness and your beliefs would have been completely different.

Beliefs are nothing more than habits of thought experienced over time. You can choose to believe anything. When you choose beliefs that are helpful and dismiss beliefs that are not helpful, your life will change for the better. In order to experience abundance and prosperity, you must believe you are worthy of abundance and prosperity. The influences you received earlier in life have no effect on the present unless you allow them to affect your present. You can change your beliefs and you can improve your life.

VI.

Most of your ideas of abundance revolve around your work life. When you work, you earn money. You may believe that the more you work, the more money you will earn. If you enjoy your work, if it's your passion, then work feels easier. In fact, it doesn't feel like work at all. If you feel worthy in your work, you'll allow money to the extent of your feelings of worthiness. If you feel inferior to another because you believe they have more talent or experience, you create some blockage in the flow of money into your experience. Comparing yourself to others and feeling inferior to them blocks the flow of money.

If you feel you are worthy and you allow others to feel their true worthiness, you allow money to flow into your experience. You can even feel more worthy or more deserving than others if you find it helpful. Just remember that all beings are worthy. There are no levels of true worthiness, just degrees of the worthiness each individual feels on a personal basis.

You are a creator and your creation is you. You can be, do, and have anything you desire. You can create as much abundance in your life as you feel comfortable with and no more. You might believe that earning more money means certain things. If you have the desire for more money but you believe that in order to get more money you have to work more hours, you may not be comfortable sacrificing the time needed and you block the flow of more money into your life.

Comfort levels are a construct of your physical mind and your ego. You are trying to rationalize how you can get more money and what action you'll have to take in order to get it. You allow your thoughts to be specific about the details and you make up stories that feel unpleasant. Because you cannot see your way from where you are now to where you want to be, you must fabricate an imaginary path. This path is full of potholes and obstacles and you cannot see an easy road ahead.

The path to more abundance in your life is the same as the path to any desire. Simply focus on the desire, practice the feeling of what you desire, attract thoughts that revolve around the desire, understand the emotion that comes with each thought, take only inspired action, and your desire will manifest at the right time in the most elegant way possible.

Abundance does not come as a result of action alone. Creating goals for abundance, planning a route to abundance and taking action when not inspired to do so will not create true abundance in your life. Action may create temporary results and may lead to something that *is* wanted, but action alone will feel like a struggle unless it's inspired. Action alone only creates that which is temporary. True abundance comes from the aligned process to the creation of any manifested desire.

Whether you desire more money, a physical possession, a relationship, an improved physical condition, or the manifestation of a desire, it all comes from the same thought-based process. The predominance of your thoughts creates your vibrational pattern, which turns into the manifestation of the desire in your personal reality.

To create the physical manifestation of any desire you simply follow a process. We will call this the Creation Process.

The Creation Process is as follows:

1. 1. Focus on a desire
2. Practice the feeling of that desire
3. Attract thoughts around that desire
4. The emotion you feel about each thought indicates how you are moving toward or away from your desire
5. Take action when inspired

If you follow the Creation Process and practice it often, you will understand that you must first come into vibrational alignment with each of your desires in order for the desire to manifest in your physical reality. When you follow the Creation Process you are allowing the universe to modify your vibration so that it becomes a match to your desire. As soon as you are in vibrational range of your desire, it will appear in your life experience. You'll be ready for the manifestation and it will be ready for you. It is always timed perfectly. You must be patient and allow the process to work.

You would not want all of your desires to manifest instantly because you would not be ready for them as they came to you. You would end up despising your manifestations instead of appreciating them. If you did not take the journey, you would not appreciate the manifested version of your desire. You would not even understand it for what it represents. There would be no joy. As hard as this is to comprehend, the journey to the manifestation actually makes the manifestation valuable to you. Without the journey, the manifestation of your desire would carry little meaning and therefore little value.

As we have said all along, it's the journey in life that *is* life. The manifestation of your desire is simply a more obvious manifestation event. You encounter manifestation events every day in your journey toward your desire. But once the manifestation of your desire occurs, you're back on your journey to the manifestation of a new desire.

Do you now understand that the journey never stops? It never stops in this life, it never stops in your nonphysical life, and it will never stop in your next physical life. The journey is life. The sooner you can accept this concept, the more fun you'll have on the journey.

The tension you feel now is the vibrational difference between your current vibration and the vibration you'll need for the desire to manifest.

You're on your way to the manifestation of all your dreams. You might as well release the tension and enjoy the ride. There's nothing you can do but play the game as it unfolds. Look for the positive in your current situation, be happy, find joy in the journey, and you'll have a good life on the way to financial abundance.

VII.

Your beliefs form your reality. Your beliefs about money create the flow of money or a blockage in the flow of money. Money is neither positive nor negative. Money is a concept and you, as humans, have created the agreement of money. Your beliefs determine what meaning money has in your life.

If you believe the wealthy are greedy or the poor are lazy, these beliefs form your reality. Your life is unfolding as a result of your specific and individual collection of beliefs. If you believe that money cannot buy happiness or that it is difficult for a rich man to enter the kingdom of heaven, then the flow of money into your reality will be hindered by these beliefs.

If you believe you are worthy of success and great wealth, you have a belief pattern that is helpful. Beliefs around each subject, each desire, are either helpful or not helpful. Since you have the complete control to change your beliefs, you can choose the helpful beliefs over limiting ones. You can modify the intensity of your beliefs by ramping up your beliefs when they're helpful and lowering the intensity of your hindering beliefs.

Many of your beliefs are so intense and powerful that you do not consider them to be beliefs; you regard them as facts or the truth. The truth is nothing more than a very intense belief. When you are able to understand this concept, you will have more power over your beliefs.

In general, beliefs are helpful. They are an integral piece of the mechanism of reality. Without beliefs, the fabric of reality would unravel. However, you can use your belief system to your advantage. By understanding that any belief can be altered, you are actually altering the fabric of reality. You can alter your beliefs so that they serve you well.

A Perception of Reality

Humans consider what they believe to be true. They will even argue the point. Few people will allow their beliefs to be questioned. When confronted with a concept that goes against a strongly held belief, people will tend to avoid the subject altogether. They will change the channel, call the idea stupid, or just leave the room. If you are to navigate reality toward the life experience you desire, your beliefs must be malleable. You must not hold onto any hindering belief, whether you consider it to be fact, the truth, or the law.

As the universe brings you closer to your desires, it must wind its way around the obstacle course you have created with your belief system. It cannot bring you straight to your desire because you do not yet believe your desire is really possible to the degree needed for your vibration to be a match to it. Therefore, the universe must shape your belief system through a series of manifestation events so that your beliefs are altered in such a way that you allow the manifestation of your desire.

If your belief system can be easily modified through one or several manifestation events, your desire will manifest quickly. If your beliefs are rigid and firm, your desire will not manifest easily. You cannot change your vibration unless you can learn to change your beliefs. However, you are already one of the very few people who are open to a new belief system. We know you are able to easily shape your beliefs to your own individual benefit.

You already possess one of the greatest talents known to mankind and that is the talent for shifting your beliefs based on your desires. We know this is true of you specifically because you would not have made it this far in reading this material had your belief system been too rigid. You have the ability to understand and allow new concepts to flow into your experience. You already realize the resonance of this material and your beliefs about the nature of reality are swiftly changing from non-beneficial beliefs to helpful ones.

Now let us help you shift your beliefs about money. We are going to give you a series of statements that if you read and believe will allow you to turn on the flow of money into your physical experience. Read these statements over and over until you believe each one. Take note of the emotions you feel after reading each statement. Write down how you feel and analyze your beliefs about each statement. If you take the time to write each statement in your own hand and analyze your beliefs about each statement, you will shape your belief system so that it will allow money to flow into your life. If you don't believe in writing down your analysis of your beliefs about each statement, then this is the first belief you must alter.

Start now: Write each statement in a notebook, then describe, in writing, how you feel emotionally about each statement.

I believe I am more than just the flesh and bones that are represented by my physical body.

I believe there is more to this world than meets the eye.

I believe I am the creator of my life experience and the creation is me.

I believe I can have, be, and do anything I truly desire as long as I follow the Creation Process.

I understand that my beliefs shape my reality.

I know I am in control of my beliefs and I can raise or lower the intensity of any belief.

I am able to analyze, through introspection, the benefits or detriments of any particular belief.

I now know that as I allow my beliefs to be altered, I allow my life to change, my perspective to be modified, and my dreams to manifest into my physical experience.

I believe money is good.

I believe I am a worthy being, as worthy as any who have ever existed.

I believe I am now worthy of receiving more money than ever to flow into my physical experience.

I understand that my thoughts control the flow of all desires into my life and I know that my emotions indicate whether the thoughts are leading me toward or away from my desires.

I know I have total control of the thoughts I attract by the way I decide to feel.

I know that action does not bring great abundance unless it is inspired action.

I have faith that the universe has the power to bring money into my life.

I know the first step in the Creation Process regarding the subject of money is to focus on bringing more money into my life.

I do not need to plan how the money will come, for I am aware that I cannot see the path to more money from my current perspective.

I know that when the time is right, I'll be inspired to take the action that will bring more money into my life.

I know that the universe will bring money into my life as a constant flow and that it is not necessary or even practical for me to hoard money.

I know that money is not a physical, tangible thing but a flow of energy.

I can feel for the feeling of abundance and I practice that feeling around things that are currently abundant in my life.

I write down lists of general ideas of abundance that are in my current life experience and write words and think thoughts of appreciation on a daily basis.

I meditate for a few minutes every day and I start my day off feeling good and at ease.

I release the tension around money by knowing that the universe will bring me as much as I allow it to.

I pay attention to the manifestation events that occur, understanding the lessons in each one, and I allow the events to mold my vibrational pattern through the shaping of my beliefs.

I am patient and allow the flow of money to come at its own pace.

I am not hurried because I understand that time is an illusion and I will be ready for the money as it comes.

As the money starts to flow, I notice it immediately and appreciate it. I am not worried that the flow will shut off; instead, I know the universe always provides more of whatever I put my attention to. I see the flow as just the beginning of something much larger.

I anticipate that the flow will grow larger and larger.

I modify and expand my beliefs every step of the way.

I expand as the money flows more and more, and I am grateful for the expansion the money creates in my life.

I never tire of the expansion of money into my life and as it comes, I am ready. I know I can limit the flow if I want, but even if at times I feel overwhelmed, I understand that this is simply tension caused by the gap of vibration and I will close the gap.

After reading these statements and analyzing your beliefs, you have now come to the place where you are able to allow the free flow of money into your life without resistance. You have been changed by the words you have just read and the analysis you have completed. Your vibration has been permanently altered and you have come to a new understanding of the power of abundance.

Money is energy. Abundance is the basis of the universe. You were born into an abundant world. Abundance is your birthright. You are worthy of all the money you desire. Now get ready because here it comes.

Chapter Eleven

The Art of Simplicity and Balance

The universe is a simple place. You live in a complex environment, not a complicated one. Simplicity is the key to joy in life. Balance is the key to harmony. As you create a simpler life, you introduce balance.

You live in the most intense time in human history. You are able to do and experience things today that were not dreamt of a century ago. Your world is moving fast. You do not have to keep up to speed. You have the power to slow it down to your speed. The art of simplicity is in maintaining a balance in your life so your vibrational pattern is in concert with the natural ease and flow of life.

You have had many experiences up to this point and the universe has shaped your vibrational pattern so that you have arrived where you now stand in life. Where you are now is the starting point, not the ending point. You are beginning a new chapter in your life and it is time to assess where you now stand. It's time to take inventory of your beliefs, feelings, and predominance of thoughts. It's now time to simplify.

As a result of your life experience, you have arrived at the state of being you are now experiencing in this exact moment in time. Where are you? What is your life like now? What do you see around you? Everyone is different. There are no grades or judgments. You are where you are. Everything in your life has brought you to this point. It has unfolded perfectly so that you are here now and ready for the next step. What is that next step going to be?

Your current state of being is unique in all of history and time. No one else, no form of consciousness, has ever beamed the vibrational pattern you are now sending out into the universe. What you are sending has never before been sent and the universe is responding to you in this moment. What will the universe bring you based on your current vibrational pattern? What do you want it to bring?

The future is in your hands. You know enough now to shape your own reality. What do you want that reality to look like? You may not have known that you had the power to create your reality before, but you know it now. What do you truly want?

You have been influenced greatly by the lives of your peers and the society in which you live. It is time now for you to go on your own and ignore the trappings of society and listen to your inner self. Thus far, you have lived an unbalanced life. You have been paying far too much attention to the physical world. The physical world outside was simply designed to be a mirror to your inside world. Instead, your inside world has been affected by what you've observed on the outside world. This is the reverse of what was intended prior to your birth.

You intended to feel your way to the reality that pleases you most. You were designed to create your reality from the inside. You were not meant to observe and then react. You were designed to create from the inside and then be pleased by what you created as it manifested into physical reality.

If you were an artist, you would imagine a painting and then create it with brushes and paint on canvas. You would not take someone else's painting and copy it. Yet that is what you've been doing for most of your life. You've listened to the aspirations of others and made them your own. You've desired what others have created and you've either created those desires for yourself and felt empty or noticed your lack of what you wanted and created more lack. Either way you created that which was not truly wanted.

You are now aware that you are on your own path to discovering and exploring your world in your own way. No one else can create in your universe, so you get to choose whatever it is you want. You do not choose what you truly want by looking to the outside world, you choose by listening to your inside world.

There is a great balance in physical reality that must be kept between the inside world and the outside world. There are two hemispheres in your brain. There are two sides to any subject. There is the wanted and the unwanted. There is a balance to everything in the universe. There must be balance in your life as well. The first level of balance in your life is the balance that must be maintained between the inner and outer worlds.

A Perception of Reality

There is much to be offered and received from listening to your inner world. You are receiving constant communication and guidance from within. However, when you are too focused on the sensory play of the outer world, you miss the communication from the inner world. This is communication you need and deserve. The messages being sent from your inner self are valuable and necessary for you to receive so that you are able to shape the reality that pleases you.

As a child, you were in touch with your inner self and you received the guidance and well-being your inner self delivered. You accepted the knowledge that came from within as absolute. You did not doubt the messages you heard. Since then, however, you've lost confidence in the communication you're constantly receiving. You dismiss it as random thoughts your mind is creating. But if you listen deeper, you'll hear a truth that will resonate within you.

The first step to receiving communication from your inner self is to realize that this communication exists. It has always existed. It comes from a deeper, larger part of you that sees your life from a higher and wider perspective. Your inner self is fully aware of every aspect of the real you, even when you are not. Your inner self can read and fully understand your vibrational pattern at every moment even if you cannot. Your inner self knows what the universe is going to bring to your reality based on your present vibrational pattern and it knows whether you're going to like it or not. You inner self can and does offer guidance to move you into a vibrational pattern that will receive the benefit of what you truly desire. But you have to listen.

You were not sent here alone. You were sent here with your inner self. Before your birth, you were given a system whereby your inner self could guide you through life experience so you could navigate reality and learn to create your world as you want it to be. It is perfect in its design and is perfectly simple. You simply lost full connection to your inner self.

The way to regain that connection as you stand in this moment in time is to simplify your life. If you were a monk living in a monastery high in a mountain, you would have an easier time connecting to your inner self. There would be less distraction from the outside world. There would be a balance between the outside world and the inner world.

However, you live here in the modern world, which is full of distraction. Most of it is fun and interesting, but it is distraction nonetheless. You deserve the communication that comes from your inner self and when you connect with that communication your life will be transformed. You must understand that distraction can prevent or at least hinder your ability to connect with your inner self.

Much of the distraction you encounter is created by you yourself. You might enjoy drama at some level and engage in the problems of others. You might enjoy watching or reading the news for this reason and rationalize your behavior by explaining it away with the excuse of wanting or even needing to be informed. The only information you need comes from your inner self. No news from outside sources is needed. You may enjoy watching TV or movies in which drama is depicted. This too is a distraction. We're not saying you must avoid all distraction. We are simply trying to change your perspective on the value of such distraction. We want you to consider that aspect of balance. We want you to consider the value of the inner communication you might be sacrificing.

Through your life experiences to this point, you have been conditioned to believe that some behaviors are acceptable and some are not. These behaviors are considered to be social norms and for you to fit into society you must follow these behaviors yourself. These are man's rules and they are fabricated due to man's fearful nature. You do not have to follow the norms of society. You are here to live your own experience as you see fit. You can decide that some outside distraction is not necessary. You can be one of the few humans alive today who can strike a balance between the inside world and the outside world.

So we ask you to consider the art of simplification. You must do whatever is right for you. We are not asking you to give up your possessions and move to a solitary cabin out in the country. This drastic change would not work to your benefit anyway. We simply ask that you consider ways in which your life has become more complicated than is necessary and for you to consider the means to simplify your life.

Simple pleasures lead you to a simpler life. Before there was IMAX and 3D, there was the sunset. There was the sky and the rain and nature. There are rainbows and mountains and streams. There are animals and life all around. There are close conversations rather than texts or email. There are casual meals with loved ones made together in the home. There is soft music and warm fires. There is reading that is uplifting and inspirational. There is time for solitude, meditation, and connection. There is a way of life that is softer, slower and easier. There is a benefit to be gained from the attention to a simpler way of life.

II.

There is simplicity in design within the universe, both in the physical and the nonphysical realities. You will notice, as your science will soon discover, that the human is as simple a design as an insect or an elephant. Simplicity is the basis of all design. To achieve greatness, one must accomplish simplicity first because it is the precursor to achievement.

How do you come to understand simplicity in the complex environment in which you reside? You must start by seeing that which is the basis of anything. You must strip away the confusion and see the elegance of the design. The map of anything is hidden within its design. You must ask yourself, "Why is anything the way it is?" and "What is the purpose?" Once you understand the purpose, you can understand the design.

Everything comes from the vibrational pattern of its source. The unfolding of life is a result of vibration. One vibration leads to the next. If you can see the vibration, you can see the design. Strip away the after effects and you'll discover simplicity.

Let's start at the beginning. Physical reality, like anything, started as a feeling. The feeling attracted thoughts. The thoughts manifested first into emotion and then into physical reality. Physical reality has a design and a purpose. The design is simple. Physical reality allows for expression, creation, and expansion of a different nature than nonphysical reality. In nonphysical reality, manifestation does not involve the lag of time, does not provide the same level of expansion, and involves different qualities of creativity.

Your physical environment is to be cherished. It is the ultimate playground. What is possible in this environment is truly extraordinary. It is thrilling, exhilarating, and should be filled with joy and fun. When you see it from our perspective, which we hope you will soon, you'll see it as the magnificent arena that it really is.

You can do anything in physical reality. That is the basis of the design. You are only limited by your imagination. The brilliance of this design is how your dreams unfold. In physical reality, you are able to use your feelings to attract thoughts. The thoughts manifest first into emotion that indicates your direction, and then into physical manifestation. As you witness the physical manifestation of your desires, you gain new feelings. This is expansion. These new feelings attract new thoughts that are accompanied by emotion and then new manifestations occur. The exhilaration you receive from the understanding of your power is how it feels to be aligned with your dreams and your inner self. This is the design of physical reality.

Your life has become rather complicated, but it need not be. It can be simple and still be exhilarating. If you are having trouble understanding or believing this concept, your belief systems must be altered. It is unlikely that these words will alter your beliefs on their own. It is more likely that you will have to experience a simpler life before your beliefs will change. You can achieve a certain change in perspective as these words resonate with you. But in order for you to understand that your life can be less complicated and still remain stimulating, you'll have to have a little faith in us.

We ask that you think about the simplification of your life over the next few weeks. We ask that you do certain things to uncomplicate your life. If you are inspired to take the action we suggest, you'll find the benefit immediately. When you see the benefit, the change to a simpler life will be easy.

We suggest the following changes in your behavior over the next several weeks:

Meditate every day for a few minutes. The duration of the meditation is not important but at first it should be no more than fifteen minutes.

Drink at least five glasses of water every day.

Eat meals that you prepare yourself. Think about the ingredients. Understand where they are coming from. Make the meals simple, with as few ingredients as you can. Reflect on the way your body feels after each meal. Adjust ingredients according to how you feel.

Enjoy nature every day.

Move your body in some form of exercise every day.

Avoid television and newspapers throughout the next few weeks. Notice that you will not miss anything of importance.

Connect with others in person, not via electronic devices if possible.

Discover your inner self through reflection and introspection.

Make it a priority to experience joy and fun.

As you apply these suggestions over the next few weeks, you will come to understand that a simpler life is a more enjoyable one. As you find balance between the inner and outer worlds, your power as a deliberate creator will expand exponentially. You will see the results of your power and your powers will grow. Your life will be transformed.

Let's examine each of the nine suggestions and see the simple, underlying reasons for each of them.

Meditate every day. There is no better way to initiate communication with your inner self than through the practice of meditation. Meditation is the first step toward creating a balance between your inner and outer worlds. Through the daily practice of meditation, you will gain confidence in your control over your thoughts. You may be completely unaware of that control, but in time, meditation will give you the control you so desire.

Your thoughts do not have to be random. You have control over them. Meditation is the key to gaining control over your thoughts. Meditation will allow you to slow down your thoughts so you can start to hear the communication coming from your inner self. Once you allow this communication, you gain access to an understanding of your guidance system. You may think you understand your guidance system as a result of reading these pages and from the teachings of others, but until you see it for yourself, it is merely theory. Meditation allows you to experience it.

Meditation takes practice. You have been unaware of your powers of thought control for a very long time. Now you must exercise a muscle that has become weak. It will take time for that muscle to gain strength. If meditation is done every day, it will lead you to having control over your thoughts. There is no right way to meditate and everyone may choose a different method. In the beginning it might help to use guided meditation. It is acceptable to use an electronic device to play a recording. This does not complicate meditation, it actually makes it simpler.

Drink at least five glasses of water every day. Your body is comprised of water, which is the basis of human construction. In order to achieve balance, you must drink more water. You will become aware of how much water you need to maintain balance. We do not suggest an amount in volume, simply an amount that is more than you are used to. Stretch your water intake and notice how you feel. It is the feeling we care about. We want you to feel good.

Eat meals that you prepare yourself. In a simpler time, man prepared most of his own meals. In modern times, many of your meals are prepared by others. In order for you to simplify your life, we suggest you prepare all of your own meals over the new few weeks. If you have a mate, prepare your meals with your mate. If you have children in the home, prepare meals with them. It is the act of preparation we want to be the focus of your attention.

Preparation includes the selection of ingredients at the market. Pay close attention to what you're selecting. Why do you select each item? What is the belief surrounding each item? Have you become aware of items you think are good for you and those you think are bad? Do you have allergies or intolerances to some items? Do you tend to prefer fresh, frozen or packaged items? Why?

The selection process, if scrutinized, will uncover many hidden beliefs. These beliefs may be so hidden that you consider them to be fact. They are not fact, simply beliefs. Since they are strongly held beliefs, they impact your version of reality. Are these beliefs helpful or hindering to your desires? What do you desire when it comes to food? Have you ever thought of this before?

As you prepare your meals, we ask that you think about the method of preparation. Do you cook your food or eat it raw? What appliances are you using and what is the method you prefer? Why do you prefer this method? Is there another way? Have you ever thought about this before?

As you prepare your meals with others, pay attention to the interactions. Are you doing it right? Are the others doing it the way you want them to? Are you controlling the situation or are you doing your best and allowing others to do their best? Are you too concerned about the result or are you not caring about the result? There is no wrong answer. We simply ask that you become aware of your interactions within the process.

As you eat your meals, we ask that you think about your thoughts. What thoughts are coming to you? Can you hear any communication from your inner self? Are you speaking to another at the table? What is the conversation? Is it pleasant or is there tension? Are you focused on the meal, your own thoughts, the conversation with others, or are there distractions? Can you make it simpler?

Enjoy nature every day. Nature has a calming and soothing effect on your consciousness. You find balance as you interact with nature. You hold no agenda and you are not resistant to nature. You find beauty and peace within it.

If you can interact with nature at least once a day, it will help you to see the benefits of simplification. If you like to garden, we believe that will be of great benefit. When you can immerse your senses in the soil, touching the ground and smelling the dirt, you can realize the simplicity of nature. You could walk along the beach and step into the ocean. You could hike a mountain trail. You could visit an orchard and pick fruit from the trees and eat the fruit. It matters not what you do, but only that you do something every day that involves interaction with nature.

Move your body in some form of exercise every day. Your body is the vehicle that carries your consciousness. It enjoys physical activity. It enjoys flexibility. It enjoys deep breathing, perspiration, and muscle contraction. It likes to work. Use your body in some form of exercise, as little as thirty minutes, every day.

If you are active in your work, we ask that you do not consider this activity to be exercise. Consciously choose some form of activity involving movement that is quite different from your work activity. If you stand all day and walk around your place of work, we think it might be appropriate for you to lie on the floor and stretch. Use muscles in the abdomen and upper body.

If you are primarily lifting or using your muscles at work, we ask that you also stretch and walk during your exercise. If you are sedentary, working from a chair, then stretching and walking will also be beneficial with the addition of muscle exercises. You can do all of these exercises from home which will be simpler since they do not involve transportation to another physical location or the interaction with others.

Avoid television and newspapers throughout the next few weeks. Since your vibration is affected by your observation and the influences of the outer world, we ask that you avoid all potentially negative influences. Most of what you call news is simply the drama of others. You view the news (as opposed to fictional television or movies), as reality and you are therefore influenced by it to a greater extent. When you see a tragedy that happens to another, you believe that it can happen to you and so you add it to your vibration. You are not understanding that everything happens as a direct result of one's personal, individual vibration. If you do not want to attract that which is unwanted, it is easier if you avoid the influences of the unwanted.

In general, you understand that fictional television shows and movies are not reality. If you can watch a show and know it's simply a fictionalization and not reality, it may have little effect on your vibration. However, your technology has made your entertainment so realistic that many shows are having some effect on your vibration. Therefore, we ask that you play close attention to what you are watching over the next few weeks. It would be even better to avoid television altogether if possible.

Even if the shows are uplifting or you can understand the uplifting potential within every vibrationally accurate TV show or movie, you must be aware of the commercials. The advertising that is presented to you in a barrage of words, music, and images often contains extremely negative messages. These messages also have the ability to impact your vibration. While their impact is small and you now have more control over your vibration than ever before, we ask that during these next few weeks you avoid all advertising.

We are not asking for a radical, permanent change in your activities. We are simply asking for a simplification of your life over the next few weeks. It is up to you to determine the extent and duration of this simplification process. We want you to experience the effects of simplification and to see for yourself if the benefits are worth the change in behavior. We believe you have been conditioned to live your life as you currently do. However, had you not been affected by the influences of others and your society, we believe you would prefer to live in a simpler manner.

Connect with others in person. You came here to explore the world at this time with others. You have a physical and spiritual connection with others on your planet. We ask that over the next few weeks you attempt more of a face-to-face connection with others in your life.

Your present technology allows you quick and short communication with others. But much meaning is lost in this type of electronic communication. While it is effective in communicating surface meanings or instructions, it does not convey depth of meaning. Personal interaction involves a much greater connection. Be with friends, family, co-workers, and even strangers over the next few weeks and see what a difference that makes in your life. Simplify the communication by connecting in person.

Discover yourself through reflection and introspection. Over the next few weeks we ask you to create a balance in your life through reflection and attention to your inner world and your inner self. Sit quietly every day and observe the thoughts that you are thinking. Ask yourself questions and listen for the answers. What are the answers? Do they make sense? Who is providing the answers? Is it you or is it your inner self?

Start to question your beliefs. Anytime you feel negative emotion, question the basis of that emotion. Your negative emotion lets you know you're thinking about something in a way that is not aligned with your desires. Why is that? How are you seeing the present condition in a way that is not true to what you really want? Simplify your life and you will begin to understand your true path in this life.

Make it a priority to experience joy and fun. You are here to have a good time. A happy life is built on many moments of joy and fun. You have the ability to make everything fun. As you make things fun, others around you will naturally join in and have fun themselves. Fun is contagious. There is a momentum to it. Keep it going and ask to have fun at every occasion. Make fun the basis of your life.

You can experience joy in every moment you choose regardless of the present condition. Start seeing the positive in everything. Over the next few weeks, as you wake up in the morning, ask to experience joy as the day unfolds. Pay attention to the times when you feel joy and keep track. Write it down or take note of your experiences of joy in some other manner. As you notice joy, you'll experience more joy.

As you simplify your life over the next few weeks, you'll gain momentum. Take this time now to simplify. It matters not your plans, your work, or others in your life; you can simplify your present life experience. Notice how you feel in the simplification process. Notice how you feel better. Notice how your life becomes richer and more effective. Notice the benefits and you'll change your perspective. Ignore the opinions of others during this time and notice the feeling that comes from the art of simplification.

III.

Balance is the key to creating the reality you desire. In order to deliberately create reality, you must be aware of the inner world that lies within your very being. The inner world is where your dreams are born and where you concoct your recipe for a happy life. Your inner self will communicate with you and guide you along your journey to the unfolding of your desires and the life experiences you are here to explore.

Without an understanding of your inner world, you live only half of a life experience. You live out of balance. Your life is haphazard in the way it unfolds. Events seem to be random occurrences. You are completely absorbed by the facade of reality you observe in the outer world. You are at the mercy of the influences of the outer world and of your reactions to what you observe.

You were not designed to react to what you observe in the outer world; you were designed to be a proactive creator. Your creation is your own reality and the outer world was designed to yield to you. It was designed to reflect your creation. Your creativity impacts the outer world and you were designed to understand and appreciate your creation. You are the creator of your reality; it is not the creator of you.

Now that you are aware of the inner world that lies within your mind, we will give it a name. We choose at this time to call the entity that lies within you, "the inner self." We call it this because it *is* you. It is a larger aspect of you that remains nonphysical, but it *is* you, nonetheless. It is your core personality. It is the you that you will come to know when you die. You can also come to know the inner you right now while you're focused in physical reality.

You may be more comfortable or familiar with a term like "soul." From our perspective, this term implies separation. We want you to know that you are never separated from your inner self. Even if you are not aware of your inner self, your inner self is fully and completely aware of you in every moment. Your inner self *is* you, but from a broader perspective. This much broader perspective has access to all physical reality in every moment and fully understands the workings of universal forces. Your inner self knows why you're here and what your intentions were prior to your birth.

A Perception of Reality

Your inner self offers no judgment, only love. There is no wrong anywhere in the universe and you, here in physical reality, can do no wrong. You are here as an explorer in this specific space-time reality. Your inner self has lived many lives on earth but has never before lived the life you are living.

Your expansion causes the expansion of your inner self and your inner self is exhilarated by the expansion you are both achieving. You are here for the direct and complete benefit of your inner self, which is pleased with your every move. Your inner self would greatly appreciate more opportunity to assist you in your expansion. You only have to be aware that your inner self exists and simply ask for more guidance.

As you create a balance in your life between your inner and outer worlds, your inner self will present you with communication. When you come to understand that this communication is from a higher intelligence, from a broader perspective, you will learn to trust it. When you believe the communication is valid and has your best interests in mind, you will gain the power that comes with this communication of broader intelligence.

You cannot hear communication from within until you're ready. You must be in vibrational proximity to receive information from your inner self (or from any source, for that matter). If you are not a vibrational match to your inner self, you will not hear the communication that is being offered and will not even be aware of the existence of your inner self. Through the reading of these pages, you are being led by your inner self to a new awareness. You have been guided by your inner self to this material so that you can become a vibrational match to the communication being offered. You want balance in your life. Your inner self knows this and is guiding you to that balance whether you are consciously aware of it or not.

Your inner self finds it extremely exciting to see your progress and is filled with anticipation for the day you are ready to receive communication. You have been searching for a new understanding of reality and the mechanism of creation. In order to fulfill your wanting, your inner self has guided you, step by step, to all of the books and teachers you have come across in your life. Each book and each teacher led you to a new level of understanding and a new desire for greater understanding. Your vibrational pattern was altered every step along the way, which led you to this new point in time. You are on the verge of being ready to truly connect with your inner self.

The next step is for you to shift your beliefs about reality so you can come to realize that your inner self exists on a nonphysical level but is also focused here, in physical reality, with you. If you can believe this concept and understand its purpose, you are one step closer to the connection you so desire. The words on these pages may have altered your belief system enough so that you are open to the idea of a deeper connection with your inner self. But until you have firsthand experience with this connection, it will remain a theory.

Therefore, you must consciously desire to create a connection with your inner self. You must want alignment with your inner self and intend to achieve it. It is from your wanting that everything, including the conscious connection to your inner self, is given. The act of wanting is the first step to the physical manifestation of your desires. If you want conscious connection and communication with your inner self, it will come if you believe in it and allow it.

How will you create your conscious connection with your inner self? What action can you take? What do you need to know for this experience to become a reality in your life? What is it that your inner self wants you to know?

First, your inner self wants you to know you are truly and completely loved unconditionally. Your inner self has a deepness of love for you that you have only glimpsed in physical reality. When you feel love for another, what you are feeling is a small part of the love your inner self has for you. You can do no wrong, there is no judgment, everything you do is considered perfect, and you are truly loved.

Second, your inner self is here to guide you only if and when you ask for guidance. You do not need guidance from your inner self. You are completely capable of navigating and creating the world however you choose. Your inner self is happy either way. There is nothing important going on in this life and most humans will never fully understand the existence of their inner selves. However, once you've made a connection with your inner self, your life experiences become fuller and richer and you'll gain the power you were born with. The difference between a life experience with conscious connection to your inner self and one without that connection is like the difference between a foggy day and a clear day.

Third, your inner self has only positive guidance for you. Your inner self will answer only the questions you are ready to hear. Your inner self will only guide you toward that which you want and never away from the unwanted. If you choose the unwanted, your inner self will not attempt to stop you and will never tell you that you are wrong in any way. You can choose any direction in life and, since there is no wrong, your inner self will always support your decisions. We will talk more about this subject later. For now, we want you to understand the balance between the inner and outer worlds and about the importance of a conscious connection to your inner self.

If you have reached the vibrational readiness to hear your inner self, you must simply become quiet, calm yourself, ask a question, and then simply and patiently listen for the answer. The answer will come quickly if you are vibrationally prepared. The communication will often sound like your own inner thoughts. These thoughts have always been a form of communication and nothing has changed now other than your awareness of their origin. If you listen to the answers and accept them as valid, you will come to a clear connection with your inner self. When you realize that the communication and intelligence, is real, valid, and tangible, your belief system will be altered in such a way that you will have created a conscious connection with your inner self.

There is no trick to this. The connection is always there and always has been. You were just oblivious to it. Now that you have become aware and you are in the same vibrational vicinity, your communication lines are open. It's as simple as that. And the more communication you allow to flow, the greater the connection will become. Just like everything else in the universe, the Law of Attraction compounds that which is given attention to and appreciated.

IV.

God is something different. We see what you call "God" as the All That Is. We see that which you call God not as a personality, but as the overall being of the universe. It is not singular, yet it is not plural either. It is all and it is one. *It is All That Is.* You are a part of that, as we all are.

Your idea of God can lead you to a misunderstanding of the role of your inner world and your inner self. Most of your feelings about God are positive, such as love and appreciation. However, depending on your specific religious background, you might have been given the impression that there could be a negative side to God. There is not.

Judgment is a trapping of certain religions and is not a valid aspect of All That Is or of any conception of God. There is no judgment that is of a Godly nature. Judgment does not exist in the nonphysical realm. While you may want to review your life experience after you have transcended into the nonphysical, neither you nor another will ever judge any part of your physical existence. You will not judge the actions or lives or decisions of others. There is no God or force of any kind that will judge your physical life once you transcend into the nonphysical. There is only joy and love and all that is positive.

Therefore, in order to gain a balance and understanding of your inner world and your inner self, you might want to modify your beliefs about God, heaven, the afterlife, judgment, sin, etc. You are welcome to believe whatever you want, just remember that some beliefs are helpful while others may hinder your expansion. Ask yourself what you truly want and give yourself permission to alter, modify, or even suspend beliefs for a little while.

The concept you might find most surprising is that we who reside in the nonphysical realm are completely focused on your physical reality here on earth. We are not up in heaven simply existing. We are interested, passionate, and consumed by your existence. We enjoy all the aspects of physical reality that you find most pleasing. We live through you, through the animals, and through all of nature. We support your environment and your world. We are focused here with you and find what you're doing to be thrilling and fascinating. The lives you are living in this time have never been lived before.

We love all that is new and there is so much that's new to physical reality. This is the greatest time man has ever experienced. And while there is great contrast and disparity in human existence, there has never been a more interesting time to be alive. There has also never been a more interesting time to be nonphysical.

A Perception of Reality

This is the time of awakening, which is really the time of connection with your inner self. You are awakening to the reality that there is more to life than the outer world you are translating with your senses. As you awaken to the reality of your inner world, your outer world will blossom into a new level of experience. The depth of expansion that is to be gained through the balance between your inner and outer worlds is never-ending.

As you delve deeper into an understanding of your inner self and your inner world, you gain a perspective on reality that is empowering. You are now living fully as you intended prior to your birth. You are becoming aware of your powers within reality and you can now use your powers to effectively and deliberately create the life and experiences you most desire.

When you feel positive emotion of any kind, you are feeling your connection with your inner self. When you feel joy, it is because your inner self is also feeling joy. The physical you who resides here on earth in this space-time reality has a connection with the larger, older, wiser part of you that resides in the nonphysical realm. Your inner self is aware of you, your vibrational offering and your desires, and it knows how to get you to everything you want in life. When you feel positive emotion of any kind, you are feeling the positive connection with your inner self.

When you look on another with love, your inner self is also looking on that person with love. You and your inner self agree. The feeling of love is the feeling that you and your inner self are in alignment. You are feeling what your inner self is feeling at this moment in time.

Your inner self sees physical reality from a larger, broader, wiser perspective. This perspective allows for only the positive to be shown. There is no negative in the nonphysical. There are no negative emotions in the nonphysical because there is no wrong anywhere in the universe. The idea of negativity is an aspect of human existence that deals with your specific ability to prefer one thing over another. Your ability to see what you do not want and call it negative is a product of your exploration and expansion. Seeing the negative or unwanted side of a subject is a human creation. Your inner self does not give any attention to the unwanted.

When you see something wanted and feel positive emotion of any kind, that emotion is your agreement or alignment with the way your inner self sees the positive aspects of that specific subject. However, when you see the negative side of anything and feel negative emotion, you are feeling the disagreement or nonalignment with your inner self. Your inner self can only see the positive, while you have the choice to see the positive or negative aspect of anything.

Negativity is a human trait. Since we can only see the positive side of everything, we can only see the positive aspects of negativity as well and we simply say that negativity is your choice. Choice is the basis of human existence and we are exhilarated by your ability to choose what is wanted over what is unwanted. Your inner self will always guide you toward what you want and never away from what it knows you do not want. Why is that?

If you were to create a guidance system from your human perspective, this system would be designed to guide you toward what you want and guide you away from what you do not want. However, your human-created guidance system would be flawed. Often, to get where you want to go, you must journey through what is unwanted. The unwanted events in your life have helped you gain clarity about what you truly want. Without occasional experiences with unwanted conditions, your vision of your true desires could never be fully realized.

From your perspective, you would like to avoid the negative aspects of life and wish to be guided directly to what you think you want. However, this is not how expansion works. You cannot live a meaningful, expansive life by simply lying in bed, watching movies, and being waited on by servants. Although at times this vision seems appealing, you would become bored very quickly because you would not experience expansion as you intended.

As you explore your world intending to gain knowledge and expansion around certain topics of interest, you expand as you make choices. Your choices, and expansion, come from interacting with the unwanted so that you know what is wanted. If you were in poor health as a child, you may have gained a new appreciation, and thus a powerful desire, for health. This experience of poor health as a child was something unwanted. This experience forced you to want the opposite of poor health, which is excellent health. When you desired excellent health and aligned with that desire, your inner self led you to higher and greater levels of excellent health. Now, due to your experiences as a child, you live in excellent health.

Had your inner self led you away from poor health as a child, knowing poor health was unwanted, you would not have created the desire for excellent health. You had to experience the unwanted to really understand what was wanted. This was what you intended prior to your birth and your inner self is fully aware of your intentions because your inner self *is* you. Your inner self knows why you are here and what you're here to explore. Your inner self knows your true path and your true desires. Your inner self is guiding you to the fullest and most elegant life experience. Your inner self is your true partner in this life.

Your inner self will allow you to fail, knowing there is no such thing as failure in life. Failure is a human misunderstanding of the nature of reality. There is only success. As an infant learns to walk, there is no failure when it stumbles and plops back down. The infant tries again until one day it walks. There is no failure in this life experience; there is only exploration and expansion. You are exploring life experience every day you are alive. No one has ever explored the life you live in the way you experience it.

You are a magnificent explorer and through your exploration of this life, you provide for your personal expansion, the expansion of your inner self, and for the expansion of the entire universe as well. We understand that it is your nature, as you observe the world around you, to minimize the magnitude of your individual contribution. You tend to see yourself as a tiny piece of an unimaginably large universe and therefore as somewhat insignificant. This could not be further from the truth. The reality we see and know is that of your integral and instrumental role as a leading-edge explorer. Without the benefit of your experience in this life, the universe would be completely different. Your individual contribution allows the universe to unfold and expand perfectly as it is unfolding and expanding. Without you and your unique life experience, this version of the universe would simply not exist.

Your individual contribution to All That Is is necessary. We are all in this together and we could not do it without you. You are a being of incredible value and importance. Your inner self is fully aware of and absolutely appreciates your worthiness. It is time for you to appreciate yourself as well.

When you create a balance between your outer world and inner world, you'll come into alignment more often with your inner self. This alignment will cause harmony in your life. Harmony will add momentum to your ability to create deliberately. Deliberate creation will confirm your powers and you will gain a greater appreciation of your worthiness.

If you could understand your value and worthiness now, rather than later, you could change your life now, rather than later. Your understanding of your own worthiness will coincide with your inner self's knowing of your worthiness and you'll feel good. Feeling good precedes the manifestation of your desires. Being in alignment keeps you on your intended path. The simplicity of alignment is all you need to live your fullest, richest life while here in the physical realm. When you die, you'll regain full and complete alignment with your inner self. You can accomplish this alignment while you're here focused in physical reality.

Right now, in this moment, you can connect with and align with your inner self. Take a moment to clear your thoughts. Take a deep breath and we'll help you find your connection with your inner self. Close your eyes, breathe deeply, and allow the thought of something or someone you love to enter your mind. You might think of your mate, your child, or even a pet. As you think the thought of the one you love, pay attention to how you feel. Do you feel good? Do you feel love? If so, this is the mutual feeling you are sharing with your inner self. This is the same feeling your inner self is feeling in this moment. You are connected with your inner self.

Remember that your inner self is always connected to you no matter what. It is you we are guiding to your personal connection with your inner self. Your inner self is now and has always been aware of you fully in every moment. You are now becoming aware of your inner self. You can now be aware of the presence of your inner self in every moment.

As you close your eyes again and you reach for the connection with your inner self, pay close attention to your thoughts. When you think of the object of your love and feel that love, what do you see? Close your eyes and notice the images that come into your mind. Your inner self is providing these images for you. Your inner self is communicating with you through mental images. Your mind is the screen and your inner self is the projector. As you feel for thoughts of the one you love, your inner self brings you those thoughts and those mental images. It is two-way communication.

So what are the images your inner self has displayed for you regarding the feeling of love you have conjured? You will start with images in your mind of the one you love and your inner self will provide you with mental pictures that most reflect that love. The images may be from the past during a special event. You may get other mental pictures that convey love of a different nature with another person. These pictures of love expand. Were you given a mental picture of yourself? If so, this is your inner self telling you that you are loved also. Your inner self is trying to tell you something. Are you listening?

V.

Your inner self feels only positive emotions, such as exhilaration, interest, love, passion, joy, bliss, excitement, fun, understanding, peace, happiness, pride, success, empathy, hope, etc. When you feel any positive emotion, you are aligning with your inner self. That is part of your guidance system. Anytime you feel positive emotion of any variety, you are feeling the connection between the physical you and the nonphysical you.

That connection is what you're striving for and feeling good allows you to connect more often. When you place your attention on something, your inner self is paying attention to it as well. If you feel positive emotion regarding the object of your attention, your inner self has that same feeling. You and your inner being agree on this subject. Thus, you are moving on your intended path toward your desire. In this moment, you are in full alignment.

Your inner self can only feel positive emotion about anything, yet you have the choice to decide whether you like something or whether you dislike something. Since your inner self always likes everything, you might believe there is no real purpose to this guidance system. What is the value of a life experience where you are asked to like everything by your inner self? You are here to choose what pleases you most, and since everything cannot be pleasing, what good is it to know that your inner self likes everything?

Your guidance system works to show you when you and your inner self agree and when you disagree. When you see something you like and feel positive emotion, you and your inner self are feeling the same thing and agree on that subject. When you see something you dislike and feel negative emotion, you and your inner self disagree.

But your inner self approves of everything and can find no wrong in anything. Your inner self loves everything and everybody. Because of your ability to sort what is preferable and what is not liked, you can choose hate, pity, envy, apathy, boredom, etc. Your inner self does not choose or even attempt to feel these emotions. So when you say you hate something or somebody, you feel negative emotion and to the degree of intensity that this negative emotion is felt by you is the degree to which you and your inner self disagree on the subject at hand.

Does this mean that you, with your ability to choose, must always choose to love everything and never dislike anything so that you can maintain your connection with your inner self? The answer is yes and no. Let's talk about how this system was designed and how it works in the real world.

In your physical reality, you are an explorer. In order for you to expand, for your inner self to expand, and for the universe to expand, you intended to experience what you liked and what you disliked. What you liked was the easy part. What you disliked was where your guidance system comes in. Since reality is bound by the Law of Attraction, you get what you pay attention to. That works well when your attention is focused on what you like. You like something and the Law of Attraction brings you more of it.

However, when you focus your attention on what you don't like, two things happen simultaneously. One, you learn more clearly what you do like, and two, you attract more of what you don't like. On one hand, the experience of what you don't like causes expansion because it makes you know more clearly what you do like. On the other hand, because you are focused on what you don't like, you attract more of it into your physical reality.

Through the guidance system of your emotions, your inner self was designed to keep your attention focused on the positive aspects of what you do not like. Does this make sense to you? You are here to understand and utilize the laws of the universe in a very powerful way. Physical reality is a simple design and was created for you to master the manipulation of universal forces for your own pleasure. You can avoid the attraction of what you do not want by focusing on the positive aspects of anything you do not like.

Let's give you a real-world example. Let's say you have two bottles of wine in front of you. One bottle costs $10 and the other costs $100. You taste the less expensive one and it is pleasant. You taste the more expensive one and it is much more complex and delicious. You can tell the differences between the two easily. You understand that one bottle is more pleasurable than the other. You choose one over the other.

Then you think about the price of each bottle and your choice becomes more complex. You now think the $10 bottle is a bargain for the price compared to the $100 bottle. You begin to feel that the more expensive bottle is not nearly ten times more pleasing. In fact, it's not worth the money at all.

In this example, you looked at both the negative and positive aspects of each of the wines. You were making a judgment and this is the process that humans have been using to weigh the balance of the positives and negatives of any decision. This process, however, is counterproductive.

Imagine now that you only looked at the positive aspects of each wine and ignored the negative aspects. You see only the value in the $10 wine and only the incredible taste and complexity of the $100 bottle of wine. Because you now understand the Law of Attraction, your focus of attention on the positive aspects will ultimately bring you value *and* taste. The Law of Attraction, due to your focus on the positive aspects of each wine, must deliver to you a new wine that has both value and taste in your opinion. You will receive the perfect wine for you.

Had you maintained your focus on both the positive and negative aspects of each wine, the universe would simply bring you a mix of what you do and do not like. You would not move forward. Your expansion would be somewhat stalled. You would continue life as you are living it. Nothing new would happen in this one aspect of your life.

Now you can more fully understand your guidance system and how it is operated by your inner self to keep your focus only on the positive aspects of everything. When you see the birth of a child and feel joy, your inner self agrees because you are seeing the positive aspects of this event. You see how the child will bring happiness to the parents and the family. You are focused on the wonderful life experience the child will enjoy. You see the potential for expansion and all the good that comes from it. You are focused on everything positive and feel joy as a result because your inner self agrees with you.

You could look at that same birth and focus on its negative aspects. You could see the child being born to parents who, in your opinion, are not ready for the child. You see the parents as not having enough money to raise the child properly. Maybe one of the parents is not participating in the life of the child and you feel pity for the single parent. When you are focused on the negative aspects of the event, you feel negative emotion. This is your indication that your inner self does not agree with you. It is not because you are wrong and should not have these feelings. It's because your inner self does not want what you are projecting on the event to be attracted into **your** life.

If you feel pity for another, it does not stick to them, it comes back to you. If you feel anger toward another, the Law of Attraction brings anger to you. If you feel love for another, the Law of Attraction brings more love to you. You live in an attractive universe. You get what you put out. If you focus on the negative aspects of anything, you attract those negative aspects to yourself.

You get to decide what is negative and what is positive and your inner self agrees with **your** definition. Your inner self does not have an opinion about the goodness or badness of anything. Your inner self simply focuses on what you deem positive.

You might hate the taste of watermelon when almost everyone else on the planet loves it. If you simply avoid watermelon while allowing others to enjoy it, watermelon will not be an issue in your life. However, if you rail against watermelon, if you belittle others who eat it, then it will become a bigger issue in your life. You will be given positive feedback from your inner self when you allow others to enjoy watermelon and you'll receive negative emotion when you fight against watermelon.

Therefore, you are truly free to explore and make your own choices. Since you have already developed your ideas of the positive and the negative, we do not need to discuss this concept any further. Just understand that your inner self is always focused on the positive aspects of everything and that because of the attractive properties of your attention, it wants you to be focused on the positive aspects as well.

The more you focus on what you want in every situation, the more you will get what you want. The less attention you give to anything you might consider negative, the fewer unwanted things you will attract into your life. Your inner self fully understands what you want and what you do not want and helps you, through your guidance system, to focus on what you want. It's a simple and elegant system.

Chapter Twelve

Self-Awareness and Intuition

Your physical reality was designed to individualize that which is you. It makes the self all-important. In the nonphysical, we are much less concerned for self. We move together in and out of groups. We flow as consciousness and are a part of whatever interests us. We move more as one, or more as a group, than we do individually. While we can understand the concept of individuality, and we can achieve it, as we can achieve anything if so desired, we do not focus on it.

Your individuality is a unique and important property of physical reality. Why do you think that is? We will tell you.

You are an explorer and you are here to expand. And, while others are here with you, you are focused on your individual, unique expansion and experience. While you, as a result of your life experience, help the expansion of the universe, you're here primarily to expand yourself. The universe, in this physical form of reality, literally revolves around you. You are the most important aspect of your reality.

Everyone else is the most important aspect of their own reality as well. Others are ultimately focused on their own reality. They see the world from their unique perspective and you see the world from yours. You are here to create you and they are here to create themselves.

In this chapter, we want you to gain a new, higher, broader perspective of you. You may see yourself as one of billions, but really you are one of one and one of infinity at the same time. You are unique in all of the universe, yet you are also one with all of the universe. This is balance played out in physical reality. You can never be apart from All That Is, yet you live an individual experience in physical reality. That's an interesting concept, isn't it?

The reason we find physical reality so fun is because you get to do whatever you want and when it's all over you return to the nonphysical realm. You can also return to physical reality anytime you like. You can't go wrong with this.

So, if physical reality is an individual experience and you cannot experience the lives of anyone else, why not make it all about you? Oh, you would consider that selfish, wouldn't you? You wouldn't want to be selfish in an individual experience. That would be against the laws of man. It's not considered proper in your society to be selfish. Unfortunately, this, is a limiting belief in a physical experience that was designed to revolve around the self.

First, it is right to be selfish. Not only is it right, but that is how the system is designed. Each cell in your body is completely selfish, yet it works with all the other cells to keep your body functioning properly. You can be selfish and work with others. If you take a broader view of your world, you will realize that everyone is acting in their own best interests. There are people who like to be doctors and people who like to be custodians and people who like to fish and people who like to play golf. Everyone likes to do something and they're all working together to make everyone else's likes available. Every point of consciousness is primarily focused on self.

The focus on self and the attention to what you want does not make you a selfish person. You are meant to determine what you want and to attract it to you. The physical world was not designed for you to notice what others do not have or for you to give it to them. You focus on yourself and allow others to focus on themselves and everything will work out perfectly.

First, we will talk about you and later we will discuss others.

There are many aspects of self-awareness. Let's see if we can list some of them here:

1. You are a vibrational being living in a physical world.
2. You are not your body. Your body is simply the vehicle of your mind and your mind controls and shapes your body.
3. You are not in a physical world; you simply see the reflection of your inner world projected into a physical reality you can translate with your senses.

4. You are much more than you sense in physical reality for there is a larger part of you that remains nonphysically focused and is fully aware of you.
5. Your inner self is you as well.

Shall we explore each of these aspects of self?

One: you are a vibrational being living in a physical world. You are vibrational in every sense of the word. You radiate vibration physically through your body. Every cell in your body is also vibrational and radiating. You are a vibrational pattern and everything responds to that pattern. Everything in the world you see around you is also vibrating and also has a unique vibrational signal. You interpret or translate vibration through your senses into sight, sound, taste, touch, and smell.

What you see as a tree is a unique vibration you are able to translate into a physical object. You can translate its visual properties by using your sense of sight. You can translate the solidity of its trunk by your sense of touch. You can even smell its blossoms, hear its leaves rustle in the wind, or even taste it if you so desire. But the tree is no more physical than you are. It is an illusion and so is everything in your physical world.

We say this not to diminish your physical experience but only to redirect your attention and slightly alter your perspective.

Every vibrational pattern has an attractive quality and would not exist in your reality if you were not a match to it in some manner. If you look out the window and see a tree, you are a vibrational match to that tree. Others who look out that window also see a tree and they are a vibrational match to the tree they see, but it is not the same tree you see. Each vibrational pattern is unique to the observer. Since you are here to explore your individual reality, we will not delve any deeper into the reality of others at this time. Just know that everything is unique to you, no matter how closely you agree with another.

Your level of agreement on the properties of what you uniquely perceive is amazing to us. We know that what you see is different from what another sees, yet you seem to agree on so many things. It is due to your highly evolved communication skills that have gone far above the verbal and on to communication on the psychic level.

Be that as it may, you are here to explore reality on your own terms and agreement is not as necessary as you may think. Much of your agreement is detrimental to your exploration. You are far too concerned with the opinions of others and you to agree too easily. Go your own way and discover for yourself what you prefer. Just understand that everything you see is unique to you and that you attracted it in some way.

Two: you are not your body. Your body is simply the vehicle of your mind and your mind controls and shapes your body. This is interesting because you may have always assumed that you *are* your body. While the experience of your body can be extremely pleasurable and intense at times, your body is no more a part of you than your car. Do you ever notice how you can feel through your car in much the same way you can feel through your body? It's because the concepts are similar.

You are the driver of your body. You move it around and command part of it, but you don't command that much of it. Most of your attention is focused away from your body while it is functioning quite well on its own. You do not command that your heart beats or your lungs breathe. They work automatically without need of your instruction. In fact, you may be able to consciously control them in a limited manner, but as soon as your attention is focused elsewhere, they automatically resume their normal functions.

You are the captain of the ship that is your body, but you could not run the ship on your own. You direct the ship and if you are aligned with its crew, the ship goes wherever you command. You must, like any good captain, see to the maintenance and proper care of your ship. You can also make modifications to your ship if you so wish.

Your body, like everything else in physical reality, is a reflection of your feelings and thoughts. If you feel fat, you are either fat or really skinny. If you feel healthy and normal, you are. If you feel beautiful, you are and if you feel ugly, you are. You can feel beautiful one day and ugly the next, and to the extent of the feedback from others, you are exactly as you feel. Start feeling better about the self and your body will transform automatically for the better.

Three: you are not in a physical world; you simply see the reflection of your inner world projected onto a physical reality you can translate with your senses. Your life is a mirror to your thoughts, feelings, beliefs, and emotions. Your inner world is experienced through the development of your outer world. Your outer world changes as your inner world changes. One is linked inseparably to the other as long as you are physically focused.

Your vibrational pattern moves with your feelings in the moment. Your outer world is a reflection in the moment as well. If you are in a high emotional state of being in the moment, you will encounter aspects of your physical world that reflect this high vibrational pattern. If you are happy, you'll meet with others who are happy. In fact, even if the others were not happy before you came into their reality, they became happy once you showed up. You attracted the happy side of them and something in them attracted you.

You cannot attract anything to which you are not a vibrational match. If you are in a happy state of being, you will attract the happy side of things. As long as your vibration is pure with the feeling of happiness flowing from you, you will encounter all that happiness represents to you personally. If the feeling is muddled with other feelings mixed in, you'll get some of whatever else is in your vibration. We shall talk more about the clarity of feelings later on. For now, you can understand that your vibration is often a mix of good feelings and not-so-good feelings and you get back a little of all of it. Clean up your feelings and you'll get more of what pleases you.

The world and physical reality were designed to be a mirror to what you're feeling. If you like what you see, you're feeling good most of the time. If you don't like what you see in the world around you, if you do not enjoy your life in its present state, you simply have to change your feelings, beliefs, and perspective. It's really very simple and it's not that difficult. Improve your mood, improve your attention to the positive, improve your beliefs about yourself and the rest of humanity, and your world will reflect improvement back to you. That's the way it was designed and that's simply how it works.

Four: you are much more than you sense in physical reality, for there is a larger part of you that remains nonphysically focused and is fully aware of you. You have a partner in this space-time reality we call your "inner self." Your inner self, as you now understand, is the larger, wiser, older, nonphysically focused part of your overall being. You see the world around you. You see your body. You can even sense the you that is inside you when you close your eyes. But most of you are not really aware of how deep your connection is with your inner self. You have complete control within this physical reality but your inner self is guiding you and working with you every step of the way.

Your inner self has the ability to lead you toward your desires and does so as long as you are willing. To be willing you must simply be in a high emotional state and listen to the inspiration you are receiving. In order to connect with your inner self, you must raise your vibration to match that of your inner self. You must feel good, be happy, and enjoy the moment. If not, your connection is tentative.

If you are in a lower vibrational state of being such as regret, despondency, boredom, lack, depression, sadness, etc., you will have difficulty connecting to your inner self. The thoughts you attract will not be communication from within. They will simply be thoughts you're attracting based on your lower state of emotion. Raise your vibration and you will once again connect with your inner self. Feel better and the connection will grow stronger.

Your inner self is always leading you to a higher vibration. When you feel positive emotion, your vibration rises. When you feel negative emotion, your vibration is temporarily lower. Seek to feel better in every moment and your inner self will help you.

Your inner self has the ability to communicate with you through your thoughts in the same manner as you would talk to any of your physical friends. You just have to realize that you have the ability and the connection that enables this communication. Your inner self will answer your questions. Simply listen for the answer when you are ready and believe in the validity of the answer coming from within. However, your communication can only come while in a positive emotional state of being.

If you are depressed or in a dire state of being, your inner being will be unable to communicate with you because your emotional state will cut you off from that communication. The thoughts you receive will match your current lower vibration. They will reinforce your current feelings. Because your inner self maintains a very high vibration at all times, you simply do not have access at this lower level. This is one of the reasons it is so important for you to reach for better feelings in each moment.

Your inner self can work with you in many ways other than simple mental communication. Your inner self can speak through you, write through you, and even drive your car for you. You can blend into one with your inner self and the harmony will create an even higher vibration. When athletes get into the "zone," they are actually summoning full cooperation with their

A Perception of Reality

inner self. They become fully blended and that blending creates a higher vibration and greatly improved performance.

If you find yourself deep in conversation with someone and the words are flowing, you're in the zone. You are fully blended with your inner self in that moment. If you find yourself writing things you didn't even know you knew and the words are flowing, this is blending with your inner self. If you find yourself driving and daydreaming and you look up and wonder how you got where you ended up, it was your inner self at the wheel. You are more in concert with your inner self than you know. If you allow the connection, if you ask for deeper connection and if you let it flow, you will improve your performance in all areas of your life.

Five: your inner self is you as well. You cannot be separated from your inner self. You are one. You are the same. There is no distinction other than your perspective. You are simply focused here while another side of you is focused both here and in the nonphysical realm. It does not matter what you call it - your inner self is you.

Since your inner self is you, your inner self knows you better than you do. Your inner self knows the real you. You may be trying to be someone you're not, but your inner self will always be guiding you to who you really are. That is why it is fruitless to pretend you are someone you are not. Be yourself and your inner self will join you and you will have the power of the universe behind you. Be someone you're not and you'll go it alone. Your inner self will never join you.

You'll know when you're being someone you are not by your emotions. If you feel negative emotion, you're acting in a way that is not true to yourself. You will have difficulty being someone you are not because the larger part of you will always stay true to who you really are. You can pretend and you may even fool other people, but you can never fool your inner self.

II.

Self-awareness is knowing who you really are. You have come here with certain intentions and you will know when you become aligned with those intentions. You have interests and desires that bubble up from within. These desires may not match the wants and needs of those in your life who may be influencing you away from those desires, but since you are the creator of your reality and are here to explore certain aspects of physical reality, you must do what you desire. Disregard the opinions of others, for they are oblivious to your intentions; they cannot see your true path.

If you do not understand who you are, who the real you is, simply follow your true interests. Your true interests are mostly natural. They were with you as a child. They are the interests you truly find fascinating. Follow those interests and you'll find your passions in life and uncover your hidden identity.

True interests revolve around the nature of physical reality and universal laws. The general intentions you made prior to your birth were for love, freedom, joy, confidence, success, happiness, passion, desire, expansion and many, many others like these. Your true interests lie within your general and your specific intentions. There are many specific intentions and because they are specific to each individual, it serves no purpose to list them here. However, in order to gain a little more clarity on the subject, we will talk about two specific intentions that many humans are here to explore; teaching and abundance.

Many of you are here as teachers and while most of you will not explore life as a teacher in a school, you will explore aspects of teaching in your daily experience. If your specific intention was to explore the concept of teaching, you come to this reality in order to better understand all aspects of the subject. You will be both a teacher and a student. You will want to work in areas where you can teach. You will want to explore ways in which the art of teaching is more effective and come to understand why teaching is often so ineffective. If you are a teacher, you will have interests that are obviously of this nature. If you're reading this material, you are in the family of teachers.

Many who come to this earth environment intend to explore the facets of abundance. One may choose to explore abundance through poverty or through wealth. Abundance is an essential concept in the universe. We live in an abundant universe, yet this subject is often misunderstood in physical reality. Some of you are here to explore this subject as well as other subjects. As you come to understand each subject more clearly, you will expand.

A Perception of Reality

You came to this physical environment with many general intentions and one or more specific intentions. Your true path lies along these areas of interest. You'll know when you're on your intended path when you're involved in something that captures your interest and is accompanied by positive emotion. That is your guidance system lighting your path.

You may have an interest that is not a true interest but that simply alleviates feelings of fear, doubt, and insecurity. If you feel unworthy and engage in gossip, for instance, you might notice a moment of relief from your negative feelings, but in general you are living in a lower emotional state of being. The lives of others only seem interesting from a lower emotional state. Your intended path cannot be followed from a lower vibrational or emotional state. If what you're doing is accompanied by joy, you've found a passion. If what you're doing is accompanied by feelings of revenge, pity, ambivalence, drama, sorrow, etc., you've not yet found that which truly interests you.

The real you can be found only from a higher emotional state. You won't find the real you by digging around in the basement and analyzing your problems. The real you will emerge once you start feeling good. Everything you want is delivered at a higher vibration. Raise your chronic state of being and you'll find the real you inside your shell.

There are no boundaries to what you can be. Any limits you feel are self-induced. If you do not feel the freedom to express yourself in the way that pleases you most, it is only because you do not allow it. You have the key to your freedom and happiness and you can keep the door locked or open it anytime you like. No one else has the power to create in your reality. Therefore, it can only be you who is allowing or disallowing the real you to emerge.

You have experienced the influences of those around you your entire life. You have felt that they have some control over you. You have learned a behavior and a way of life that seems acceptable to them, but they do not matter. You are here only to live a life and behave in a way that is acceptable to you. Remove the shackles of influence from others and begin anew. You control your ability to create the life you want.

The first step is to accept yourself for who you are. You have always known what you want and who you are at some deep level. You are now finally ready to come forth as the unique, individual personality you truly are.

Be yourself fully and you will experience a life of passion, fulfillment, and happiness. You must become aware of the real you that was born into this environment to thrive. Once you discover the real you and start living your life from that perspective, you will find your true path, you will find your true interests and passions, and you will gain the full benefit of expansion, as you had intended prior to your birth.

III.

Your inner self communicates with you constantly. If you can tune into that communication, you will gain the benefit of a higher, broader perspective. Your conscious mind is in sync with your inner self. What your conscious mind thinks, your inner self knows at the time you are thinking it. If your inner self agrees with your thoughts, you'll feel positive emotion. If your inner self disagrees with your thoughts in the moment, you will feel negative emotion. Pay attention to your thoughts and emotions and you'll discover the knowledge and wisdom of your inner self.

Your conscious mind attracts thoughts and receives thoughts. Your mind also sends thoughts. Your mind is a receiver and a transmitter. Your feelings attract your thoughts. As you feel loved, you attract thoughts of love. When you feel sorrow, you attract thoughts of sorrow. As your feelings change, your thoughts change. Your inner self also sends you thoughts as a form of communication.

You inner self will always send you positive thoughts. If you are in a higher emotional state of being, you can comprehend these thoughts. The thoughts align with your higher vibrational pattern and you are more likely to be aware of the thoughts being sent to you from your inner self. You can ask questions and your inner self will respond with the answers. If you are in a happy emotional state, you have the ability to easily understand the answers. You can now move forward.

If you are in a lower emotional state, such as anger, you will attract thoughts that match that anger. You might receive two thoughts at the same time. One thought is of punching a wall. This thought seems reasonable in your state of anger. Another thought is of forgiveness. This thought does not seem as reasonable as the first thought. How does this work?

A Perception of Reality

The Law of Attraction will always bring you a match to what you are feeling. The first manifestation of that match is your immediate thoughts. At this point in time you have the ability to contemplate them without taking action. You can choose, in the next few moments, to punch the wall or not. If you punch the wall (or if someone comes along and they punch you), this is a physical manifestation of your feelings of anger. It is a direct result of the Law of Attraction.

The Law of Attraction is like gravity; it does not know if something is good or bad, it is just a law of the universe. Like gravity, it always works regardless of the situation. It attracts negativity when negativity is felt and it attracts positivity when positivity is felt.

However, at the same time you are receiving thoughts that match your feeling of anger, your inner self is sending you thoughts that might help ease your feelings. If you can be soothed, you can gain perspective on the situation and release the anger, or at least soften it. Your inner self wants to stop any negative momentum you may be creating through your feelings. If you can stop the momentum, the feelings will not manifest physically. If you can see the thought of forgiveness that was delivered by your inner self, you can stop the momentum and it will not manifest into physical reality. You will not punch the wall. Instead, you might realize what has happened and you might even consciously change your emotional state of being.

You will also attract thoughts that are a match to your feelings when you are in a high emotional state. In this case, your inner self sends you thoughts that increase your momentum so that your thoughts manifest into physical reality. In a high emotional state, your inner self sends you thoughts that increase your level of vibration.

You are much more likely to be able to accept and understand those thoughts being sent from your inner self when you are in a high emotional state. When you are in a low emotional state, the positive or soothing thoughts coming from your inner self do not feel as satisfying as the thoughts that match your feelings. When you are in a rage, thoughts of forgiveness seem off. Thoughts of violence seem more appropriate.

However, now that you are aware of the communication that comes from your inner self in times of lower emotional states of being, you can stop yourself and listen to the communication. You can stop the negative emotion and realize that it is simply unnecessary to dwell on negative thoughts even though they feel right in the moment. You can adjust and turn in the direction of better-feeling thoughts at any time. This is the communication your inner self is sending.

Your inner self will always direct you to a better emotional state of being. If you find yourself living in sorrow and depression, your inner self will be completely focused on helping you to feel better. Your inner self cannot guide you to your passion in life because before you are ready for that guidance, your inner self must guide you to a higher emotional state. Only when you are on stable footing can your inner self start guiding you toward your true path.

Guidance starts by helping you gain and then maintain a higher emotional state of being. Before you can receive the real power of communication, you must achieve a consistently high emotional state of being. You must be happy more often to move forward.

This is the opposite of how you think life works. You think that once you find your passion, you'll be happy. Typically, this is not the case. You don't stumble across the subject of your fascination when you are feeling angry or depressed. You are led to your passion through a series of manifestation events that raise your vibration to such an extent that when you finally come across your passion, you are ready for it and see it for what it is.

You can see that your inner self has its work cut out with you. First, your inner self must somehow help you raise your chronic state of being to one of happiness, or at least contentment. Then your inner self must lead you step by step through the use of many manifestation events to a higher vibration. Once you have reached that higher vibration, your path will unfold and your inner self will help guide you along that path.

In order to be happy, you must be happy. You gain happiness by realizing that you should not be influenced by the world you see and then feel good or bad as a result of that manifested world. Feel good and the world will reflect your good feelings. The only reason you are unhappy now is because the world you see displeases you in some way. You are reacting to a world you created.

If you were a painter and painted a great work of art, you could look at it in two ways. You could view it as the incredible work it is and appreciate it. You know you can paint another painting tomorrow, but it will never be this painting. You look forward to your next paintings, as they are the way you express yourself as a creator. You appreciate this painting and anticipate even better paintings to follow as you grow and expand as a skilled painter. You do not compare your paintings to others', for you realize that you are unique in all the world. While others may have opinions of your art, you paint simply because it pleases you and you disregard their opinions.

On the other hand, you could look at your painting and see only the flaws. You look at it and see that the colors are not perfect and the brushstrokes are uneven. You could compare your painting to others' and feel inferior in your talent. You could listen to the opinion of others and feel a further lack of talent as a result. You might listen to their advice and paint in a way that does not match your style and takes you away from who you really are. You may then assume you have no talent as a painter and give up painting completely. It is the same magnificent painting, but your perspective makes the difference.

Your life, the one you've created with the predominance of your thoughts and beliefs to this moment in time, is your painting. Whether you believe it or not, it is a masterpiece. It is completely original and there has never been one like it in all of history. Regardless of what you or others think about the quality of your life, there are countless of us in the nonphysical world who consider your life to be a truly great masterpiece. It is time you start seeing your life the way we see it.

You create a new work of art every day of your life. Every day is a new painting. You have complete control of the tools of your artistry. You have the powers of the universe and the guidance of your inner self at your disposal. You can create your life in a way that pleases you without comparing yourself to or heeding the influence of others. You create simply that which pleases you and your creation will be a masterpiece. Look forward to creating a new masterpiece every day.

Become happy and in time your world will reflect that new, higher emotional state. As you raise your emotional state, you raise your vibration. As your vibration increases, your level of readiness and awareness increases. You become more in tune with the guidance of your inner self. As you follow that guidance, your true path will unfold perfectly. Reacting to what you have created in a negative way will cause you to feel only negative emotion because your inner self will not agree with you. Reacting to your world in a positive way will cause positive emotion and enable you to create an even better world tomorrow.

Remember that you are the creator of your world. You can see your creation, or any individual aspect of it, as either positive or negative. If you notice the negative aspects, you make them more prolific in your life. When you place your attention on the positive aspects, you make the entire creation more positive. If you are going to react to your creation, do so only in a positive way or do not react at all. In essence, you are the proactive creator of your life.

IV.

There are many indications that you are on your true path. One of these indications comes in the form of your conscious awareness of your powers of intuition. Intuition is strong guidance from your inner self. You must be emotionally ready for this type of guidance. You must be vibrating at a higher emotional state of being to receive intuition on a consistent basis. You must also trust that the information received as intuition is coming from a higher realm. It comes from the nonphysical realm through your inner self.

Intuition happens in the moment, so you must be aware of the moment. You cannot be thinking of the past or the future. You must be present. You cannot be in a state of fear or doubt, but rather a state of confidence and ease. When you receive the intuition, you must act on it in the moment and not second guess yourself. Intuition is sent in the moment it is needed and not before. It requires a response. It is inspiration to act.

Intuition cannot be properly received while in a low emotional state of being and anything you deem as intuition at these times is probably not coming from your inner self. It is difficult to be inspired to act in a positive manner from a lower state of being. You must pay careful attention to how you're feeling in the moment for intuition to be recognized as inspiration to act. If you're feeling good, it's intuition. If you're not feeling good, it's likely a manifestation of your feelings in the form of fear or doubt.

There will be times when you simply know something is true. You do not know how you know it; you just feel it. This is intuition. It is the feeling of knowing something despite a lack of evidence or even in spite of evidence to the contrary. It is what you call a gut feeling and, when you are aligned with your inner self and stand in a good-feeling place, you can rely on this feeling.

You have five senses that help you navigate your physical world. But there is another sense that comes from within. You were born with the ability to use all your senses and, as you grew, your senses improved. However, since you reside in a physical world, your five physical senses evolved to translate information to your brain in a stunningly vivid and powerful way. Many of you lost touch with your nonphysical sense of intuition. You must recognize that this sense is real and valid and you must exercise it.

When you pay attention to your feelings of knowing, in the moment, when you're feeling good, you exercise your sense of intuition. When you witness an event and experience it with your five physical senses, think about the feeling that comes from that event. Many times your physical senses will show you one thing and your intuition will tell you another. Start adding your feeling sense into each situation and see if you can find more clarity in the situation.

You can sense vibration as we do. It is not something you can see, hear, touch, taste, or smell, but vibration can be felt through intuition. As you now know, everything is vibration. All events have their own overall vibration. Your physical senses might tell you one thing, but your feelings, your intuition, might tell you something different. The truth of anything is its vibration. You are simply translating vibration into physical realty using your physical senses. They do not always tell you the whole truth.

In a very simple example, you can look at a glass and see it filled with water. If you were to touch it with your finger, your sense of touch would confirm that it is indeed a glass of water. If you hit the glass with a spoon and heard the tone the glass made, your ears would also agree that it was a glass of water. If you stopped there, you would leave with the belief that it was a glass of water.

However, if you tasted or smelled the liquid, you would know it was something else. It could be any number of clear liquids and your sense of smell and taste would override your three other physical senses. Your intuition works in the same way. Your physical senses can be used in observance of a physical event that may seem to indicate one truth. But your intuition, or nonphysical sense, can perceive the vibration of the object or event. Your intuition can override your physical senses. In many situations, your intuitional sense is the only sense that can see the vibration of the entire event and thus see the truth.

Because your intuition is the broader sense, since it can perceive the vibrational nature of the event, it can become the most useful and powerful sense. But you have to add it to your array of senses. This is not easily accomplished because you have tuned your physical senses so brilliantly to your physical environment that they have become automatic. You open your eyes in the morning and you can see. You take in the world with your eyes first. Sight is your strongest and most obvious sense.

When you lie in bed and open your eyes, you see your room. You may not hear anything unless you consciously listen for sounds or a bird sings outside your window. You may not smell anything unless you consciously seek to smell the aromas of your room or your coffee maker has started brewing coffee. You may not feel anything unless you consciously feel the sheets of your bed or your mate or pet moves next to you. And you certainly may not taste anything unless you consciously seek a taste or your mate wakes you up with a fresh cup of coffee. In that case all your senses are awakened.

But the sense of intuition lies in the inner world. It is not an obvious sense and may even go unnoticed consciously for much of your physical life. However, it is the sense that stays with you when you transition to the nonphysical and is it therefore your most trustworthy and valuable sense. Start being aware of it now and it can help you as much as your other senses. Practice it now and it will grow in strength and confidence. Trust it and you can navigate your world with more ease than ever before.

V.

In conversation, you cannot listen when you are doing all of the talking. The same is true of intuition. If you're doing all of the thinking, if your mind is flooded with the chatter of random thoughts, you cannot hear the messages coming forth from your inner self. You cannot utilize intuition for your benefit.

A Perception of Reality

The first step in developing your sense of intuition, like the first step in developing any skill, is being aware that it exists and recognizing its benefit to your life. When you know that your inner self is guiding you to your desires through inner communication, you become more ready and able to receive the communication.

The second step is being aware of the messages and differentiating them from other thoughts. When you can identify a thought as a message from your inner self as opposed to a random thought that is simply taking up space in your mind, you will gain clarity. Because at first all thoughts sound the same in your mind, you'll have to feel for the difference. You'll have to distinguish one thought from another. You'll have to notice the differences in quality of thought to know that they are coming from your inner self.

The third step toward strengthening your ability to receive intuition is being able to trust that the message is true for you. In order to gain trust in your abilities of intuition, you must gain a larger perspective. You must see your life from the eyes of your inner self. You must understand the overall development of your life here on Earth. Once you gain that perspective, you will have the trust you need to fully utilize your powers of intuition in the most beneficial manner possible.

Imagine you are your inner self are fully aware of every aspect of your life from an all-encompassing, broad viewpoint. You know every moment of your life, even though the physical you in your body can only remember small instances of your past and can only imagine the future. Pretend, if you can, that your inner self knows every instant of your past. Your inner self knows exactly what happened every step of the way to bring you to this moment. Your inner self knows your current vibration and knows exactly what you want moving forward. In that sense, your inner self knows your future as well, or at least the future that you desire at this moment in time.

So, now that you are pretending to be your inner self looking down at the physical you from your perspective above, what would you tell yourself? That will certainly depend on where you stand in life at this moment. If the physical you was happy and had found passion in life, then the inner you would send messages that would help the physical you move along, maintaining a happy life full of passion. You would not advise the physical you, you would maintain positive affirmations while the physical you was doing well.

Occasionally, you would help to bring clarity to a decision the physical you was facing. You would help the physical you in the moment of making a decision. From your broader view, you can recognize the vibration of the event and each involved person's vibration as well. You can help the physical you interpret the vibrational reality of every situation. You can send a sense of knowing even though the physical you is unable to understand the entire story of the event. Through the sending of the message, you can help the physical you make the right decision as you know it to be from your broader perspective.

What does this mean for the physical you? It means the intuition must be trusted even if in the moment it seems like a mistake.

If you are maintaining a high emotional state of being and receive intuition that you can recognize and you act on that intuition in the moment, you can trust that the decision or action will work out for your higher benefit. Even if it turns out that the decision you made based on the intuition you received at the time seems wrong, it is not wrong from a higher perspective. It was meant to benefit you in a stronger, broader way. It was meant to lead you ultimately to a better place than you would have traveled to had you not acted on the intuition.

Generally speaking, intuition is mostly in alignment with your desires in the moment and you recognize that the intuition was correct. You deem it to be a positive outcome based on your perspective in the moment. Most of this is true because you are moving along nicely with your life and the intuition is there to keep you on track, so you build confidence in your intuitive abilities. However, once in a while you'll have intuition that seems wrong from your perspective. It is not that the message or the subsequent decision is wrong, just that it seemed wrong in the moment from your point of view. However, once you are able to trace your path from a broader perspective of time, you will come to see that the intuition led to a decision that brought you to where you now stand.

You might wallow in regret for what might have been. But had you not made that decision, you would not be here now. You might not have been led to this material so quickly and easily. From here, your life will improve faster and you will expand to a greater degree than if you had made a different decision.

This is why regret does not work. You can only see the path you've traveled. When you look at what might have been, you do so wearing rose-colored glasses. Ironically, you tend to see only the positive in that which you did not experience and you tend to focus on the negative in that which you did experience. If you do the opposite, you will have no regrets. If you look back and imagine all the terrible things that might have happened on the path you **did not** travel and instead looked at all the wonderful things that **did** happen on the path you **did** travel, regret would not exist in your reality. It is all a matter of how you choose to see your life. It is all a matter of perspective.

Now that you understand that all intuition is given in a manner that is fully aligned with your highest benefit, you can begin to trust the messages you are receiving. You can be confident that the decisions you make as you receive clear intuition are the right decisions for you. However, you must be in a positive emotional state and be aware of the messages. This takes some practice, but it is a natural ability within you and in all other humans.

VI.

You have more intuitive ability than you know. You may see others in your society with incredible intuitive abilities. Most of your society does not believe that these abilities are real even in the face of uncompromising demonstration. Without a basic belief in one's own intuitive abilities, the powers of intuition become unavailable. Most of those in your Western society have cut themselves off from a powerful sense they were born with. This demonstrates the powerful and potentially limiting aspects of beliefs.

As long as you believe you have powerful intuitive abilities, you have access to this sixth sense. When you practice your abilities, your powers will grow. The ultimate power of intuition is the ability to merge or blend with your inner self. The extent to which you are able to accomplish this is the extent to which you can access the infinite intelligence of the universe and gain the perspective of a much broader point of view. Imagine the benefit of having these abilities in your life.

Your inner self desires to become one with you in this physical reality. You already merge with your inner self at various times in your life. When you are asleep, you are fully merged with the nonphysical and with your inner self. When you are exhilarated, when you're passionately involved in something, and when you're having the time of your life, you are merged with your inner self. You have the ability to merge more often if you choose.

You have total control over your life and can choose to merge more often with your inner self. You can also decide to go it alone if you wish. It's always your choice. Your inner self has no desire to control your life. Your inner self knows what you want and is only there to help you achieve your dreams. If you choose to merge with your inner self, you'll unlock the key to finding joy in every moment.

So how do you merge with your inner self? By acting as your inner self would act if it was living your physical life. Your inner self, when blended with you, would only focus on the positive aspects of every single piece of daily life. Your inner self would be elated upon waking and feeling the world through all six senses. Your inner self would feel the joy of being alive in every single moment. The taste of food, the ability to move around the planet so easily, and interacting with other physical beings would be so exciting. Each day and every moment would be filled with depth and beauty.

As a physical being, your inner self would only look at the positive aspects of everything in physical life, knowing that the Law of Attraction will bring more of those positive aspects. Your inner self would not allow itself to notice anything negative because it does not recognize the negative side of anything. While your inner self could develop preferences in a physical world, as you can, the preferences would be in favor of one set of positive aspects over another set of positive aspects.

You might call this way of being living as a "Pollyanna." However, because you are now aware of the nature and the power of the Law of Attraction, you realize that you get what you focus on so you focus on what you want. You do not get what you want by giving your attention to things you do not like. You get what you give your attention to. To get more of what you want, you must notice and observe only what you want. Your inner self knows this fully. Your inner self does not attempt to perceive the negative side of anything. Your inner self has such a highly developed understanding of the Law of Attraction and all other universal properties that it is unnatural to look upon the negative aspect of any situation.

If you want to develop your powers of intuition and merge more often with your inner self, you must start looking at the positives and ignoring what might be perceived as negative. Start making a game of it. Start analyzing everything, not in terms of pluses and minuses but in terms of pluses alone. Forget the minuses and ignore the negatives. Start being silly and just concentrate on good things.

Be crazy and go against the grain of your society. When someone mentions something negative, turn it around. Be ridiculous. Make them stare at you in a strange way. Hope that they see how truly odd you are. Laugh in the face of negativity and don't take anything too seriously.

From our nonphysical view, we think it's funny how you are in sorrow at funerals, but you celebrate at weddings. From our perspective, we see the funeral, or the death experience, in terms of freedom and joy, and we see the marriage as bondage and suffering. Not really - we only see the positive side of everything and we can make jokes, too.

From the larger perspective from which we view your world, your history, and the well-being that we know is available to all, we see no downsides to life. We understand how your expansion and the expansion of the universe is allowed through your ability to experience what is not wanted so that you can expand into what is wanted. We just don't understand why you spend so much time in consideration and contemplation of the unwanted. We would simply move on to what is wanted and forget about the rest.

VII.

You were meant to live this life with the understanding that there is a nonphysical presence in all that is physical. Nonphysical energies move through you and all around you. In this time of awakening, you are now becoming aware of much that has been hidden from humanity throughout time. It was not that it was intentionally hidden; it was that humans decided to ignore what they could not perceive. Once you're aware of your inner world and the fact of the nonphysical presence in your outer world, you're going to see and feel things you have never experienced before.

Your inner self flows the force of life to you and through you at every moment of your life. Your inner self is the reason you are focused here in physical reality. The inner you is responsible for all the energy and vitality you feel at this present moment and for much more as well. If you allow the full flow of energy from your inner self, you will feel tremendous energy and well-being.

You can allow the energy to flow freely to you or you can limit the energy that is being given to you. It's your choice. You allow energy to flow through your thoughts, feelings, emotions and beliefs. We want you to start believing that life force is flowing to you in an inexhaustible supply. You need only to allow it to flow. The force of life is generous and you can have all you want.

In your mind, picture your inner self sending a beam of light and sound that flows into your body from above. This is the energy of life force and your inner self has been sending it to you from the moment you stepped into physical reality. It is always flowing in the same never-ending supply. You control the flow with your feelings. When you feel good, you allow more to flow. When you feel bad, you restrict the flow. Your general mood has a lot to do with the flow. When you're having fun, life force is flowing. When you're sad or angry, life force is flowing a little less.

This is just some of what is given to you from your inner self. Your inner self flows life force to you, communicates with you through intuition, and guides you to whatever it is that you desire. Your awareness of your inner self is the ultimate in self-awareness. We want you to understand the depth of connection you have and have always had with your inner self and we want you to cultivate that connection. Once you can achieve more and more moments of blending, you will gain powers to create in this reality that you have never before dreamt of.

Chapter Thirteen

The Perception of Vibration Through Your Beliefs

Everything in your physical world is vibrating. You translate that vibration with your physical senses and with your nonphysical senses. The chair you are sitting on, as we have said before, is vibrating and you translate that vibration into that of a chair. We also said the vibration is unique to you and that what you see is different from what others see. This is because you are a vibration as well and your vibration affects the vibration of everything else.

We are asking you to perceive reality from a new place. You have established certain rules in the physical world in which you live. These are man-made rules and they help you navigate the world around you. You are aware that these rules are broken from time to time and when the fabric of your reality is torn away, you see the nonphysical behind the physical. In these times, you either don't recognize what has happened or you explain it away in some fashion.

For your benefit in this life, we want you to know that there is much more to the world that you cannot see unless you are aware of it. We won't go into too much detail here, just enough to let you know the reality behind your reality. You are awakening to a new understanding of reality and your broader understanding will be beneficial to your physical experience.

You are here to pursue joyous expansion and this is your playground. Everything here is meant to be fun. There is nothing inherently serious happening. Your perspective, which is limited, makes you look at certain aspects of your life and you make them serious on your own. However, from the larger view of our perspective, it is all good.

The Perception of Vibration Through Your Beliefs

By understanding the construction of this playground, you become aware that certain rules you have established are unnecessary. When you realize why you're here and what you're here to do, you will come to understand that there is no need for fear, doubt, or worry. You can do, be, and have whatever you want in this experience. You are the creator and this world was designed to allow you to have full creative capabilities. You were given all the tools you need and the connection to your inner self for any guidance you might desire.

The first rule you have created is the rule of beliefs. You have a set of beliefs that assist you in navigating your environment. As you know, many of these beliefs are limiting. You need only to glimpse your history to see many of the limiting beliefs that hindered the improvement and quality of life over the ages. You do not need beliefs in the way you think you do. You can dismantle all of your beliefs, and if you do, you will come to live a much freer existence.

Let's start with the belief in the solidity of your world. You see a tree and think it's solid. You see a building and cannot pass through it without a door. You see a boulder and it will not move without great force. These are your beliefs and they are limiting. You see no reason why these are limiting beliefs and that is a limiting belief in itself. We want you to see the reality behind your reality.

We are taking you to a new perspective of understanding of the physical world by challenging your beliefs. We want you to see the world in a new way. We want you to see the energy within everything. We want you to know that everything is vibrating and that everything is nothing at the same time. The thing you gaze upon is no thing at all, simply a vibration you interpret with your physical senses based on your unique perspective. There is nothing without your unique perspective. It is all energy and it forms once you are ready to perceive it. It does not exist unless you reach vibrational alignment with whatever it is you perceive.

If you were not a vibrational match to your chair, you would be sitting on the floor, or maybe on another chair. If you were not a vibrational match to your home, or your city, or your world, you would be living elsewhere. If you were not a vibrational match to your mate, to your children, to your friends, or to your pets, they would not exist. You created all of it and if you were not a vibrational match to any of it, it would not exist in your reality.

A Perception of Reality

So let's look at that which you *are* a vibrational match. Look at your life. Why are you a vibrational match to the dwelling you currently occupy? What are the beliefs that led you here? Why are you not a vibrational match to a mansion on the beach or an apartment in the city? It is due to your set of beliefs and nothing more.

Why do you drive the car that's parked in your driveway? How does it compare with your previous cars? What beliefs do you have now that are different from the beliefs you had when you drove your previous car? You are different therefore your car is different. If you have owned your car for a long time, why have you not purchased a new car? What are your beliefs telling you?

You can ask these questions about every single object or relationship that exists in your physical reality. You are a vibrational match to everything you have in your life and you are not yet a match to anything that is not already in your life. That which does not exist in your physical reality does not exist until you come within some vibrational frequency that allows it to manifest. Until then, it does not exist for you.

It is important to note that there are things, people, and places all over the world that you can imagine and to that extent they exist in your imagination and thus they have the potential to manifest into your reality. For instance, you know that Paris exists even if you have never been there. You can imagine the buildings and the famous landmarks you have read about or seen on television, in movies, or in photos. But for you, Paris only exists in this fashion. When you dream about a trip to Paris, you are working on the creation of the city in your physical experience. Eventually, depending on your beliefs, you will either manifest a trip to Paris or not. But until then, the reality of Paris for you is just in your imagination.

Once you travel to Paris and experience it physically, Paris has now manifested in your reality. However, it is always *your* Paris and the Paris you experience is unique to you. You might talk about Paris with another person and discuss your agreements and even your disagreements about your individual experience, but it is never the same Paris you are discussing. What you discuss is just a minute fragment of your complete experience. You do not have the ability to describe what you experienced to another. Even if you did, it would funnel through the filter of *their* reality, not yours.

The Perception of Vibration Through Your Beliefs

Everything you experience is unique to you and does not exist for anyone else, even if you agree that it does. This is the illusion of reality. You have a conversation with someone and completely agree on every topic of conversation. You and the other person are a vibrational match to begin with, so you may find it easy to agree on many things. But everything is different for every person. You only think you're seeing the same thing.

If you can understand that everything is different for every person, then you can free yourself from the need to be right. You are always right and they are always right. There is no wrong anywhere in the universe because everyone is seeing what they perceive as right, or at least what exists to them. Since each individual is unique in all of existence and has a unique vibration, then every subject is unique to that individual. What you perceive is unique to you and what another perceives is unique to them. If you and the other person agree, that's fine. If you disagree, that's fine too, because ultimately you can never really understand what they perceive.

The message we are trying to send is that you need not strive for another's agreement because it is very unlikely that anyone can agree with you to the extent of your knowing. You know what you know, but others know what they know. What exists for you does not exist for anyone else in the same way. You and everything you perceive is unique to you. Everyone perceives everything differently than you do. When you agree, you have no real idea of what you are agreeing with. If you could perceive life through the vibration of another, you would be quite shocked to see how different their experience is from yours.

You assume you have a certain view of the world and that everyone else has a similar view. Actually, everyone has a different view and each individual perceives the world in a unique way. What is right for you may not be right for another who is very different from you. You have opinions based on your current set of beliefs. When you change your perception, your beliefs will change and then your opinions will change. The more you can change your perception of reality, the more you can alter your beliefs. Once you have lessened the strength of your beliefs, you are able to give up your opinions altogether.

What is the value of your opinions when they come from a set of beliefs that are unique to you and valid to no one else? If every individual lives a unique life and perceives reality in a unique way, what is the point of agreement? Is it simply to validate your existence? You are the center of your universe. You do not need validation. You are unique in all the world and all of history. You are worthy beyond belief and you do not need anyone to agree with your opinions. Nor do you need to force your opinions on others. They are here to expand on their own and have an inner guidance system just like you do. Follow your path and allow others to follow theirs.

II.

You are here to joyously expand as you intended prior to your birth. You are here to follow your own unique path. You may co-create with others if you wish, but it is not necessary. You have the ability to create your life on your own terms. Do not allow others to influence you to travel too far from your path and realize that you do not need to influence others. If others come to you seeking help, you are able to see them for who they really are even if they do not. You are able to see the most positive aspects and have confidence in them even if they do not yet feel the same confidence.

If you can allow yourself freedom from the unnecessary need to agree with others and allow them to disagree with you, you will gain tremendous freedom and will benefit from this new way of life. Allow others to go their own way and you will find that you gain much more harmony with others. You only demand agreement out of fear and doubt. You believe that negative outcomes follow disagreement. This is an illusion based on fear and doubt. If you are going with the flow of life, you do not need to control your present circumstances or conditions through agreement. The universe will always deliver to you that which you desire in the most elegant way, as long as you allow it to.

If you try to control the conditions through agreement, you hinder the power of the Law of Attraction. You are not allowing your desires to manifest because you think you know better and that you can control the situation. If you allow everything to flow as it is meant to and do not block the flow, you will allow the universe to deliver everything you want in the most exhilarating manner possible. It is only when you force events to change their natural course that you block creation.

The Perception of Vibration Through Your Beliefs

You have the ability to allow the universe to deliver to you every desire you hold. You also have the ability to completely block the universe from delivering that which you most desire. When you exercise your beliefs of how things should be rather than allowing them to flow as they are flowing, you block your own desires from manifesting into your reality. You are not allowing the universe to alter your vibration so that you become a match to your desires.

When you allow the universe to alter your vibration, you will receive everything you desire. You do not need to control anything, even when you think you're right. You are only right from your point of view, and you cannot see what another perceives. They will do whatever is right for them. You may believe what they are doing is wrong, or you may fear it will hurt you in some way, but this is only an illusion. If you allow fear to interrupt the natural course of events, you block the universe from delivering your desires to you. The universe will continue to attempt to modify your vibration, but if you keep trying to control the situation, you'll keep blocking the universe and your desires will be kept apart from you until you start to go with the flow of life.

You must concede power to the universe. You must trust that the universe, your inner self, and All That Is are working together to bring you whatever you want. Your beliefs may be holding you apart from what you want. Your current beliefs have allowed all you have now to exist in your reality and these same set of beliefs have kept all that you want from entering your reality. If it does not exist in your reality, it is because you do not yet believe that it can.

Your beliefs form your world in such a tight and controlled manner that they literally change your perception of reality. They shape the world around you. You can only see what you believe. You can only understand what is in alignment with your beliefs. This is a natural and necessary aspect of being human, for without beliefs, you might not believe in gravity, and therefore you might fall off a cliff. But you do not have to believe in anything limiting. You can decide what to believe.

Much of your beliefs were formed during childhood. You adopted many limiting beliefs from your parents, teachers, and peers. You lost connection with your inner self and the influence of others and society led you to a set of beliefs that is limiting in many ways.

A Perception of Reality

Now, in this moment, you have absolute control over your beliefs. You have the ability to alter your beliefs and thus alter your perception of reality. If you can lower the intensity of your limiting beliefs, you can allow for new, beneficial beliefs to take hold and grow.

III.

Your beliefs determine what information gets through. While you are reading this book, you are translating it so that it harmonizes with your unique set of beliefs. There are certain sets or packets of information contained in this material that come through from us to you in exactly the manner and meaning we intend. You are in alignment with those specific packets of information. You fully understand certain chapters of this book. Your beliefs allow you to receive our message exactly as we intend.

However, there are portions of this material that you will not understand or even notice. Because your beliefs are so rigid in certain areas, you will miss this information entirely. You will not understand it as you are reading it and will not remember it after. Your beliefs shape your vibration and you are not a match to certain subjects or ideas contained in this book.

You have to be a vibrational match to what is manifested into your reality. At least, you must be in the vibrational vicinity of it. Because your beliefs help to create and shape your vibrational pattern, they control much of what comes to you. If you believe in something, you cannot receive any information contrary to that belief.

When you alter your beliefs, you alter the type and quality of information that can come to you. When you alter the attractive nature of your mind, new information can flow in more easily. When you stand rigid in your beliefs, you do not allow new information to enter. Your life cannot change unless and until you allow your beliefs to change.

The main reason people do not change is because of their inability to alter their beliefs. If you keep the same set of beliefs, you will keep attracting the same things over and over. As the world changes around you, your world stays the same. If your belief system is empowering, your world is a nice place to live. If your beliefs are limiting, your experience of the world is limited.

Let's say, for instance, that you have a very rigid religious belief system. You believe in a heaven and you believe that you will be judged for your life in the afterlife. You can see that how you act in this life is greatly determined by your beliefs. You live a very specific lifestyle based on this fear of judgment. When we tell you there is no judgment in the nonphysical afterlife, you do not hear us. You either miss that idea completely, or as you read it you omit the word "*no*." What you actually read and understand is the sentence you read as "There *is* judgment in the nonphysical afterlife." This statement now fits with your belief and you carry on reading the rest of the book.

If you do read the sentence as we wrote it and it does not fit with your belief system, you might simply stop reading the book right then and there. Since the book is not a match to your set of beliefs, you consider it untrue or misguided and feel no reason to continue reading. Since this book comes from infinite intelligence, however, we would say there is great value in all of the ideas contained within these pages. It matters not what we say, for if anything does not match with your beliefs and your beliefs are rigid, you will not understand what we have to say as we intended.

If your beliefs are rigid, what you read, hear, and experience will be physically altered by your beliefs. Everything you experience is a match to your beliefs because the Law of Attraction brings you more of what you believe. Therefore, your beliefs are reinforced and become even more rigid. You can see that this is a powerful cycle that is hard to break.

However, if you hold the belief that you are open to new ideas, then new ideas can flow to you. You can say to yourself that you are a person who seeks more information and then more information will flow to you. You can start to call yourself an "innovator" and you will see the world in new ways. You can call yourself "lucky" and then watch all the ways you experience what you consider to be luck. When you adopt beneficial beliefs, you lessen the intensity of limiting beliefs.

The Law of Attraction will always agree with whatever term you use to describe yourself. So you might as well describe yourself in a way that benefits your experience of reality. You could just as easily see yourself as a cheerful person or a grumpy one. You can choose to be either an optimist or a realist. You can choose to believe in the laws of the universe exactly as we describe them or in a way that suits your set of beliefs. You can view the world as flat or as round as you like. It's up to you.

IV.

Ideas, like chairs, or buildings, or people, are vibrational as well. Words are also vibrational. You are a vibrational match to all the words you know. You are not a vibrational match to all ideas. You are a match to some ideas but not to others. It is interesting to note that you are a match to most, if not all, of the words in this book, but not to all of the ideas.

You are a match to some of the ideas and you gain a new perspective on reality based on your ability to accept new ideas and to recognize the deeper level of understanding you already possess. Depending on your level of understanding of the universal laws, you accept some ideas fully and completely. They may be stated in a new way, but you understood a lot of these ideas all along. You knew all of this information when you were born and now it's coming back to you. If there is anything you do not believe fully, it is due to a limiting belief that you've picked up along the way.

If your belief system is challenged because we use the term "limiting," it is a sign that your beliefs are too rigid. There is really no reason to fear the loss of a limiting belief. You can simply give it up. You can release it to the universe. No harm will come to you unless you believe it will. Fear and doubt keep limiting beliefs in place.

While you read this book, take note of what comes up that you find difficult to believe. Why do you find this particular idea unbelievable? What is it about your belief system that makes the idea untrue for you? Is this a limiting belief? When asked why you do not believe it, what do you say? What is your evidence? The evidence will lead you to your limiting belief.

Let's say again that you believe that how you behaved in this life will be judged in the afterlife. You believe that if you live a good life, you will get some reward in the afterlife. If you behaved in a manner that your society deems inappropriate, you will be punished in the afterlife. We tell you there is no judgment and you do not believe us. Why not? Wouldn't it be nicer to live without the burden of judgment? Wouldn't that give you more freedom in this life? Your belief in this judgment is a limiting one and there is no evidence to support it. So why do you still hold on so tightly to this belief?

Fear is the answer to every limiting belief you hold. You fear that if you let go of this or any limiting belief, you will suffer dire consequences. If you were to let go of your belief in a judgment day and started living life as you pleased, you might ultimately face eternal damnation. What if we're wrong? It's just not worth the risk. Or what if you let go of the belief and start living as you please. Your life might spin out of control. You might start doing things you would not normally do and that thought frightens you. More fear and doubt enter your mind.

You might not believe us, but we are here to tell you that you can release all limiting beliefs without fear of negative consequences. If you question something we say in this material without having evidence to the contrary, you have uncovered a limiting belief. When you contemplate the release of that belief and you experience fear and doubt, you know it is a limiting belief. Release it anyway and allow for a new, beneficial belief. Once you do, your life will begin to change immediately.

Finish reading this book and then re-read it immediately. Many of you will take notes the first time through. If you underline or highlight any sentence or section, it is because you currently believe in the idea being presented. It reinforces a current belief. It justifies what you already believe and you feel good about it. It may even give you chills down your spine or goose bumps on your arms.

We want you to focus on what you did not underline. That is what you do not believe, understand or, as you say, "are not ready to hear." These are the ideas you don't believe. You have limiting beliefs in these areas. We want you to closely examine your beliefs on these topics. Why don't you understand the words? Why did you miss this information the first time around? Why did you not highlight those sentences? It's due to a limiting belief.

When you understand the existence of the limiting belief, you can release it. When you can look back on the nature of the limiting belief, you can see how it got started and realize you simply fell into a habit of thought that led to this rigid belief you now carry along with you wherever you go.

Why would a person believe they will face a judgment day? This is a limiting belief because it causes people to act in a manner that was not intended prior to birth. All humans intended freedom and this belief restricts that freedom by forcing people to conform with behavior that is considered acceptable. If you understand that the belief exists and realize it is limiting, you can release it. Since there is no evidence to support this belief, there is no reason for its existence. You have evidence to support a belief in gravity, but not a belief that you will be judged.

If you trace the origin of the limiting belief, you can understand how and why it was adopted in the first place. Afterlife judgment is a commonly held belief in your society based on many religious teachings. Your parents may have believed this. Your religious leaders may have held this belief. However, if you were not exposed to this belief, you would not carry it. It is not a natural belief and was only created by man to control the actions of others. It only works to control the actions of those who believe it and does nothing to control the actions of those who do not share this belief.

All limiting beliefs are simply unnatural beliefs you would not carry unless you were exposed to them through the influence of others. Let's look at the most commonly held limiting belief in your society: the belief that you are not worthy. Nearly all humans share this belief in some way. The older you are, the more likely it is that you hold this belief. The younger you are, the less rigid the belief. Babies do not generally believe in the concept of unworthiness.

You adopt the belief of unworthiness through the influence of others. Usually you start to believe in your unworthiness as a result of some punishment you received as a child. The more severe and prolonged the punishment or mistreatment, either physical or emotional, the more intense the belief in unworthiness.

Your belief in your own unworthiness is directly related to your levels of comfort. When you feel safe, you feel more worthy. When you feel exposed, you feel less worthy. As you rise to higher levels of achievement, the belief in your own worthiness comes into play. You either achieve or fail based on your belief in your worthiness. If you believe you are worthy of this particular achievement, you succeed. If you believe you're unworthy in some way, you will fail. In competition, those with the highest feelings of worthiness, in the moment, succeed.

You try new things based on your individual, specific feelings of worthiness at the time. Your belief limits what you experience to the degree you believe it. When we say you are as worthy as anyone who has ever lived, there is no evidence to the contrary. If you believe there is, you hold this limiting belief. If you can show evidence that someone else is more worthy than you, you hold the limiting and untrue belief that you are not worthy. Your evidence is false. You created the evidence in your mind. This is a limiting belief and the opposite belief is what you must adopt. You are as worthy as anyone who has ever lived a physical existence.

We are starting to see that your society is changing their beliefs in this regard. Children are allowed more freedom to develop and parents are not seeing the need to punish children in a way that might cause a belief in unworthiness to grow. When children are cherished and loved unconditionally, they adopt the true and natural belief in their own worthiness and the worthiness of others. With this belief, all things are possible.

V.

There are many limiting beliefs common among people in your society, as well as many that are beneficial. Mass beliefs within countries shape the nation more than the workings of its government. Your country is what you as a people believe it is, not what your government tries to make it. When you go to war, you go as a population, not as a government. Your beliefs shape policy, not the politicians. There are mass beliefs within cultures that also shape periods of time. Each decade has an individual feeling due to the beliefs of the population at that time.

As you move forward as a people, you develop new beliefs that allow you to expand as a culture. Your beliefs in freedom shape your laws. Your beliefs shape your education system. Your mass beliefs allow for the evolution of your society. Your beliefs determine whether you create technology or whether you adopt the technology of other nations. Each region of the world is shaped by the beliefs of its people.

There are regions of the world where the people hold onto old beliefs. These cultures are slow to move forward and evolve. There are also regions of the world where the people adopt new, more beneficial beliefs and are therefore evolving at a faster rate. There are areas of the world where the people are mostly pessimistic in their beliefs and there are areas of the world where the people are mostly optimistic. If you look at the history of nations and find that its people were explorers, you can see that those beliefs shaped those nations in certain specific ways and that many of the beliefs of these nations are still held by its people. If you look at the development of any nation, or any region within a nation, you can see that certain beliefs have been a predominant aspect it.

This illustration was made to change your perspective on the nature of belief. You might have assumed that you adopted the set of beliefs you now carry around with you on your own. You might think that your beliefs are unique to you because you have a unique life experience. But now you might also come to understand that many of your beliefs have been adopted due to the influences of others or of your society. You do not simply experience something and then adopt a belief based on your personal experience. Many of your beliefs are based solely on the teaching or transference of others' beliefs. Your beliefs are not based on any specific evidence. Instead, they are just picked up like baggage along your path.

If you can see that your limiting beliefs are often the result of fear or doubt that has been transferred from others to you, you can alter the intensity of these beliefs. If you believe that your nation is superior to all other nations and should dictate to the world how the rest of the world should operate, this is due to the influence of patriotism. You have not visited every other nation and have thus concluded that your nation is superior; you simply adopted this belief from the transference of those who believe in the separation of nations by the use of borders.

This perceived need for borders is a belief rooted in fear, just like any other limiting belief. Your society, like others around the world, holds onto the limiting belief in its superiority. These societies are fearful that their "way of life" would be altered by the hordes of people who would flood the country if not for its borders. However, it is the Law of Attraction that causes others to be drawn to or leave any country. No borders are stronger than the Law of Attraction.

If you could just allow the Law of Attraction to bring you what you desire as a people, you would not need borders. If you focused on what you wanted rather than fearing the unwanted, you would have only peace and no need for an army. But because what you focus on grows larger, your army grows larger and your walls grow higher. Since what you focus on grows more, your police force and prison system grow as well. Imagine the benefit to your nation's economy and to the economy of the world if you had no need for a military, no need for a police force, and no need for a prison system.

But the need for these things exists because your limiting beliefs exist. Change your beliefs as a society and you'll change the nature of your society. When you embrace other nations and allow them to develop as they must in the manner they choose and at the pace they choose, you allow yourselves the benefits of a new, more tolerant belief system. When you empower others to be as they are while shining your example of success and love, you inspire others to their own success and love. When you condemn others for the beliefs of their society, since you know how deeply these beliefs are rooted, you do not help to alter their beliefs; you only harden them.

The Law of Attraction works to bring evidence of any belief you hold. If as a society, you believe that one particular religion is wrong or one form of government is wrong and you work to change the beliefs of another society, the Law of Attraction will show you evidence of their wrongness and reinforce your beliefs. The other society that sees that your society is calling their way of life wrong will see you in a negative manner, which will reinforce their own beliefs. When you attack, they cannot see that you are a peaceful people. They only see what they believe.

The path to change is by example alone. You cannot force a society to change its beliefs; you can only **allow** a society to change its beliefs. When you shine as an example of the qualities you aspire to, you allow others to see those qualities in you and inspire them to want those qualities for themselves. When you see only the positive aspects of a society, those positive aspects are reflected back to you through the Law of Attraction.

As a society, you also have many beneficial beliefs and positive qualities. These qualities shine as a beacon to others around the world who aspire to those same qualities. Those who are within the vibrational vicinity of these qualities see the tremendous benefits; those who are not within the vibrational vicinity cannot see the benefit of your way of life.

To many cultures, your way of life is very desirable. To many other cultures, your way of life is something to be avoided. This disparity is due to the belief system of other societies. As those societies evolve, their belief systems also evolve and they may move toward a society such as yours or they may maintain their beliefs but adopt a belief in tolerance and peace. However, it is up to your society to adopt beliefs that allow for peace and tolerance first. Like the outer world of your personal experience, which is a mirror to your personal set of beliefs, the world outside your society is a reflection of your society's mass beliefs. Alter society's beliefs and the rest of the world will change to mirror the new beliefs.

Your society's beliefs change with history. You can see other nations that were once bitter enemies are now great allies. You can see perceptions held by the society in the past that were quite different from what they are now. You can see what was once a great fear of society is no longer feared at all. The same will be true in your future as well. From your perspective, you might not be able to see the change that will come, just as those of a previous era could not imagine the change that has taken place up to this present time.

What you fear today will not be feared a generation from now. Change is occurring quickly in these times and the sooner you release your fears, the easier these changes will be. Those you think of as enemies will one day be your friends. They could be your friends sooner if you simply allowed it.

Your ability to influence the rest of the world does not come from a place of fear. You cannot use your military or your police unless you harbor fearful thoughts. You cannot write laws unless they are based on fear. Anything done out of fear is not done out of inspiration. When you see how beliefs shape your society, you can see how you are also individually shaped by your beliefs. When you see how your society is held back by its limiting beliefs, you also see how you as an individual are held back by your limiting beliefs. Remove a limiting belief and you gain freedom. Remove several limiting beliefs and you gain ease. Remove all limiting beliefs and you gain the full and absolute power of the universe.

You may not be able to alter all of your society's limiting beliefs on your own, but as you remove your limiting beliefs, you inspire others to remove theirs. If you stopped to think about what you're saying, what you're voting for, and what you're believing, you'll inspire others to do the same. Others have influenced you to adopt limiting beliefs. You can influence others to replace their limiting beliefs with empowering beliefs. As you change, others will change. As you influence another, they will influence scores of others. One change leads to cascading change throughout a society, and the society as a whole will also change.

VI.

Your beliefs carry with them levels of intensity. You might hold a limiting belief at a low intensity. That is, the belief is there, but since you don't think too much about it, it has less of an impact on your life. Other limiting beliefs carry very high levels of intensity and your life is greatly impacted by these beliefs. If you believe you are a good singer but not as good as many pop stars, you might sing in front of a small group of others and not be too concerned with their reaction. If, however, you believe you are a terrible singer, you will never sing in front of anyone.

You might look at any talent you possess and judge yourself against others. To the degree you feel confident under the scrutiny of that self-judgment you will allow the talent to flow forth. You have the ability to do, be, and have whatever you can imagine, but your judgment, which is based on the intensity of a limiting belief, will determine how far you go. The intensity of your beliefs accounts for the degree to which your desires manifest. If you have a low-intensity limiting belief, you might experience much of that which you desire. If you have a high-intensity limiting belief, you will experience none of that which you desire.

If you consider yourself excellent at something, you have no intense limiting beliefs in that area. This allows you to blend fully with your inner self to achieve whatever you desire with regard to that talent. If you believe you are the best in the world at something, you have a highly intense beneficial belief and no limiting beliefs. Therefore, you can achieve greatness through alignment with your inner self on this subject. Your high-intensity beneficial belief with no limiting belief present allows you to experience the fullness of your desires in this area.

All champions have this combination of high-intensity beneficial beliefs with no limiting beliefs. As long as this combination of beliefs is maintained, the individual will maintain their greatness. As soon as a limiting belief arises, the champion will experience the diminishment of their desires.

As limiting beliefs gain in intensity, beneficial beliefs diminish in intensity. This causes the diminishing of the experience the champion once enjoyed.

You have the ability to enjoy high-intensity beneficial beliefs with the absence of limiting beliefs in any and all areas of your life. When you allow the highly intense beneficial belief to arrive in your experience, you gain the full blending of your inner self and leverage the powers of the universe. You can explore the fullest manifestation of your desires. To the extent you entertain a limiting belief, you lessen the intensity of your connection with your inner self and limit the extent of your desire. You may experience some success, but not as much as you could have had you let go of the limiting belief.

All limiting beliefs are based in fear and doubt and can be reduced in their intensity. When you realize that the power of the universe is at your disposal, you have nothing to fear. When you understand that everything is here to serve you and was designed for you to achieve your dreams, you need not worry. You are the creator of your life and the only thing holding you back is your limiting beliefs. You adopted these beliefs without careful consideration. You harbor these beliefs without inspection. They carry negative energy, yet you allow them to exist. Once you come to know the weight of these beliefs, you can drop them, as you would any unnecessary baggage.

VII.

You are able to dismantle any limiting belief you may be unconsciously carrying. Most of your limiting beliefs are hidden from you. You accept them as truth or fact, even though you have never analyzed any of them. When you think you cannot do, have, or be anything you want due to fear or doubt, it is a limiting belief and it is not true. It is not fact.

If you have a true passion, you can follow it to great success. Only doubt stands in your way. Doubt is the evidence of a limiting belief. Doubt and fear expose limiting beliefs and bring them to the surface. As you experience doubt, you must analyze the belief. As you bring the belief to conscious awareness, you can gain insight about its intensity. The more limiting the belief, the more intense the fear or doubt associated with it. You can lower its intensity and thus lower its ability to hold you back from the fullest experience of your desires.

You can lower the intensity of a limiting belief by raising the intensity of a beneficial belief. Imagine that you are an actor and your true passion is acting. You have found what it is you are here to explore and you want to experience the fullest manifestation of your craft. Your dream is to become the lead in a Broadway play.

When you are an actor beginning your journey to your desire, you hold a set of beliefs that are both empowering and limiting. When you experience success in your craft, you automatically allow your beneficial beliefs to increase in intensity. As you experience a setback (which exists only in your mind), you automatically allow your limiting beliefs to increase in intensity. The degree to which your reaction to your outer world affects both your beneficial and limiting beliefs has, up to this point, been automatic. You have not consciously worked to increase the intensity of beneficial beliefs or reduce the intensity of limiting beliefs.

When you as an actor experience success as you are awarded a desired part in a play, you might believe that it is appropriate to be humble about the success for fear of hurting others. This action does not increase the intensity of your beneficial beliefs. If you experience a setback, such as being cut from a scene, you may experience anger, frustration, or unworthiness, all of which work to intensify the limiting belief. Soon your limiting beliefs will be so intense that you can no longer pursue your passion and you might give up on your dreams altogether.

Now that you are consciously aware of the existence of both your beneficial and limiting beliefs you can knowingly work to ramp up your empowering beliefs and also minimize the intensity of your limiting beliefs.

When you experience a success, you must willfully place your focus on all of the positive aspects of that success. You tell yourself, "Well done." You give yourself credit for the success. You take time to play the success over and over in your mind. When you raise the intensity of the success while you're in the moment of the success, you positively affirm your success. You take note of the high vibrational feeling of the success and re-run that feeling over and over. You have successfully increased the intensity of the beneficial belief greatly and have simultaneously minimized the intensity of any limiting beliefs.

When you experience a setback, you consciously work to reduce the intensity of your limiting beliefs. You tell yourself that the setback is simply in your mind and it is not a setback at all, just part of the process of gaining more clarity. You focus on the **positive** aspects of the setback. You imagine that the setback was designed to move you along your path, and if the event did not occur, something truly unpleasant might have happened instead. You no longer call the event a setback or a failure, but rather a defining moment. You have deliberately minimized the intensity of your limiting belief and have widened the path to a fuller manifestation of your desire.

Beliefs affect your perspective and your perspective affects your beliefs. If you change your perspective on a subject, you can change your beliefs about that subject. What you consider to be true is what you believe. What you consider to be false is what you do not believe. If you can change your perspective about the nature of truth and falsehood, you can change your beliefs. What you agree with you believe and what you disagree with you do not believe. Start agreeing more and you will alter the intensity of your beliefs.

Let's look at a real-world example and see if we can view it from a new perspective and thereby alter some beliefs. Let's imagine you believe that suicide is wrong. You vote to insure that all forms of suicide remain illegal. You agree with others who argue that suicide is wrong and you disagree with those who believe the decision to end one's own life should be left to the individual.

However, you also believe in much of what we are teaching you from our nonphysical perspective. You believe that what we have told you about the nature of beliefs is true. You believe that we have a clearer understanding of the nature of the universe, of the reality you're living, and of the nonphysical realm to which you will all return. Then we tell you that **"All death is suicide"** and that the manner in which you die matters not. When you are ready to transcend to the nonphysical, you will go one way or another. You might prolong the transition through the experience of illness, or you might make it quick and painless through suicide. It's always your choice.

If you can alter your perspective on this subject, you can lower the intensity of this limiting belief. When you can understand that this belief stems from fear, you can deem it limiting and realize it is an unnecessary belief. What you fear is the potential loss of someone you love. What you fear is that children may commit suicide. What you fear is the unknown ramifications of tolerating suicide. However, there is never anything to fear. Simply lower the intensity of the belief by gaining a new, broader perspective on the subject.

You can lower the intensity of any limiting belief by realizing that it exists, that it is based in fear, and that there is no evidence to support the belief. If you believe that suicide is wrong, then realize that this is a belief that does not serve you and is limiting. You know you cannot create in the lives of others and since your opinion in this regard involves others, you accept that it is not your concern. You have now lowered the intensity of this belief. Even if you knew someone who committed suicide, your relationship is now eased with that event and with that person because you have gained a new perspective. You now see it as less wrong than you previously believed it to be and that brings relief.

Your limiting beliefs affect *you* negatively, not the people you cast your judgment on. They do not care about your opinions. Your limiting beliefs only make *your* life less pleasant, not theirs. You gain freedom, connection, and alignment by reducing the intensity of limiting beliefs.

Let's look at another limiting belief that people in your society once believed in strongly: the belief that same-sex marriages should be illegal. This is a belief that is making its way out of your society and will soon be long forgotten. If you hold this belief, it is limiting to you, not to them. They believe they should be allowed the freedom to marry and that is a beneficial belief for them. If you held the belief that all people should be allowed the freedom to marry, it would be a beneficial belief for you. If you believe that you should create in the lives of others, you carry a limiting belief. It holds you back from what you truly desire. Once you lower the intensity of this belief, you move along your true path. This belief no longer holds you apart from many of your desires.

If you can realize that a limiting belief exists within yourself, you can change your perspective and reduce the intensity of the belief. If you can see any subject from a broader view, you can see it in a new light and then

A Perception of Reality

lower the intensity of your negative belief. If you can see the point of view of the other side in any disagreement, you can change your perspective and then alter the belief.

When in disagreement with another, one believes he is right and the other is wrong. It does not matter on which side of the argument you sit. Since the truth lies in the eye of the believer, there is no real truth as you know it. Truth is an illusion based on belief. Change the belief and you alter the truth. Change your belief regarding the nature of truth and you allow yourself to easily alter your limiting beliefs.

When we tell you that you are worthy beyond compare, we are telling you an absolute truth. Why is it the truth? Because we know it to be true. Why can you believe that it is true? Because it's a highly beneficial belief. If the belief is beneficial, then calling it truth is also beneficial. This will strengthen the intensity of the beneficial belief. If the belief is limiting then you can call it false. This will reduce the intensity of the limiting belief.

Everything we have ever told you can be labeled true because it is all beneficial. When any information is presented to you, whether you considered it fact or fiction, you can determine the information to be true or false based on the beneficial or limiting nature it. If an airplane crashes and it is labeled a tragedy, you can realize that the label of tragedy is limiting and then alter your perspective to find a new beneficial belief. Your ability to see things from a new perspective is for your benefit alone and you do not need to share your unique views with others, for they will attempt to transfer their limiting beliefs to you.

Your beliefs control your version of reality. Beneficial beliefs brighten your world and make life more enjoyable and easier. Limiting beliefs hold you apart from your desires. Reduce the intensity of your limiting beliefs and pour all your focus and energy into increasing the intensity of your beneficial beliefs and you will live the life of your dreams.

Chapter Fourteen

The Magical Power of Creation Through Intention

Intention is the basis of all creation. It is what created the physical version of you. Your life, as you are living it, was intended prior to your birth. Many of the wonderful aspects of your life were intended by you before you entered physical reality. Intention is a magical power you possess even in your physical form.

What you intend you must believe. The stronger your belief, the more powerful your intention. Your intention has the power, when backed by a high-intensity belief, to create a physical representation of that intention. Before anything physical exists, there is thought. When intention is coupled with thought, powerful positive manifestations occur in physical reality. Focused thought, high-intensity belief, and conscious intention work together utilizing the leverage of the universe to create the physical manifestation of a desire.

In order for intention to be powerful, it must be in alignment with your set of beliefs. You must believe in the basis of the intention. You must know that the intention will manifest. You cannot have a limiting belief that is in conflict with the intention. This muddles the vibration and reduces the manifestational power of the intention. Alignment with beliefs is crucial for the intention to manifest physically.

You can intend to do, have, or be anything. Clarity of intent focuses your mental abilities onto your creation. What you intend must be created by your thoughts before it manifests into physical reality. Once you set your intention, you focus your thoughts on the creation of that intention. Your thoughts must be clear and free from doubt and fear. Doubt and fear arise from a conflicting set of limiting beliefs. If you encounter fear and doubt when building your intention through thought, you must stop and find the limiting belief. Once you have reduced the intensity of the limiting belief you can resume thoughts that build your intention.

You can intend to create an empire and you can intend to enjoy a meal. What you intend does not matter, only the clarity of your intention. Smaller things are easier to manifest because the intensity of limiting beliefs is relatively lower. When you set intentions regarding what you consider to be big goals or accomplishments, you will face more limiting beliefs of higher intensity. However, the process of intention is the same.

Focus your thoughts on the intention.

Clarify the intention by noticing fear and doubt.

Identify the existence of a limiting belief.

Change your perspective on that limiting belief and reduce its intensity.

Resume thinking about your intention and clarify further.

This simple process will help you clarify any intention, large or small.

You intend many things throughout your day of which you are not consciously aware of . You intend to be safe while driving. You intend to eat during the day. You intend to sleep at night. You may intend to go to work. You may intend to get the children off to school on time so they won't miss the bus. All of these intentions are routine and are accomplished without much thought.

But you can become more specific in your intentions and thereby raise your vibrational frequency so that what you intend manifests into a better, richer experience and does so to your benefit.

For instance, let's say that today you will eat lunch, as you do every day. Normally you do not give lunch much consideration. It is more of a habit than an intention. You've eaten lunch most days of your life and today will be no exception - except that today you will consciously intend to have lunch. What does this intention entail? Let's say you have one intention for health and another for friendship. Today you will intend to have a healthy, delicious lunch with a friend. This is the intention you set before you get out of bed.

Your intention might be very specific or rather general. The difference depends on how you're feeling. You may want to set the intention to eat a specific dish at a specific restaurant with a specific friend. If you fully believe all of these specifics can and will occur and you do not notice any fear or doubt, your specific intention will likely manifest.

If, on the other hand, you experience any fear or doubt when specifically intending this lunch, you might adjust your intention and become less specific. You might simply think about eating something healthy at any restaurant with any one of your friends. You let the universe decide how it will play out for you.

In either case, when the new and improved manifestation of lunch occurs, you can revel in your ability to create a manifestation that is richer and fuller than if you had you not set your intention. You can see that a little thought about what you want will improve anything you do on a regular basis. This intention-setting procedure can and should be done prior to any activity. If you go to the gym you can set an intention to feel stronger, to utilize your muscles better, and to gain more from the exercise experience. You could set your intentions for the machines to be available exactly when you need them.

When going to the grocery store you could set your intentions on buying the best food for your family. You could intend to be inspired to buy the ingredients for a wonderful meal you will prepare later. You could intend to recognize products that are the best for you. Intentions set before any routine activity increase the beneficial experience of that activity.

When you set your intentions prior to any normal activity, you raise your vibrational frequency. As your vibration rises you build momentum. This momentum carries forth into other routine experiences and improves them as well. As you consciously consider the impact of your intentions on routine activities you increase the vibrational experience of your entire life. Everything becomes fuller and richer.

Setting your intentions prior to any normal activity helps you gain confidence in your ability to set intentions around those events you consider small and large. It works the same way. When you think about a large event, let's say a wedding or a job interview, you think about what it is you want. Why do you want this event to happen? What are the outcomes you desire? Do you notice any fear or doubt? Must you clarify the intention further?

If you are planning a wedding, what are your intentions? We will assume you intend for the event to allow your friends and family to witness a special day in your life. You want the environment to be beautiful. You intend for the food to be delicious and prepared perfectly. You want the guests to enjoy themselves. You want the music to be lively so everyone will dance. You want the celebration of your love to carry you forth into your marriage. You desire the wedding to symbolize your love for each other. When you set these intentions, they do not raise any feelings of fear or doubt. They are less specific intentions and since fear and doubt are not present, the intentions will manifest into your physical reality. Your intentions create a wonderful wedding.

A wedding with fewer specifics will be easier for you to think about and therefore easier to manifest. But what if you wanted something more? What if it was your dream to be married on the beach in Hawaii? As you ponder this and set your intentions, you see yourself at sunset on a beach with all your friends and family gathered around as you take your vows. You think about the beautiful ceremony with everyone standing in the sand. Now you might add chairs so that everyone is sitting. You might add an arbor beneath which you will recite your vows. You see a cloudless sky and a mild balmy breeze. Everything looks wonderful.

As you delve deeper into your scene, you think about your aunts and uncles who live on the East Coast of the United States. You wonder if they will be willing to travel all the way to Hawaii. Doubt creeps in and it's time to clarify your intention. What is the limiting belief? Is it that you are not important enough for them to come? Is it that you do not have the money to pay for their travel costs? Are you worried they will resent you for being selfish by having your wedding so far away? If any of these fears or doubts arise, you must discover the limiting belief and change your perspective. If you cannot lower the intensity of the limiting belief, your wedding will not manifest as you intend.

If you fear that others will see you as selfish for having your wedding in Hawaii, you must change your perspective. You may realize that your wedding is all about you. You are meant to be selfish on your wedding day. If you're going to be selfish on any day of your life, this is the one day to do it. Other people get married in Hawaii and you can as well if that is your dream. Those who really want to come to your wedding will find a way to do it. It will be good for everyone to be together in such a beautiful environment celebrating a special day. You realize that they love you and if they can't come to the wedding you will understand. You'll take lots of photos

The Magical Power of Creation Through Intention

and videos you'll send to them. You will include them in your wedding even if they cannot be there in person.

You have now changed your perspective, removed most of the fear and doubt, lowered the intensity of a limiting belief, and clarified your intention. Your intention is now much more likely to manifest in your reality. As you get closer to the day and make more specific decisions as to what you intend you will continue this process each time a fear or doubt surfaces.

Now let us take a look at your intentions prior to a job interview. Let's say you have a desire to become a chef and begin by setting a general intention with few specifics. At this point you are simply embarking on a new journey to become a chef and you realize you must start by cooking in a restaurant. You set an intention to work in an established restaurant that will have the ability to train you so you can learn everything you need to know to become a chef.

Your intention does not involve a specific income, specific hours, or a certain type of restaurant. You only desire to become employed and have the opportunity to learn. As you sit down to your first interview, you have little fear or doubt that you will get a job. You are not too concerned about receiving the job as a result of this interview because you have several interviews lined up and you know there are many restaurants in need of cooks. Your intention is clear, the interview goes well, and you are hired for a position that allows you to learn how to cook in a restaurant.

Now let's imagine you have been working at this restaurant for a while and are ready to become the executive chef of an upscale restaurant. Your intentions become more specific due to your experiences up to this point. You are now aware of your talents and you set very specific intentions. You will demand a certain salary. You want to stay in the area in which you live. You want to cook a specific type of cuisine. You want control over the kitchen. You also want to work in an environment that allows you to train aspiring chefs just as you were trained.

A position become available in one of the top restaurants in your area and you schedule an interview. As you think about the job and dream about the perfect position your mind is filled with images. You see yourself in your chef's coat working with your team in the kitchen. You see the food being prepared and plated. Everything looks wonderful. You think about the increased income that comes with the new position and imagine a new home and a new car. Then your mind wanders and you see a waiter bringing food back from a displeased customer. You see the owner of the restaurant and he looks worried. He may have made the wrong decision in hiring you.

Fear and doubt have crept into your intention. It is time to clarify. What is the limiting belief? Are you not ready for this position? Are you not worthy of the additional income? Is this restaurant too big to handle? Now is the time to recognize the limiting belief and change your perspective. Let's say you have uncovered the limiting belief that you might not be ready for such a large and well-known restaurant. How can you change your perspective?

As you ponder working in the new restaurant, you can reduce the intensity of your limiting belief by reminding yourself of several things you do believe. You are an excellent cook at your current job and have become even better than your current executive chef. Everyone raves about your food. The new restaurant is designed to handle more people and you will adapt to the environment easily. You know you're an excellent chef and that you deserve the added income. It is the same as any chef would be paid for such a position. The owner knows what is right for his restaurant and if he should hire you, it will be the right decision.

You have just clarified your intentions by changing your perspective and reducing the intensity of the limiting belief. You now have an excellent chance that your intention will manifest and you will be hired for the new position.

General intentions manifest more easily because doubt and fear are less likely to arise. Specific intentions will always encounter some thoughts of fear and doubt and therefore must be clarified every step of the way. General intentions moderately raise the vibration of the event just enough so that the general desire can manifest into physical reality. A specific desire requires a higher vibration and therefore requires more focus and clarity.

II.

Thoughts have a vibrational pattern and attract other thoughts with complementary vibrational patterns. Intentions also carry unique vibrational patterns and attract events that resonate with the vibration. The Law of

Attraction puts it all together. If the vibrational pattern of the intention is focused and the signal is strong, it will attract the physical representation of the specific intention. If the vibrational pattern of the intention is muddled by doubt and fear, the attractive power of the intention is weak. The physical representation of the intention as it manifests will be weak as well.

Clarity is the key to the preferred physical manifestation of the intention. The clearer the intent, the stronger the signal. An intent is a signal broadcast from you out into the universe and has a strong power of attraction. The event that most closely corresponds to the signal will manifest in your reality.

The beneficial belief you must have at a very high level of intensity is that this process is true. You must believe that your intentions have the power to create the physical representation of what you desire.

If you do not understand or believe that intentions carry tremendous powers of attraction, the Law of Attraction will prove you right. You are always correct in your beliefs as far as the Law of Attraction is concerned. You always receive physical evidence that supports your beliefs. Unless you strongly believe in the power of your intentions, your intentions will have no power.

If you set a specific intention for the manifestation of a certain outcome and that outcome does not manifest, your intention was too specific for your set of beliefs. The frequency of the intention was muddled by fear and doubt. The intention was not focused. A limiting belief was vibrating at a high intensity and prevented the physical manifestation of your intention. This is the mechanism of intention. The more you believe that it works, the better it will work for you. If you doubt it, it will not work.

You increase the intensity of your belief that intention is a powerful and creative tool through practice. As you succeed, you gain confidence in your abilities and the intensity of this highly beneficial belief increases. You must start with general intentions and only move to more specific intentions when your belief in the power of intention has been established. If you move too quickly to specific intentions, your intentions will not manifest in the manner you desire and you will lose faith in your powers of intention. When you see signs of failure, your confidence diminishes and the intensity of your belief dwindles. Soon you make up excuses. You justify your lack of skill by creating limiting beliefs.

A Perception of Reality

If you can intend to enjoy your day, you can begin the practice of intention. As you go through your day enjoying many moments and finding pleasure in small things, you practice your intention. Each time you find an aspect of your day to enjoy you practice your intention. As you are enjoying your day and appreciating the manifestation of your intention, you're practicing intention. Enjoying your day is a very general intention. When you find yourself actually enjoying your day as you intended, you build confidence in your ability to set an intention. You have also experienced your ability to allow the universe to provide you with the physical manifestation of your intention.

You might say that intention is a self-fulfilling prophecy. We agree. You might be thinking that the only reason you're enjoying the day is because you're consciously paying attention to things that occur during the day that you enjoy. We concur. However, you say, it is no different than any other day. The day is the same, It's just that I'm becoming aware of things I enjoy because of the intention I set. The universe didn't do anything different. I was the only change. And we say, "Now you've got it!"

The universe doesn't change for you; you change for the universe. You are the one with the power of focus. As your perspective changes, you change and the world around you represents that change. Things do not magically materialize. They were there all the time. However, once you've placed your attention on them, it seems like they materialized into your reality. And if it seems like they did, then for you, they did. That's how this reality works.

When you decide to love someone, you see the wonderful aspects of the person that were always there. You love someone, but another may not love that person. It's the same person. To you, he or she is very lovable. To another, he or she is not particularly more or less lovable than anyone else. This other person did not change, your perception of this person changed. You changed your focus on that person in such a way that you saw qualities that gave you the feeling of love.

When you decide to hate another person for something they did that you feel is wrong, the other person did not change, you changed so that what you saw in that person gave you the feeling of hate. You can focus on either the positive or negative aspects of anything. The object of your attention is neutral. You decide how you will see this object. When you decide to see all of the wonderful aspects of this object, your perception has changed. You have changed. The object has not changed.

The next day you may notice something you do not like about the object. The object did not change, your perspective changed. Now you are focused on a negative aspect and the negativity grows. It matters not what the object is; you determine what you focus your attention on.

When you set an intention, you ask yourself to observe the positive aspects of something in advance. You tell yourself to look for the best. You come into alignment with your inner self. You intend to see the object of your attention from the perspective of your inner self. You change your perspective from one of a casual observer, noticing the good and the bad in everything, to one of an intentional observer noticing only that which you intend to notice.

By predetermining your point of focus through intention, you give your attention to that which is wanted and you withdraw your attention from that which is unwanted. The Law of Attraction will give you more of what you focus your attention on. Therefore, your intention activates your attention and you align with that which you desire.

When you start with a general intention, you will find it easy to place your attention on it. When you intend to enjoy your day, you find it easy to notice things you are enjoying. You might believe your day is filled with many things to enjoy. As you encounter these things, people, events, etc., you acknowledge and appreciate them. This creates momentum. The next day, when you again intend to enjoy your day, you will find even more things to enjoy.

If you can go through your day taking mental notes of what you enjoy, you will have achieved the manifestation of your intention. If you go through your day and also notice things you do not enjoy, you will slow the momentum you have created. If you place your attention on things you enjoy and also notice everything you do not enjoy, and you tally up the score on two columns, you will bring more things you do not enjoy. You will, by default, set an intention to discover things you do not enjoy.

So, as you set your intention, it is important not to take score. Don't look at the opposite of what you intend and use that as an indicator that your powers of intention are lacking. You are new to this and it will take some time to develop your skill. You will not become a master of intention overnight. The practice is part of the journey. When you start slowly, you'll gain confidence and momentum. Start small and work your way up gradually. Be patient and allow your skills to develop. Soon you will be able to move on to more specific and therefore more powerful intentions.

III.

Intention is the tool for creating a reality you desire. Before the physical world existed there was an intention. Before you existed there were many intentions. You create the physical manifestation of everything through the creative use of intention. Intention is creative. Like anything else, your creation is intended through thought first. As you build the idea, through your thoughts, you begin to automatically set intentions. However, in the past you've set many intentions without much conscious awareness of the process. What you intend often plays out as you believed it would. Sometimes your experience is quite different than your intention. Why is this?

Let's say you have the intention of buying a new vehicle. You dream about the car you really want but your intentions are not clearly defined. The car that will actually manifest into your experience is out there somewhere. You do not have that car now in your experience, but one day soon you will have a car parked in your driveway and that car will be the physical representation of your intentions whether you consciously and deliberately set those intentions or not.

There are truly limitless possible cars that have the potential to manifest in your driveway. Which car ultimately arrives depends on your intentions. Prior to your understanding of the power of intentions, you created a mental version of the car you wanted based on aspects of other cars you liked and one's you didn't. Therefore, you ended up with a vehicle that represented both the positive and negative aspects of other cars. The car that showed up in your driveway had some aspects you wanted and some you did not. You accidentally or unconsciously set intentions without really knowing what you were doing.

We will continue the example of a vehicle purchase. Assume you want a brand-new red convertible sports car. You look at the car and say, "This is a beautiful car!" Then you see the car up close and realize it has a back seat no one could fit into; you are noticing a negative aspect of the car. Then you look at the price of the car and doubt you can afford it. Then you notice it is low to the ground and you fear you will not be able to see around other cars and worry about its safety.

Now you've turned your attention away from the car of your desires and look for vehicles that combine the aspects of utility, affordability, and safety. These were the missing aspects of the car of your dreams. Thus, you end up with a used minivan in your driveway. This is the result of a muddled set of intentions.

If you can come to appreciate your minivan for its positive aspects of utility, safety, and affordability, you will have a wonderful experience with it. If, however, you resent the minivan because it is not the car you truly desire, you will experience nothing but problems. The minivan did not change; you changed your perspective and the Law of Attraction provided you with evidence of your feelings.

You now have a new understanding of intention, perception, and the Law of Attraction, and you have the ability to focus your attention on what you desire. The next time you intend to manifest a new vehicle, you will use your power of intention and receive the vehicle you really want.

Let's start with your new understanding of intentions and revisit your desire for a brand-new red convertible sports car. You know the make, model, and price. You know right where they sell it and you set your intentions prior to your arrival. You set your intentions by saying to yourself, "I want a brand-new red convertible sports car." You continue with your intentions: "I intend to purchase this car at a price I can afford and I know the universe will provide me with the income that will allow me to easily afford this car." You keep going: "I intend to buy a car that is safe and I know the universe will allow me to drive safely in this new car. I need not worry about the backseat because there will always be alternate means of transportation anytime I require the use of a back seat or cargo area. I have many friends and family members and can always borrow a vehicle if the need arises. I can even rent a car easily if I want to. I intend to buy the car of my dreams and I intend only to see the positive aspects of this car until I desire a different one."

With those intentions fully set and from your place of alignment with your desire you will manifest the car of your dreams into your reality. You took the time to align with your desires and lowered the intensity of any limiting beliefs by altering your perception before walking into the showroom. You could not be swayed from your intentions, for they were firmly set in advance. You allowed the universe to deliver your dream car in an elegant way and the process unfolded beautifully.

IV.

As you lay in your bed in the morning soon after you have opened your eyes, you can think about the day ahead. You have a general idea of what will happen during the day and you can envision each event beforehand. As you think about the things you are going to do that day, you can set your intentions.

Your intentions prior to your birth were mostly general, though one or more were specific. Think of each new day as a whole new lifetime. As you lie in your bed prior to getting up and starting your day, think of this time as your gestation period. When you get out of bed, you are born. So your intentions for the day should be mostly general, with some specific ones.

Your general intentions for the day are similar to your general intentions for your life. You intend to feel good. You intend to have fun and experience joy. You intend to be safe and make good decisions. You intend to allow guidance from your inner self and to blend with your inner self as much as you can throughout the day. You intend to appreciate your life for the abundance you now experience. You intend to appreciate all the benefits of this life experience and all the things that are going well. You intend to place your attention on what is wanted and withdraw your attention from the unwanted. You intend to love and appreciate others and to see only the best in everyone around you.

If you have something specific planned for the day, you might intend something more specific regarding that event. If you are going to a business meeting, you might intend to communicate your presentation so your audience fully understands your proposal and sees the benefits of your ideas. You might be playing a round of golf and intend to have fun, for the weather to be clear, and for your best score to be broken. If you plan to cook dinner for friends, you might intend for the meal to be cooked perfectly with the right timing and for everyone to enjoy themselves. You have the ability to set intentions for all of the specific events of the day from the comfort of your bed in the morning.

As you go through your day and notice how each of your intentions are unfolding perfectly you can feel positive emotion flowing through you. This is guidance that shows you proof you're on the right path. Prior to each event you reaffirm your intention for that event. In your car on the way to your business meeting you will restate your intention for that meeting. See yourself in the meeting and feel the feeling of success. Picture everything going the way you want it to.

Before you start your round of golf, while you're at the first tee, see yourself swinging easily and picture the ball in the fairway and on the green. See your putts going with the slope of the green into the hole. Feel the feeling of joy as you best your own record. Imagine the look your friends will give you when they see how well you're playing.

Intentions should be set in advance of each day and in advance of each event. The outcome of your day and each event within your day will be greatly improved due to the focus of your thoughts. Intentions are simply a method of creating focus within your thoughts. Without intention your thoughts are less focused. Focused thought is what deliberate creation is all about.

As you set your intentions on the short-term you change your physical reality in the moment. In each moment lies the power of your creative abilities. Each moment of focused thought causes the manifestation of wanted things into your physical reality. Generally, your thought is unfocused for much of your day and therefore there is no great movement either forward or backward. If you had the ability to focus solely on what you want in every moment without the muddling effects of fear or doubt, you would constantly and continually manifest everything you desired.

Your life is a series of moments that seem to flow, just as a film is a series of slightly different photos that give the illusion of movement. If you can maintain thoughts about what is wanted for moment after moment after moment, you can create great power in your thoughts. Your thoughts would create momentum. Your emotional state determines whether you are more likely to attract positive or negative thoughts in the moment, but the power is in that moment. If you become distracted and your thought wanders, you lose momentum.

Focus is the ability to keep your thoughts on one topic. After moments of thinking about a certain topic, you will attract new thoughts relating to that topic. These thoughts, though different from previous thoughts, remain on the same subject. The longer you can keep these thoughts going on the same subject, the more momentum you build around the subject and the more power you give it. After just seconds of focused thought, the vibration you have created around that thought will be strong enough to start attracting the building blocks of physical manifestation.

Intention keeps your mind focused on what is wanted. The longer you keep your thoughts on your intention, the more powerful your intentions become and the more likely it is that your intentions will manifest in the manner you have intended.

Every intention has within it a level of intensity. The more time you spend envisioning your intention, the more intensity it gathers. As long as your thoughts around your intention are pure and focused, your intention becomes more powerful and gains momentum. As long as your intention is set with clarity of thought and focus, there is a high degree of probability that it will physically manifest as you intend. If, however, you entertain contrasting thoughts, your intention loses its intensity and its focus, and the probability of manifestation is diminished.

Clarity of thought in setting intentions is crucial for the intention to gain the intensity needed to allow the physical manifestation of that intention. If you experience worry, fear, or doubt, you are really setting another intention that contradicts your first intention. You now have two opposing intentions operating simultaneously. Each intention has the power to manifest, but it's likely that neither will manifest in the face of its opposite. Therefore, your intentions must be complementary and must work together in harmony.

Let's say you've set your intention on your golf game, as we have discussed earlier. It is a bright, sunny day with little wind and the course is in excellent condition. Everything is working out as you intended and you've just finished setting your intentions as you get up to tee off. One of your friends suggests making a little wager on the match and your thoughts scramble. Your clarity has been compromised by this new proposal.

The Magical Power of Creation Through Intention

You are feeling brave and decide to accept the bet. Now, thoughts of fear, doubt, and worry enter your mind. You've glimpsed a future in which you have lost the bet. You picture your frustration while you play poorly and your friend plays well. You can see yourself reaching into your wallet and handing over the money. You've automatically set your intention to play poorly and lose the bet. You must regain your focus and reset your intentions.

It is unlikely that you can excuse yourself and go somewhere quiet to set new intentions. You will simply have to do the best you can in the moment. If you have the ability to focus and maintain your thoughts on the wanted aspects of this event, you will have an easier time allowing your desires to manifest. However, if you have not practiced focus of thought, you will encounter thoughts of what you want and thoughts of what you do not want simultaneously. You have lost focus and your intentions have lost their power and intensity.

If you can maintain your focus on what you want better than your friend, you will win. If your friend can maintain his or her focus better than you, he or she will win. Your ability to play golf (or anything else) is mainly guided by your beliefs, expectations, and focused thoughts, not by any specific talent. If you and your competitor have similar beliefs and expectations, the winner that day will be decided by the one who maintains focus on what is wanted. The loser will be the one who cannot maintain focus on what is wanted.

It does not matter whether you can keep your focus on what is wanted long enough for it to manifest. This is a journey and you are just beginning to practice focused thought for the first time in your life. If you are an Olympic athlete, you have likely been taught to focus your thoughts on what is wanted and that is the reason you excell. Your entire being is vibrating at a level that brings you to the physical manifestation of the experience of a champion.

If you are a champion and have practiced focused thought your entire life, you have built your success though powerful intention. Others will look at you and see a God-given talent, a talent that few humans possess. It is not an ability given by any deity, it is simply the result of highly focused thought over many years. The focusing of thought has led the champion to believe in his or her capabilities and to expect a certain level of performance. The champion's body has changed physically to reflect these beliefs. Actual chemical and hormonal changes have taken place within the body so that it grows to the perfect proportions for their sport.

You might look at an Olympic swimmer and see the long arms and broad shoulders and see that the body is perfect for swimming. You might imagine or assume the training created the muscles so that the body took a specific shape as a result of hours of practice. Actually, it is the mind that shapes the body so that it conforms to the desires of the individual.

If you lined up a champion swimmer next to a champion weightlifter next to a champion gymnast, you could tell which person competed at each specific sport with no other cues than the shape of their bodies. Yet if you were to line up these people as they existed prior to training for their sport, you would see little difference. The mind, the predominance of thought, the individual's specific intentions, beliefs, and desires, are responsible for the changes to the shape and form of the physical body. The body is just part of the overall manifestation of the champion's desires.

Your intentions set off the changes necessary to cast your desires into physical reality. Some of these changes occur in the form of changes to your perspective. Some of the changes occur within your physical environment and physical body. At this point it is not really helpful for you to understand the process in its entirety. Simply understand that intentions help you focus your thoughts and that focused thought creates your reality.

V.

It may be helpful for some to discuss here the subject of prayer as it relates to intention. Many humans around the world engage in the practice of prayer and experience the beneficial qualities of this practice. Prayer is often similar in essence to intention. When an individual prays for health, peace, or appreciation for a meal, the prayer is focusing thoughts on what is wanted.

When prayer is based on an individual's desire for what is wanted in his or her own life, it has an effect similar to intention. As long as the prayer revolves around something wanted in the individual's own experience, the manifestation of that desire has the same probability of occuring as an intention. If the individual's belief that God will bring that which is wanted is strong, the desire will manifest easily. However, if the individual leaves it up to God to decide whether the individual is deserving of the request, the prayer loses its power.

Coupled with belief and expectation, intention has tremendous power. If prayer is coupled with the belief that God will provide what is wanted and the individual expects God to provide it, then the prayer becomes a powerful intention. However, when the individual prays for what is wanted and believes God will decide whether the individual is worthy of receiving it, he removes expectation and the intention has little power.

When one prays for another person, one is trying to manifest in another's reality, which is not possible. You can pray for yourself and thereby set an intention in your reality. You cannot pray for another or set an intention for someone else to receive anything because you cannot create for another. Everyone creates their own unique experience and you do not know what the experience of another entails. You may, from your perspective, believe that one desires what you desire, but you cannot **know** what is right for anyone else.

If you pray for someone and it makes you feel good and you find comfort, then we agree that this a good thing. When you pray for someone and find that your prayers have gone unanswered because you cannot create for another, you may feel disappointment. This is an indication from your guidance system that your thoughts are not focused on your own desires but on another's. Once you give up trying to help others in ways you think they need your help, you will gain freedom. When you see another in need, it is *you* who is seeing the negative aspects of their experience. You cannot help someone by giving your attention to what you perceive as negative, missing, or lacking; by doing so you only attract that negative aspect into your own experience.

When prayer is offered because it is expected of you or because you believe you owe homage to some divine entity more powerful than yourself, you are giving away your own power. It may be difficult for many of you to accept the fact that you are here to create your life in any way that pleases you. You are not here to serve the make-believe wishes of any deity. The God we know, the All That Is that powers the universe, has designed this physical environment for you to experience joy and growth on your own terms. You are the divine one that we shower with our attention and love.

Your religious training has many powerful and wonderful qualities. However, in that training, the true message has been lost, or corrupted to a degree. You are not here to prove your worthiness or to be judged. You are not here to earn salvation, because you already have eternal salvation and cannot experience anything else. You are here to be, do, and have anything you desire and to expand through the growth that comes from achieving your desires yourself.

We are here to guide you, but we do not give you anything but our guidance, attention and love. You earn everything you get through your own powers of intention and focus. Do not give away your control by believing a higher power will give you what you want only when the higher power decides you deserve it. You already deserve everything you can imagine. Now we want you to use your own powers of thought to come into alignment with what you want.

You are not required to alter your behavior in a way that will suit someone else or even in a way that will suit God. The demands of God were created by man and no such demands exist in the nonphysical realm. You can live your life in any manner that pleases you. All man's laws intended to guide your behavior were written by people who felt lack or fear. Anything done out of lack or fear has not come from inspired action and has little effect on changing the behavior of those who do not recognize these laws. There are no rules of behavior that come from above.

Intention must come from a place of true desire. It must be focused on what is truly wanted. You must believe your intentions will manifest into physical reality and you must expect to witness the results of your intentions. You have the sole power to create in your own reality. You have the sole power to set your intentions and you have the power to align with your desires and watch them manifest into your physical reality. No one else, not even God, not even us, has the power to create in your reality.

VI.

Even when cast away, Intentions, never cease to exist. All the intentions that have ever existed still exist. In that way, intentions are like thoughts and ideas: they always exist. Once you set an intention, it will keep working long after you have forgotten all about it. It is always working to bring you that which you have intended. This is why long after you set an intention, it will show up as a physical manifestation. In fact, sometimes it is easier for the intention to physically manifest once you've lost conscious consideration of the manifestation.

When you intend for something that you strongly want, you might be delaying its manifestation by noticing that it has not yet manifested. When you place your attention on the fact that the object of your desire has not yet arrived, you keep it from manifestating. It cannot come when you notice it is not here.

Let's say you desire a mate. You decide to set your intention to find a mate and fall in love. Each day when you wake up and notice you're alone you place your attention on being alone. Therefore, since your attention is on being alone, you cannot bring in a mate. You cannot have the feeling of loneliness and have the feeling of being in a loving relationship at the same time. The stronger feeling will always win. Once you give up the feeling of loneliness and stop noticing that your mate is not in your bed, you will allow the manifestation of the mate.

When you set your intention to have a partner to share your life with, you must strive for the feeling of what that experience would be. What would it feel like to wake up in the morning next to someone you love? What would it feel like to love someone and share your life with them? What would it feel like to co-create with someone as partners in life? Would it feel like loneliness? No; it would feel like fun. It would feel comfortable and easy. It would feel exciting and joyous. It would be interesting and stimulating.

When you wish for a mate because you do not want the feeling of loneliness, you put your attention on what is not wanted rather than what is wanted. You cannot rid yourself of what is not wanted by noticing how strongly you do not want what you have. You can only get that which is wanted by practicing the feelings of it. You remove the unwanted by allowing it to be as it is and removing your attention from it. You cannot remove the unwanted by wishing it away for that only gives it more power. Allow the unwanted to be as it is and you remove your attention from it. Gradually, it will remove itself from your physical experience.

The feeling of loneliness will dissipate when you change your perspective. Loneliness, like unworthiness, is an illusion based on a flawed premise. In the case of loneliness you are never alone. It is not possible to be alone. Your inner self and all those who love you and are eternally connected to you are with you every moment of every day of your life. If you knew how many nonphysical entities surrounded you in each moment you would be amazed. The feeling of loneliness would leave you forever.

Just because you have another to share your life with does not mean you will lose the feeling of loneliness. Many people have very strong feelings of loneliness even though they live in homes with a mate and a large family or with parents and siblings. The feeling of loneliness has nothing to do with your proximity to other people; it has everything to do with your lack of connection with your inner self.

When you wish for an end of loneliness by wanting its opposite, a mate, you do not alleviate the feeling of loneliness. You may find a mate, but you'll still feel lonely. You must connect with your inner self and then the feeling of loneliness will dissipate on its own. You cannot be connected to your inner self and still have feelings of loneliness.

When you set your intentions you must consider what it is you truly want and not that which you do not want. The removal of what you do not want is not a true desire. You cannot remove failure from your life by wishing for success. You cannot remove fear from your life by wishing for God to save you. When created to solve illusions of lack, your desires are not true desires.

When you feel unworthy, you may have a desire that when manifested proves to the world your worthiness. This desire cannot manifest in the way you truly want because you are already worthy. Your focus, however, is on unworthiness. Do you see the difference?

If you feel unworthy and desire feelings of worthiness, they will not manifest no matter how successful you become. You might desire recognition so your feelings of unworthiness will be eased. If others saw your greatness, surely you would see it too. But that is never the case. No matter what others see in you, you have to see it in yourself first.

If you were to achieve fame and the adoration of others in order to gain the feeling of worthiness, you would feel even less worthy. You would feel even more disparity between how you should be feeling and how you really feel. This is the reason so many famous people commit suicide or die young. They see the adoration of others but cannot feel it for themselves. This disparity causes them to experience even greater pain. They often search for relief in illicit substances, but to no avail. Any relief is only temporary.

You must feel worthy yourself before you can accept the love of others. When you set your intentions to remove the feeling of unworthiness, you can see that they are the intentions for false desires. You must seek the feeling of worthiness and intend only that which you truly desire. Ask to feel worthy and the universe will show you just how worthy you are. When you start slowly seeing yourself as worthy, you will begin to see small signs of your worthiness.

When you smile at someone and they smile back, this is a sign that you are worthy. When you wave to someoner and they wave back, you can know you are worthy. But you must smile and wave first. The world around you is a reflection of your feelings. Like a mirror, the image does not move until you move first.

When you have poor health, you cannot remove it by wishing for good health. Your focus is still on your poor health. You cannot remove the obstacle by wishing for its opposite and assuming that this alone will remove the obstacle. You must flow past the obstacle, allowing it to be there and not trying to remove it.

The body will move toward well-being on its own. You cannot help the body toward health by hating it in times of poor health. You must love your body and its condition, whether healthy or not in this moment. You cannot love your body when it feels healthy and hate your body in times of poor health. You cannot manipulate your body to good health the way you might try to manipulate a child to good behavior. You cannot reward your body with love when it feels good and punish your body with hate or anger when it feels bad. You cannot change the conditions in the moment; you can only love whatever the conditions are.

A Perception of Reality

How can you love your body in times of poor health when you feel bad? How can you love your child when your child is acting in a way that makes you feel bad? You can ease your feelings by changing your perspective. When you notice a condition in your body that causes you to feel bad, realize that the conditions cannot make you feel anything. You already felt that way and the Law of Attraction is simply giving you evidence of what you've been feeling for a long time.

If you feel physically bad, this is a physical manifestation of how you've been feeling for a long time. It's a physical representation of your predominant feelings and thoughts over a long period of time. It is a message the universe has sent you so you can become aware of your habit of feelings and start the process of change. The physical manifestation of poor health, however slight or pronounced, is a gift from the universe. You are now aware of your habit of thought. You are aware of the vibration you have been offering. You have been given a wonderful gift and now you can change your habit of thought.

The new perspective this bodily condition is giving you is insight into your habits of thought which is very powerful. If you can see your condition as the gift it is, you can see your way to an incredibly healthy and balanced body. Your habit of thought actually coincides with the exact manifestation of any bodily condition. If you have a headache, it is the manifestation of certain thoughts, feelings, and beliefs you've been practicing over time. If you have a cancer, it is the manifestation of another unique set of thoughts, feelings, and beliefs. Every physical condition, whether it is good or bad from your perspective, is the result of a unique set of thoughts, feelings, and beliefs.

If you have a physical condition present in your family, you did not inherit it. You inherited the same set of thoughts, feelings, and beliefs. You are not predetermined to receive the same condition because you share a set of genes; you can only receive the same condition because you share the same set of beliefs.

If you are overweight, you have a certain practiced set of thoughts, feelings, and beliefs. If you are skinny, you have a very different set of thoughts, feelings, and beliefs, and you will not gain weight until your set of thoughts, feelings, and beliefs changes. Any physical condition is the physical manifestation of your habit of thought over a period of time. Change your habit of thought and you change your condition, be it your physical body or your physical world.

VII.

Intention works to bring to you anything you desire. Intention cannot stop anything unwanted. An intention to remove unwanted conditions from your life brings more of the unwanted into your life due to the Law of Attraction,. If you intend to win the lottery to ease the condition of poverty, you simply introduce conflict into your life. The desire to win the lottery is not a true desire. It is a false desire and is only present to stop the unwanted experience of poverty. If you were to win the lottery without uncovering the feelings that led you to poverty, you would simply lose your money and return to poverty. This would increase the feelings you held before and cause your experience to be even more painful.

You cannot set your intentions to attain a false desire and have it work out to solve your problems. It will not work in the way you expect. By trying to remove the unpleasant condition, you make the condition larger. You make it more intense in your physical experience. You must make peace with the unwanted conditions that currently exist in your life. You must allow them to be and not try to remove them. You must move yourself from the present condition slowly and carefully toward that which you truly desire.

Imagine you are hiking along a trail in the forest and you encounter a snake in your path. What are you to do? Are you to fight the snake? Must you kill the snake in order to continue on your path? Must you fight and kill every snake in the forest before you can move forward? Or could you simply allow the snake to be and take a wider path around the snake? Even if you fear and loathe snakes, can you come to appreciate the beauty of the snake and see it for the benefit it offers the overall environment?

If you cannot come to appreciate all conditions for the balance and integrity they offer to your physical reality, you cannot easily move around the present conditions and on to conditions you prefer. If you cannot love the snake for the beautiful creature so beneficial to the environment that it is, the snake will simply follow you and place itself in your path at every turn.

A Perception of Reality

Not only are you unable to intend to remove conditions you do not like, but you must actually come to love and appreciate these conditions. You must see the beauty and the benefit in the circumstances you despise. You cannot fake this. You must truly change your perspective to see the inherent benefit in even the most despicable people in your life. You must see the beauty in the most rancid environment. You must come to love the pain for what it is really there to offer you. You are being given messages regarding your predominance of thoughts and feelings over time. These messages are gifts to behold. Once you can change your perspective, you can change your thoughts, feelings, and beliefs.

Let's imagine you hold a job you despise. You believe that in order for you to leave this job, you must intend to receive a better job. Your intention is not that of a true desire. You simply desire a new job as an escape from your current job. There is something in your current job you do not want. You are intending the opposite of what you do not want and attempting to annihilate it instead of intending a true desire. You cannot possibly rid yourself of what you do not want because you will receive more of that which you are placing your attention on.

You attracted your current job through your feelings, just as you attract anything. The condition that exists in your current job that you hate is the result of your precise feelings, thoughts, and beliefs. It comes to you in response to your vibrational offering. You must ask yourself what it is you hate and what feeling you get when you think of this aspect of your job.

Let's say you hate your boss. Why? What is it about this person that causes you to feel hatred or anger? Think about why you in particular despise this person. Don't worry too much about what others think of you or your boss. Their opinions are clouded by your opinions. Remember: this is your universe and you are the center of attraction. Others' opinions will either line up with your opinion or oppose it depending on your point of view.

You must focus inside deeply and identify the core feeling that leads you to hate your boss. Does your boss make you feel inferior? Does he give you reason to doubt yourself? Does he make you feel unworthy? Does he fail to praise and appreciate your contribution? If so, why? Do you see that your boss is simply offering the physical representation of your innermost feelings about yourself?

If you felt worthy and powerful, you would love whatever job you attracted. You would not look for another job if you felt good about yourself. Your job, like your life, is simply a reflection of the way you feel. If you feel good, you receive positive feedback from the universe in direct proportion to your intensity of feeling. If you feel confident, powerful, and worthy, you do not need to seek better jobs or better conditions - they will seek you.

If you feel unworthy, bitter, or resentful, you will not be able to escape these feelings by changing the conditions. You will come to find that all bosses, co-workers, and customers will treat you in the exact manner that reflects the way you feel about yourself.

Can you change your feelings about yourself? Absolutely. Can you change your feelings in this moment? Absolutely. Is it more likely you will have to alter your feelings, thoughts, and beliefs over time? That will be up to you. You live in each moment whether you know it or not. Your power is always in the moment. You can think good-feeling thoughts in each moment and as you do, you gain momentum.

But first you must love that person you hate. You must love your boss for the message he is sending you. How else would you discover your feelings if not for such an obvious example? You must see your boss as a gift from the universe, for that is exactly what he or she is.

Any condition in your life that you want to be rid of is a message from the universe that tells the story of your predominance of thoughts and feelings. Messages come in beautifully wrapped packages as well. If you are receiving wonderful people, conditions, and experiences in your life in a constant flow, you are being shown that your feelings, thoughts, and emotions are positive in their entirety. If there are small areas of discomfort, these are simply brief messages intended to help you clean up some of your uneasy lingering thought patterns.

Embrace the conditions you dislike and simply flow around them to conditions you prefer. See them as messages and not something you must fight. You have no battles in life, only alterations of perspective that can help improve your predominant patterns of feelings, thoughts, and beliefs. Nothing is here to get in your way. It is all a reflection of your inner world projected on your outer world. What you see and experience is there simply to guide you toward a better-feeling place and a brighter, higher-vibrational frequency.

You are here to joyously expand. You cannot expand until you accept that your vibrational pattern can increase in frequency. As you progress in your expansion, you encounter feelings, thoughts, and beliefs that hold you apart from your expansion in some way. The universe knows this and provides you with obvious examples of the basis of your limiting thought patterns.

As you alter your thoughts to keep up with your expansion, you expand further and uncover more hindering beliefs and thoughts. This is an ongoing, never-ending process of expansion. The sooner you stop fighting it, the more rapidly you will expand. Your expansion continues throughout this life, throughout your nonphysical experience, and into your subsequent lives. Never-ending, continual expansion is the basis of all existence. Sounds like fun, doesn't it?

Chapter Fifteen

The Reality of Imagination

There are many forms of reality. You are currently involved within a physical reality. There is also the nonphysical reality, where we dwell. We have the ability to expand from our reality to your reality and to many other forms of reality. Imagination is another form of reality that exists and is as valid as any other one.

Your thoughts are real, just not tangible. Your experiences are real, just not tangible. You can remember the apple you ate yesterday just as you can remember a thought you had yesterday. In that sense, each is as real as the other.

Your imagination is a creation in a different type of reality. What you imagine, exists. It has life and experiences in and of itself. Imagination is real and therefore holds real power. Imagination is the continuation of intention.

When you intend something, you must also imagine the fruition of that intention. You must imagine the physical manifestation of that intention. If you intend to buy a new house, you will imagine not only the house in some detail, but also the process. You will imagine what it will be like to look at several homes and what you will encounter in the form of people and paperwork. You might imagine the costs involved and the collection of documents. All this is part of the manifestation process.

Your imagination is a key to the physical manifestation of everything you desire. How you use your powers of imagination greatly influences the actual representation of your desire into physical reality. What you hold in your vibrational pattern is what you truly desire. You do not fully understand what you really want or why you want it. Your vibration is the exact representation of everything you really are. It is the beacon that calls out

A Perception of Reality

to the universe. Your imagination is the mental representation of what you think you want. Your vibration works within your imagination to fine tune your intention. Here's how it works.

Let's say you want a new home. Whether or not it is a true desire matters not. If you want a house because you hate your neighbors, you will get a new house. You will also get new neighbors you will grow to hate. You still get what you think you want until you realize that the universe is trying to tell you something. Then you'll clean up your thoughts, feelings, and beliefs and get what you really want.

In this case we're talking about how you will get that new house you want (later we will talk about how to get what you really want, which is to feel good). You dream of a new house. You intend to buy or rent a new house. You imagine the house of your dreams. You then imagine your bank account and the mortgage or rent payment. You also imagine the costs of moving and of maintaining your new house and you realign your imagination with what you perceive to be possible. Your perception dictates what you will receive. Your beliefs also determine what you will receive. And your feelings will absolutely be reflected in what you actually get.

You can have anything you want if you can imagine it and feel good about it while you're imagining it. But you are so stuck in your limited concept of reality that your mind will not allow you to imagine more than what you think is possible. When you were a child, you could imagine anything and feel good. Your imagination was your playground. Because you were young and you believed in your potential, you had fun imagining things and believed it was all somehow possible. You did not get yourself entangled in the details. You understood that the details were not your concern. You understood that the universe would work it out for you.

But now, as an adult, when you imagine something you are confined by your narrow set of beliefs. You are restricted by your limited perspective of reality. You are stymied by your level of confidence and your belief in your own power. You do not yet understand that this is your world and that everyone in it is here to support you. Once you do you will unleash the power of the universe and hold it toward the sky, realizing that anything is possible and that your imagination is your reality. Until then, you will go on believing that your reality is the only reality.

The Reality of Imagination

We must work with the imagination you have at this level of your expansion. We must succumb to your beliefs and fashion a process that will stretch your imagination to its limits. The more you can comfortably imagine, the more you can actually experience in your physical reality. Once your imagination becomes uncomfortable, however, you begin limiting your powers of realization. If you can imagine the resulting manifestation of your desire without experiencing any discomfort in the form of fear or doubt, the manifestation of your desire will look similar to what you've imagined. The manifestation will come quickly and easily.

Think about something that is easy to manifest. Imagine the look of love your pet gives you. See the image in your mind. Now look at your pet and see how he loves you. This is an easy manifestation and is closely aligned with what you imagine. The same process is involved in what you consider big dreams or desires.

There are several ways in which the manifestation of a desire can be created through the use of your imagination, but as with any process, it will take a little practice. The point of practice is to slowly allow your abilities to develop by focusing your thought. When you practice something, you are actually practicing the focus of thought. Whether you practice a golf swing, a musical piece, or even the preparation of a meal, it is all done in your mind before you take action.

The practice of imagination is the focus of thoughts of your desires without the intrusion of fear or doubt. The idea is to imagine the physical manifestation of your desire through good-feeling thoughts which are pure. As soon as you entertain a fearful or worrisome thought into the picture in your mind, you must stop and refocus your attention. The worrisome or fearful thought alters the imagination to include the unwanted.

As you know by now, fearful or doubtful thoughts have the potential to manifest in your reality. Fearful and doubtful thoughts split the energy of your imagination so that your imagination loses its power. Clarity of thought within the imagination process maintains the power of your imagination. When you picture everything going right, you raise your vibration so that what you imagine becomes attractive. Once you allow a thought of fear or doubt into your imagination, you've lowered your vibration.

The key to maintaining pure positive thought is aligning with your beneficial beliefs and keeping your imagination based on the feeling of what you want. It is also important to make sure you are focused on a true desire. When you imagine what you truly want by imagining the feeling you want to achieve, steer clear of thinking about the way in which you think it should unfold. Don't think about the specific path that will take you to your goal. Instead, think of what it will feel like once you've achieved your goal.

For instance, if you want to take a vacation to Hawaii, think of how it will feel to lie on the beach. At first it may be easier to skip ahead to the feeling of the vacation. See yourself lying there on the beach, sipping a Mai Tai, feeling the breeze blowing and watching the waves crash onto the shore. If you can maintain this feeling, the universe will work out the details.

Many humans imagine the details as well as the feeling of the goal. This tends to derail your powers. If you were to imagine the drive to the airport, the long wait in the security line, the cost of the ticket, the cost of your overweight baggage, missing your connecting flight, long hours on the airplane, sitting next to a screaming child, catching a taxi from the airport to the hotel, checking in and then finally getting into your room, you would lose some of the power of your imagination. Can you see how the details reduce the luster of your desire? You might never make it to Hawaii.

Every time you dwell on a detail as you imagine your desire, you create an entry point for a fearful or doubtful thought. The fearful thought may not enter at this time, but it is more likely to. Through your imagination, you should be allowed to bask in the enjoyable aspects of your desire. You do not need to worry or concern yourself with the path that will lead to the manifestation of the desire. That is for the universe to work out. You cannot see from your perspective how the universe will get you to where you want to go.

As you practice your imaginative skills, you will gain a new ability to move with your imagination so that every aspect of the path is fun and enjoyable. The path to a manifestation is the fun part. The result is simply the indication that you have the power and ability to manifest all of your dreams into your physical reality. So imagine that the journey is filled with fun and enjoyable moments.

Now let's take a look at your trip to Hawaii after you've been practicing imagination for a while and have become more skilled. You now picture the drive to the airport free of traffic and you arrive at the perfect time. You see the security lines flowing smoothly and they take your baggage without question. You arrive at the gate right at boarding time and find your seat with ease. You see yourself sitting next to a wonderful person and the time flies as you are both lost in deep conversation. When your airplane lands, you are greeted by a hotel shuttle driver and whisked away to the hotel. Your room is ready when you arrive and the check-in process could not have been easier.

Imagination should be fun and easy. You get to create anything in your mind, so make it fun. If a troublesome thought arrives, simply replace it with a better-feeling thought. You have control over your imagination, so make it exciting, fun, and easy. There are no limits to what you can imagine, so why not take it as far as you can?

II.

Imagination need not be practiced only to achieve the manifestation of a desire. There are many other uses for your imagination. Like any muscle, imagination should be worked on and strengthened. The more you use your imagination, the more powerful and beneficial it will become.

As a child, you spent endless hours using your imagination. You used your imagination in play. You created worlds and adventures with your mind. You made up stories complete with heroes and villains. You created your own games for your delight. Your imagination was a large part of your daily experience.

When you were a child, you were closer to your nonphysical self. You had recently entered the physical world but were still tied to your nonphysical reality. In your nonphysical world you used your imagination to create. As a child in the physical world, you remembered the creative abilities of your imagination.

Over time, you lost touch with the memory of your nonphysical life before you entered the physical world. Your senses tuned you more and more to the physical world as you aged and spent more time immersed in the physical realm. As you became more reality based you considered your imagination less important. You might even have considered those who spend time in day dreams and fantasies to be out of touch with reality. The fact is that you might be a little too preoccupied with the illusion you call reality.

There is a balance to be made between what you understand as the real world, or the outer world, and what lies within. Your inner world includes your thoughts, your beliefs, your feelings, your inner self, and your imagination. You must spend time in both worlds. You must learn that the outer world is simply a reflection of your inner world. If you do not take time to organize your inner world, you will not experience an outer world that pleases you. Imagination allows you to shape and mold your inner world any way you like. Your outer world will be a pleasing reflection of your inner creation.

Imagination can and should be used to improve your feelings. You can use imagination to gain a feeling of relief. You should exercise your imagination to soothe and comfort yourself when you're feeling low. When you're really feeling good, you can use your imagination to ramp up your feelings even more. You can use your imagination to make bad feelings better and make good feelings even more wonderful.

III.

Much of your struggles in life come from your reactions to past events. These events are merely reflections of your deeper feelings, which have simply manifested in your reality. And you see them as real. You are also hurt by them and you hold them in your memory. Through the use of your imagination you can resolve these events and dissipate their power.

If you were hurt by the actions of another, whether it was a parent, a lover, or even a very good friend, you may hold resentment. If you believe the feeling you now hold as a reaction to the event was deliberately caused by the other person, it was not. The feeling was not caused by the other person, it was caused by you. Your reaction to the event caused the hurt feeling and you are the one who carries it. The other person has no power to create in your reality, only you do. Don't worry about it. You now know how this all works and from this point forward you have the knowledge, tools, and understanding to create what you want deliberately.

However, you are still burdened with the feeling of resentment regarding the actions of others and the events of a different time. These things haunt you. You try not to think of them and wish the memory would fade. It becomes easier with time, but you still hold resentment. You may even blame the troubles you are currently experiencing on these past events. This resentment is growing larger and may soon manifest into something more that is unwanted. It is time to heal yourself through the powerful practice of your imagination.

Your imagination is a healing tool. You can use it to go back and change the past. As we have said, what you create in your imagination is real. What you experienced in your past is real. They are each a form of reality, one no more valid than the other. However, your memory of past events is sketchy at best. You do not know the feelings, thoughts, and emotions that led to the event. You only have the fading memory of the event itself. You cannot remember the details. This is a good thing. It makes the event seem less real. You can't know all of the components of the event. What appeared to you as betrayal or any other significant action, was simply an illusion you interpreted through your perspective at the time.

We are not trying to discount the wrong you felt as a victim in that situation or to deny that it may have been truly painful at the time. We are saying that you are literally a completely different person now and that your only attachment to that event is through your memory of it. Thoughts that feel bad when you think them are not beneficial and there is no need to let them linger. You can reduce the intensity of these thoughts and thereby reduce their power.

Resentment, hatred, anger, and other negative feelings must be released. If not, you will continue to suffer. You might not view it as suffering because you have long ago grown accustomed to these bad feelings. But if you were to live a life of mostly good feelings, you would not be able to tolerate these bad feelings. We want you to be so familiar with good feelings that when a bad feeling arises, you can't stand it.

If you believe you have been wronged by someone in your past, by some unjust event, or even by yourself, you must ease the pain through the art of forgiveness. You do not forgive in order to release the other person of guilt or shame; you do it to release yourself from the detrimental feelings you hold onto. You allow yourself to feel good rather than continuing to feel bad. You only absolve the other to your benefit, not theirs.

We are asking you to change your perspective. We are asking you to see the event in a new way that will release you of your burdensome thoughts. We want you to recreate the event in your mind, using your powers of imagination, to actually change the reality of the event. We want you to change the past so that your present and even your future can be changed for the better.

There is no reason that an event that occurred in what you think of as the past must remain in any particular form. The past is not set in stone. The past can be changed using your imagination. When you change your past in your mind, you are actually consciously changing the past. It is your version of the past that exists and there is no specific reality tied to it. No one can describe your past but you. It is only real to you. But there is no fixed reality in anything past, just as there is no fixed reality in anything future.

If you lost your memory, would you be bothered by events that happened in your past? Would you consider yourself a victim if you had no experiences of being a victim? Would you act the way you're acting now toward the other person if you had forgotten all about the incident? Imagine how you felt about the person before the incident. If you forgot the incident, would you feel better about that person? Would you still love that person as you once did? It's interesting to think about, isn't it?

Do you think it is better to feel love or hate toward others? It certainly feels better to feel love. But is there any benefit to feeling love rather than hate? Is there any benefit to your life or to your health? What makes you think there's a difference?

We are certain by now that you can sense the beneficial aspects of feelings of love and the detrimental properties of hate and other unpleasant feelings. Not only is it more enjoyable to feel good and to think good-feeling thoughts, but it is also better for you as a person in this reality. Bad-feeling thoughts are in conflict with everything you want in this reality. Bad-feeling thoughts are your indication that you are not feeling the same as your inner self, you are not in alignment with your true desires, and you are not on your true path. If you ignore these feelings they may grow larger until you can ignore them no longer.

All diseases stem from the continuation of bad-feeling thoughts. If you carry with you feelings of resentment, anger, hatred, disappointment, victimization, or any other bad-feeling thought or belief, over the long term the thoughts will manifest into your physical reality. You might be diagnosed with a disease. The disease stems from the dis-ease within your mind. It comes from the bad-feeling thoughts. Your feelings are manifested by the Law of Attraction. If you feel bad, the Law of Attraction will manifest that specific feeling into your reality, either in your physical body or in the form of an event that closely reflects that feeling.

If you consistently feel good, the Law of Attraction will manifest those feelings into your reality as well. Good-feeling thoughts manifest into joyous, exciting, exhilarating events. If you could simply focus on feeling good, your life would be one long series of good-feeling moments.

We will help you reduce the intensity of any past event in your life that burdens you with bad-feeling thoughts. We would prefer if you could simply forget that this event ever happened but you are not inclined to do so. All we can offer is a process to reduce the intensity of the event. We want to turn your bad feelings into good feelings. If this is not practical, we would like to at least reduce the intensity of the bad feelings. We want you to feel better about everything.

You change your feelings by changing your perspective. When you look back at this event we want you to know that your version of the reality of that event is simply your own version of it. It is not the complete truth. It is not the complete reality. You do not know what you were feeling prior to the event. You do not know what the others involved were feeling prior to the event. Therefore, you are only aware of a tiny piece of the reality. Your version of this reality is all in your mind. You have the power to change your mind. You must come to realize that changing your mind and altering your beliefs as they relate to this event is for your benefit alone. You are not changing your version of reality to assist anyone but yourself.

Any event that occurred in your past has within it a similar core or nature that lies within all such events. Whether you were abandoned as a child; sexually, physically, or emotionally abused; betrayed by someone you loved; misunderstood by someone; experienced the death of a loved one; or even experienced being attacked by a stranger, these all have similar themes. All of these events involved you. You are the center of any such event and you

A Perception of Reality

feel that you've been harmed by the event in some way. Also, all of these events occurred in your past. None of the events are occurring in your present. You have survived your event and others have survived theirs. You are still here in this moment in time and right now everything is alright.

We want to change your perspective on this event that is so predominant in your life by teaching you a process, because not only do we want you to change your perspective on this large, all-encompassing, and tragic event, we also want to change your perspective on all the smaller events in your life. We want you to become an expert in this process so that you can use it to thwart such events as they occur. We want to stop the momentum of unpleasant events in your life before they manifest.

We want you to spend time using your imagination. You can practice and enjoy your imagination at any time. The more you use it, the more fun it will become. Imagination should be fun. Now we want you to think of a small event that you still hold a little resentment about. Think of an embarrassing moment. See the event as it unfolded. See all the people who were there. Did someone do something to you that caused you to feel embarrassed? Did you do something embarrassing? What do you think everyone else thought about the situation?

Use your imagination to recreate the scene. This is not a big deal; it was actually a funny moment. You had nothing to be embarrassed about; it was just the timing of the event. Did anyone really even notice? Use your imagination to slightly alter the events. See people not noticing the situation. See them focused on something else. See them not remembering the moment at all. See them thinking well of you and hoping you are doing well today. See them for the loving people they really are and remember that they have also been embarrassed at some point in their lives. They understand what happened. They have all been there before. They do not consider this a big deal. It was really nothing. You are the only one who can even remember the situation.

Do you see how your imagination can turn around a small embarrassment and soften its intensity? Use your imagination on all such small events. If someone cuts you off in traffic or pulls out in front of you, look at the event in a compassionate way. They were not trying to do anything to you. They were simply not paying attention or made a poor decision. See them for the loving person they are. You are connected to everyone else. You are all family. There are no real divisions. Everything you perceive comes from your own perspective. Broaden your perspective and you'll make life easier on yourself.

When you are ready, you can use this simple process of imagination to heal the big events in your life. When you have practiced your imagination to recreate small events and turn them to your favor, you can then work on the big events. You can go at your own pace and practice your imagination on anything you want. You can always come back to the event and take it further and further. You are actually recreating the past as you re-imagine it in your mind. You have all the power at your disposal. You have choice and you can choose how you want to view any event.

Let's say you had a parent who left you as a child. Maybe the parent died. Maybe your parents were divorced, or maybe you never knew one of them. You felt abandoned in some way and this abandonment lingers in your mind. You may have abandonment issues now as an adult. You may have lovers or friends you feel abandoned you in your time of need. You may carry resentment toward the parent you feel abandoned you. It is now time to recreate that event using the power of your imagination.

The first step is to look at the event from the broader view of your non-physical inner self. Look down on the scene as if you were floating above it. Now look at it through the eyes of the one who left you. Look at the scene from their perspective. Imagine what it must have felt like for them.

Imagine the pain and guilt they must have felt at leaving you. Imagine what must have brought them to leave. They were not as equipped to handle the situation as you are now. Don't you wish they had the comfort of knowing that you have the tools and understanding to deal with this event? Can you imagine their relief knowing that you have the ability to alter your perception and find relief yourself? Doesn't it make you feel better to see their side and forgive them for doing what must have been a very painful thing to do? Can you remember how much you loved them prior to the event?

This event led you to where you are in this moment. Without this event you would be a different person. What if they had not left? Who knows how your life would have been? You might be imagining that it would be better, but we are here to stress to you that it might not have been better. It may have been even less pleasant. It may have been even more difficult. We know you would certainly not be in this place in your life right now.

Maybe you can see that the universe caused these events to happen so you could be in this place right now. Maybe your resentment should be one of appreciation and thanks. Maybe there was a reason your parent was forced to leave. Maybe your growth and expansion was most important. Maybe your parent sacrificed their time with you so you could grow into the person you've become. Maybe they knew on some level that they had to go in order for you to thrive.

Can you look back now and see some positive aspects to their leaving? Do you see that the path you took was made possible by their absence? Can you understand how you benefited? Maybe they had no choice. Maybe it was designed to work out like this. Maybe you both had an agreement that was formed while you were in the nonphysical realm. Can you feel empathy for them? They had to experience the pain of leaving. That pain is often greater than the pain of being left.

Your memory of the event causes you to assume that the event revolved around you. It did not. It revolved around an entire group of people. It was an event that affected the paths of countless others. It may have seemed like it only affected you, but the effects of that event were like a stone being thrown into a pond; they rippled outward and touched the experiences of many others.

Without that event you would not have met your mate, you would not have birthed your children, your life would be different - you would be different. It is time you come to change your perspective and your beliefs about that event. It is time to pay homage to the event, because it created the version of you who now reads these pages. This is an excellent version of you and we would not change a thing.

IV.

Reality is in the moment. The reality of the past is the imagination of the past. The reality of your future lies in the imagination of what your future will look like. You cannot think of your future without your imagination. The reality of your present is simply the actualization or the physical manifestation of your imagination, thoughts, feelings, beliefs, expectations, and emotions.

Close your eyes and imagine the room you are sitting in. Can you see in your mind the placement of furniture, the color of the walls, the lighting, and the windows? Can you picture it all in your mind? When you open your eyes, what do you see? You see everything as it was in your mind, only now, with your eyes open, it is more vivid. Why does your environment seem more real when perceived with your eyes than with your mind? Your eyes are simply translating the vibrations of what you are seeing into your mind. Your imagination and your sight both end up in your mind. Sight is more vivid only because it is more practiced.

As you practice your imagination, you will become able to see with your mind as vividly as you see with your eyes. You will be able to hear sounds, experience tastes, smell aromas, and feel your imaginary environment just as well as you do with your five senses. However, unlike your senses, your imagination is free to see, feel, taste, touch, and hear anything it wants. Your senses are limited by your perception of reality and your beliefs. Your imagination is not.

In your imagination, you can picture yourself boarding a space shuttle, hitting a home run in the World Series or diving off a cliff into the blue Pacific Ocean. You can also use your imagination to rearrange the furniture in your room. You can take the couch, place it against the other wall, and step back to see how it looks. You can hang a piece of art you saw in a store and picture it on your wall. You can cook a meal in your mind before you go to the grocery store and purchase the ingredients. Your imagination has many practical purposes.

As you start to understand the true nature of reality, you blur the lines between what you experience with your senses and what you imagine. One is no more real, no more valid, than the other. However, you believe your reality is fixed in time and space and that you believe your imagination can be created as easily as a thought. The truth is that all reality is created in your mind. It matters not whether you create an imaginary life based on your present expectations or on your wildest imagination. It is all the same thing.

Right now your reality is bound by the chains of your expectations and beliefs. What you expect is what you get. What you believe is what you see. Your beliefs and expectations are tied together. You expect to receive the basis of your beliefs and so you do. In your imagination, however, you have no ties to expectation. You can imagine anything you believe, but you might not expect much of it to manifest in your reality. That is why the power of your imagination is muted to a large degree.

As a child, you could imagine yourself as a famous pop singer, a fashion model, or a home run hitter. As an adult, you imagine what's possible under the structure of your belief system. You might imagine a vacation to Europe or Asia because it seems possible. You might imagine driving a red sports car because it seems possible. However, you no longer imagine being a pop star because you believe that kind of life is not possible for you. Therefore, your future reality is limited to a degree.

We are not saying that we think you should imagine yourself as a pop star or a home run hitter so you can become those things. We are saying that by limiting your imagination, you limit the fun and joy of it. We are saying that if you cannot imagine yourself living in a big, beautiful house, driving a fun, fast car, or traveling to exotic places on your planet, you are limiting your future reality.

Expand the scope of your imagination and you'll expand the possibilities of your life experience. Create vivid imaginary experiences and your reality will reflect the feeling you get when you use your imagination. The more you use your powers of creation through your imagination, the easier it is to create the world you prefer. Do not draw such a sharp line between imagination and reality. They are far more similar than you currently believe.

Chapter Sixteen

Expectation

What you expect, you get. It's as simple as that. If you believe it and expect it, it will be. Your expectations play such a large role in the formation of your reality that it is often difficult to separate the two. Expectation is reality. Expectation creates reality. Expectation creates the physical world around you. What you see exists only because it is what you expect to see.

When you wake up and look around your room you expect the furniture to be in the same place it was when you went to sleep that night. And it is. You have so many expectations that you cannot identify each one. You only notice when something you expect to be there goes missing.

Since your expectations form your reality, might it be advantageous to start expecting good things and stop expecting bad ones? There are entire cultures that deliberately do not expect good things to happen, and when they don't, their expectations are realized. There are cultures that expect bad things to happen in sets of three, and so they see three tragedies happening together. Their expectations are met. There are cultures that believe that bad things always come after too many good things. So they do. The Law of Attraction provides evidence to support your beliefs and expectations.

Expectation provides the framework, the overall structure, of your reality. If your expectations are specific, the structure is filled with the details of your expectation in the way you perceive reality. If your expectations are general, the universe has more flexibility to fill in your reality, so it is easier for you to receive what you desire. The more rigid you are in your expectations, the more fixed your reality becomes. Those whose lives never change are rigid in their expectations. Those who seem to move faster than

A Perception of Reality

everyone else are more fluid in their expectations. They allow for change. They adapt to what the world gives them. They expect to be happy, to have adventure, and to experience new things.

If you could alter your life by changing your expectations, what would you change? How would you choose what you expected? What would be the basis of this choice? Let's say you expected to find the parking space nearest to the store. Would it show up? Yes, if that was a clear expectation. Could you maintain the clarity of that expectation? Yes, if you believed in the power of your expectations.

Expectations are similar to strong beliefs that occur in the moment. When you expect something, you believe it fully. There is no conflict in the belief. If you expect something and it does not occur the way you expected it to, you have included fear or doubt in your expectation. Fear and doubt lower the vibration of your expectation, just as they lower the vibration of thoughts, beliefs, desires, and anything else. You must come to trust that what you expect will manifest and then, in the moment, they will.

If you have an expectation that does not manifest, it simply means there is some doubt mixed in. Do not let this dissuade you from creating expectations of things wanted. Expect to receive what you want regardless of the evidence. This is a practiced art and your practice will take a little time. No one gets it all right at first. You have been living in the physical world blind to the laws of the universe for a very long time. As you learn to play with those laws, you are gaining the power to deliberately shape reality.

When you expect to receive the first spot in the parking lot and you do not get it, realize that your expectation was simply not yet clear enough. When you expect to get the first spot and you do get it, think of it as a wonderful accomplishment. Praise your own powers and revel in the joy they bring. To others, it is simply a random or lucky occurrence, but you see it as your control over reality. You see it as a major accomplishment - because it is.

Seeing the result of a deliberately created expectation is a baby step and like a baby learning to walk, you will fall on your butt. Do not judge your ability to wield your powers. It takes time and over time you'll gain more and greater powers. Practice your expectations on everything throughout your day. Set your intentions and expect them to be filled. See the evidence of your manifestational abilities and revel in them as they occur. Do not be humble; be proud. Do not consider yourself lucky; consider yourself a powerful creator.

Expect things to go your way. Expect to win at every turn. Expect the universe to deliver to you everything you desire and revel in the fulfillment of your expectations. You have so much control over your reality. Expect to see the results of your powers.

Expect your friends and family to be amazed by your achievements. Expect others to be awed by you. Expect them to be inspired by you. Do not let their comments interrupt the deliberate creation of your life. They simply might not understand that you are deliberately creating the life of your dreams. They may be threatened by your success, your happiness, or your joy. Do not let their influence affect your abilities. You can be a shining example of what can be created when one decides to create their own reality deliberately.

II.

In physical reality you expect certain mechanisms to be consistent. You weigh or measure something and the weights and measurements come out as expected. You may expect gravity to be consistent and for a pound to always weigh a pound. Certain aspects of your physical environment are designed to feel consistent so that your expectations will be fulfilled.

When you watch a magic show, the magician plays with your expectations. What you expect does not occur and you are caught up in the illusion. It's not that the rabbit magically appeared in the hat out of thin air; it's that you expected one thing and were given another. Your surprise comes from the magician's understanding of your expectations. He knows that you have made certain agreements about the nature of reality and he has created the illusion that your agreements have been broken.

A comedian does something very similar. A comedian will tell a story you expect to evolve in a certain manner. When the story goes in another direction, one that defies your expectation, the result is humor. When you expect one thing and receive something entirely different, your belief system is altered and the result is surprise, delight, humor, or even shock.

A Perception of Reality

Obviously, the intensity of your reaction to the missed expectation has to do primarily with the intensity of your beliefs. If, for instance, you see a magician for the first time or you're told a joke you've never heard, your reaction is more intense. The magic is surprising and the joke is funny. However, when the trick is revealed or the joke is retold, the intensity of the surprise is greatly reduced.

As you are now learning about the nature of physical reality and your current perception of your own reality, you are becoming aware of the trick. You are learning how the tricks of the universe are produced. You are coming to understand the true nature of reality. Your surprise at the fact that you create your own reality is less intense and you are coming to believe that it is possible to think your way to what you desire.

Prior to this knowledge, you were not aware of the tricks of the universe. When you experienced something that did not match up to your expectations, you called it coincidence. When something odd occurred, you made up an excuse for it. Now, as you become aware of your powers to control and affect your experience of reality, you will no longer explain away your own magical abilities. You will no longer believe in luck or coincidence. Instead you will revel in your own creative abilities.

There is no luck in the universe. Nothing is random. It has all been created, deliberately or otherwise. Nothing happens to you by chance. It is all coordinated by the laws of the universe. Your expectations will allow you to notice and understand how and why things are unfolding as they are.

When you are in a good mood, the world around you responds to the energy of your vibration. In your positive emotional state of being, you drive to the grocery store and the first parking spot is yours for the taking. If you have positive expectations that your good mood will bring you good results, you are not at all surprised by this small token of good fortune. You expect good things to happen and so they do.

As you enter the store, you are greeted by smiling faces everywhere you go. You expect this reception and are not surprised. You are consciously seeking those who are in similar moods and you connect with these other happy people in your physical reality. You have connected with these and other people in a nonphysical way as well. Your mood has lined you up for these encounters before the encounters existed in reality. These are all manifestations of your vibration. Other seemingly random events unfold, but you are aware that your vibration has led to their creation. You create through your vibration. Your expectation of your creative abilities allows you to see and comprehend the extent of your creation.

When you are in a sour mood, you are also creating. As you become aware of your vibrational power to create, you come to understand that you can create what is unwanted just as easily as what is wanted. You notice that your sour mood does not allow you to receive the first parking spot but instead one in the back of the lot under a tree filled with birds. You encounter others in similar moods who do not greet your presence with kindness but instead with similar disgruntled attitudes. You have summoned these people with your vibration in a nonphysical way and your rendezvous was nonphysically established and then manifested into your reality.

You can no longer blame others for being in a sour mood when you're in a sour mood. You can no longer blame the conditions of your environment for the quality of your mood. Once you come to understand the tone of your vibration in the present moment, you can expect your reality to resonate with your current tone. You can expect positive or negative manifestations based on your predominance of thought in the moment. You are no longer able to be surprised by what you receive.

Expect the conditions around you to reflect your thoughts. Understand that you have precisely created these conditions. If the conditions make you feel bad, know that you are experiencing an illusion. Your bad feelings are not the result of the conditions of your physical reality. The conditions are the direct result of your predominance of thought. The conditions reflect how you've been feeling.

You do not order a piece of chocolate cake at a restaurant and expect the waiter to bring you a bowl of soup. When the waiter brings the cake, you do not look at it and cry. You understand that you ordered the cake and you expected to receive cake, not soup. Your reality is similar in concept. You order the universe to bring you evidence of how you feel, and it does. When the evidence is not to your liking, you blame everyone and everything but yourself. When you blame the universe for not understanding what you really want, you experience the exact feeling that led you to this reality.

If you are feeling lonely and want a mate, the universe will provide you with one. Your feelings of isolation, however, will not be resolved simply by the appearance of a mate. Your feelings of loneliness will actually become more intense due to the presence of this mate in your life. The universe is responding to your feelings and the mate has been delivered to intensify them. Your new mate will either leave you, which will make you feel even more lonely than you did prior to his or her arrival, or will treat you in a way that makes you feel lonely even within the framework of a relationship.

You ordered loneliness by your continued feelings of loneliness and the universe delivered to you more intense feelings of loneliness. If you expected love, fulfillment, and companionship but received deeper feelings of solitude, you would be stunned by the events that have unfolded around you. If you understood that the basis of your present circumstances came from feelings of loneliness and you encountered more of that, you would not be surprised. Instead, you would have the ability to reflect and to understand that the cause of the conditions in your life stemmed from your root feelings. This is the gift of your conscious awareness. You have the ability to reflect and to understand the cause and effect of your emotional state.

Once you have the ability to take responsibility for your present conditions, you can start to change your feelings in order to change the unwanted conditions. Once you can expect that the world around you will change as a result of your change in perception, you can expect to see evidence of that change. When you see the evidence, you can come to know that what you are seeing is not a random occurrence, not a lucky accident, but a manifestation brought into physical reality by your tremendous power to create deliberately.

Expect to see signs of what you are creating in the world around you. Look for the evidence and realize what it is telling you. Look at your life and see from a new perspective how you have arrived at this point in it. What have been the dominant feelings that have led you to this place that is unique to all of creation?

When you think of the term *"creative,"* it tends to bring up images of things that are unique. You may never have thought of yourself as particularly creative, but your life is your creation and that creation is unique in all the universe. There has never been another who has created a vibration that is in any way similar to the vibration you have created. What you have attracted into your life, in the mix of good and bad events, beliefs, possessions, experiences, relationships, bodily conditions, financial standing, etc., has never existed before and will never exist again.

Your creation of your life experience may have unfolded without your full conscious awareness. You may have created many things deliberately. You chose the car you're driving, the home you're living in, your friends and the other people in your life, and even the clothes you are wearing. This is all part of your conscious creation. However, part of that creation was not made deliberately. Anything you do not like about your life was also created by you.

You create the good and you create the bad. You probably take full responsibility for the good and you may be proud of your achievements. But do you take responsibility for the bad in your life? Do you accept that you created those conditions, those experiences, those aspects you did not want? If you do take responsibility, do you judge yourself harshly or do you accept that from your perspective, anything you judge as bad is simply an illusion?

At this point in your life you are coming to a new realization that you are a creative being, that your creation is your life, that you are more creative than you thought, and that your life is unique in all of history. This allows you to revel in the creation of what is wanted and causes you to accept responsibility for the creation of things unwanted. Hopefully, you can alter your belief system and realize that judgment holds no place in the universe. You cannot judge yourself because you cannot see the big picture. Everything you have done up to this point has worked to bring you where you stand now. Everything has unfolded perfectly.

You are at the starting point of a new beginning. From this day forward you can expect the world around you to conform to your feelings, thoughts, emotions, beliefs, understandings, and deliberate creative abilities. You now know how the universe works. You understand the mechanism of physical reality. You realize that this world is designed to serve you. You are not here to serve it, anyone, or anything else. You now remember that you are a vibrational being and you are expanding your abilities to raise your vibrational pattern.

A Perception of Reality

You understand that you came here to explore. You know that life is supposed to be fun. You see yourself on a journey and the journey is to be treasured. There is no ending to the journey, just pleasurable and brief stops along the way. You are an eternal being and you are eternally growing, expanding, and living. There is no end. There is no death. There is no loss. There is no lack. There is only well-being. There is only freedom. There is only abundance. Live with joy. Make it fun. Bring in peace, compassion, and understanding. Live for exhilaration. Live the life of your dreams and if you need guidance along the way, look within. The answers are always to be found within. That's where we are and we are eternally here for you.

You are loved more than you can imagine.

Joshua

Special Section

Questions and Answers

Lili Batista - January 4, 2014

Dear Joshua

What can I do to think good thoughts about my health when I feel terrible?

Lili

Dear Lili,

We understand how powerfully you are asking this question and we want you first to know that everything you are doing is right. There is nothing wrong with you, your health, or your life. Our answer to your question can only be viewed through the filter of your overall set of beliefs and predominance of thought. You can only understand our answer to your question from your current perspective. But we know that at a vibrational level, you will receive the full benefit of our answer.

You are a very powerful creator, more powerful than you know. You understand the laws and mechanism of the universe at a very deep level. Your quest for expansion is great and you desire expansion at a fundamental level. However, given your set of beliefs, which you hold onto rather tightly, you feel overwhelmed by the expansion you have created in your life. Your energies are conflicting. You believe in the power of your ability to create and thus you create magnificently. Since you are holding back somewhat due to your limiting beliefs about your worthiness, you are in inner conflict. As you realize that you are worthy of all that you desire, you will catch up to your creations, relieve the conflict, and feel better.

You have always had a firm belief that you were healthy. You exude health from the inside and you are a remarkably healthy person. However, your conflict between your creative abilities and your feelings of unworthiness manifest themselves in the one area you have always felt most worthy; your health.

The unworthiness you feel about your creative abilities, which is completely unfounded, manifests itself in the area in which you felt most worthy; your physical body and your health.

As soon as you start believing in your true worthiness as a creator and your brilliant abilities to use the powers of the universe, you will be relieved of inner conflict and thus your physical body will return to its natural state of well-being.

Your solution, as always, lies within. Trust in your abilities, go with the flow of your life, as fast as that flow is, and you'll resolve your conflicts. See your accomplishments as the incredible achievements of manifestation they are and allow yourself to feel your own power. Believe in yourself and release the negativity of others, who can only stand back and watch you as you soar. From their perspective, they, will have either feelings of envy and jealousy or feelings of pride and inspiration. That is their issue, not yours. Live life on your terms and do not allow yourself to be influenced by others.

Over the years, the influence of others may have led you to a belief that is not helpful; the belief that you must prove yourself to others in order to get their approval. This is not the case and it is not possible anyhow. You have nothing to prove. Look for the positive in every situation and do not try to change the conditions in the moment. Momentum has led you here and momentum will lead you to an even better place. There is nothing wrong with your present condition. Simply go easier on the present conditions and you will be led to a better place. You cannot take inspired action from a place of doubt, so the only action you need to take is that of feeling better and trusting in your abilities.

You will not receive all we have intended to say in this short letter. You are now reading a book that will be very helpful to you and to others. You were a large part of the creation of the book and your great wanting helped to bring it forth into physical reality. As you read the words we've written here and in the book, you will find relief. As you re-read these words and re-read the book from an improved emotional state of being, you will gain an even deeper understanding. So re-read these words often and work on altering the hindering belief that you are not worthy. We can see your vibration and we know the complete worthiness that is you.

You are loved more than you know.

Joshua

Debra Jo Bright - April 25, 2014

Hey Joshua,

I have been paying much more attention to my energy since meeting you. I have noticed that as soon as I wake up I have a smile on my face and feel happy and alive. It does not have anything to do with what I have planned for the day or inspirational action. I do not have to have a project to complete or an intention in mind. But I feel as if all the things I ever wanted are here (not coming to me - they are here). And I think I have a physical result of this, but I want to verify this with you!

Now the moment I wake up, before I move or make a sound, my dog comes from underneath the bed to greet me. She jumps up on to the bed and runs up my body and gives me wonderful kissy licks and snuggles. This is always happens as soon as I wake up - exactly. She has never done this before in the last twelve years. Is my energy on a higher level that she can sense?

Thank you in advance for your awesome answer!

Debra Jo.

Dear Debra Jo,

You are reaching higher levels of vibration and appreciating where you stand. You are in the "in- between" phase - that phase that comes after reaching a higher vibrational level and being happy with where you are. You do not need more right now because you are thrilled with your current high-level vibration and it feels good. This is a very nice and blissful state. But it won't last long.

As soon as you're up to speed with it, you'll want a new challenge. This is why you are here in this physical reality. You're here to reach for new levels. When you reach one level, you feel satisfaction, but then you become used to this new vibration and start to look around to see what new challenge or interest presents itself. As you find something interesting, you'll move in that direction and birth a new desire. You'll then strive for that new level and upon reaching it you'll go through another phase of blissful appreciation. Then you'll be on to another new interest. This is the process of life and you are living it fully.

Many people are unaware of this game you are all here to play. If they do not find instant success, they give up. They do not allow their desires to become too big for fear of failure. They are simply stalled and life for them becomes one of struggle and monotony. Mostly they are in a rut of fear and doubt. There is nothing to fear, because this is a game you cannot lose.

What we have to say to you now is to get ready for something big. It is time to go for it. Don't worry any longer. Do what you want to and watch the universe support your next big thing. Surely you have seen your guides in action. Your dog's behavior lately is just one such indication of their constant presence and support. Ask yourself, "What's next?" Think of bold fantasies and ask yourself, "Why not?"

Spend some time imagining life at this next level. Do not try to figure out the details; simply state what you want to create and allow it to unfold. Don't be afraid that you may not be able to manifest the big desires. That is what is holding you back. You believe you are a great manifestor, but you worry that your powers of manifestation are an illusion and that if you can't manifest the big things, maybe you didn't really manifest anything. This is not true. You are a magnificent manifestor, you are a powerful creator, and you can manifest big things as well.

But there is no hurry. You have all the time in the world. Enjoy your life while you're getting used to the new energy that is flowing to you and through you. Don't brag about it, just enjoy it. Don't try to bring others up there with you. Go into your inner world now and start to communicate with your inner self. Listen to what is said. Notice coincidences and be led to the next step. Follow your interests and do not do anything that is not up to speed with where you now stand. Don't go backwards, move forwards. Move up, not down. Keep moving up. Think bigger.

Love,

Joshua

Jennifer - January, 23, 2014

Dear Joshua,

My daughter has bouts of anxiety, mostly over being separated from me. It happens mostly at bedtime, and she's had issues with sleeping her whole life (she is 5). How can I facilitate her finding her own connection with her inner being and allow her to feel more secure?

Jennifer

Dear Jennifer,

Thank you for your wonderful question. As we share our perspective with you, we know that many others share your question and are also seeking an answer. First we would like to acknowledge your brilliance as a mother and a parent. There is nothing you are doing that you could consider wrong in anyway and we are sure that you realize that your daughter's issues with insecurity are only temporary; since another cannot create in your reality, you cannot create in your daughter's reality, though you can and do influence it.

We are going to talk about what you can do to alleviate your own feelings of insecurity and as you gain a different perspective, your influence will help your daughter as well. You are an intelligent being and you are aware of many realities in your world. You are also aware that you are the creator of your reality and that the feelings you have will manifest into your reality. Your feelings of insecurity have manifested in your perception of your daughter's reality. She has manifested those same feelings as well. However, you also realize that you are in a safe and secure environment and well-being is offered and accepted by you at all times.

As you slowly come to the knowing that you are safe, that you have the ability to allow well-being, and that you can control your feelings, you will ease your own sense of insecurity for your daughter. You, like many parents, fear for the safety of your child. You wish to guide her to safety and away from danger. When she runs, you feel fear of her falling. You must realize that she has her own guidance system. She is at the age where your guidance of her actions interferes with her own sense of well-being. Your guidance is replacing her own inner guidance and that is her conflict.

As soon as you allow her to follow her own guidance system, she will return to a feeling of security and well-being. She may not yet have experienced this feeling of well-being and security in her life because she has been influenced by you. But when you allow her the freedom to fall, the freedom to explore, the freedom to experience the unwanted, she will grow more secure. Her security relies to a large extent on your own feelings of security. When you trust her guidance system, she will learn to trust it as well.

You can facilitate her connection with her own inner being by allowing her to find that connection on her own terms. You do not have to worry so much for her. You have built a safe environment for her and she will thrive in that environment. But she must be allowed to experience contrast so that she can find her guidance from within. You must align with your desire for her well-being. At present you are worried for her well-being and that negative emotion is your own guidance from within. Listen to what it is telling you. Know that there is nothing to worry about. Align with your desires, not your fears.

We know that you have the ability to understand the full and loving answer that we are offering. We would not advise you to take any particular action. We just want you to see the situation from a different, broader perspective. This is one of the most common of all situations in the lives of parents and their children. But it is also the easiest to solve and the solution lies in your ability to allow your child to experience contrast.

If you have never fallen, your fear of falling grows with each day.

Love,

Joshua

For more information or
to ask Joshua your own
question please visit

www.theteachingsofjoshua.com

Printed in Dunstable, United Kingdom